Dedication

This book is dedicated to my son, Walter Larkins IV, the most exuberant and passionate person I have ever known. Our adventures together have made my life an exquisite, unforgettable journey.

To my mother and father, Cecilia de Lusignan and Gordon Oliver, who instilled in me perseverance and who, by their example, inspired me to think innovatively and to never be afraid to see what others do not. They taught me to never give up, no matter what. And to my darling siblings, Denise, Marcus, Rory, Melissa, and Monique, whose humor, laughter, and friendship will join us forever.

And finally, this book would never have been completed or published without the vision, tireless encouragement, friendship, and ongoing assistance and perseverance of Robert S. Friedman, president of Hampton Roads Publishing Company.

Table of Contents

Editor's Introduction

This book is entitled *Calling on Extraterrestrials* for a good reason. The title has two interpretations. First, "calling on" can mean "paying a visit," as one would call on a friend for tea. Second, it can also mean "asking for," as in requesting help or guidance, as one would call on one's doctor for a diagnosis. Our neighbors, whom we call ETs, are letting us know that they are open to meeting with us, and to providing guidance when they deem it appropriate. The steps outlined here will tell you how to do it—if you're serious. But the question still remains, one that many of you will ask: Why do it *this* way? Why don't the ETs just show up as talking heads on *Larry King Live*?

The answer was addressed in the first book of the series, but in case you missed it, I will say again that evolved and enlightened beings landing on this planet in broad daylight would cause such disruptions to our cultural, religious, military, political, and economic paradigms, the resulting panic and chaos would make Orson Welles' 1938 radio program, based on H. G. Wells' novel *The War of the Worlds* look like a tractor-rusting party. Our ET friends would prefer for us to call on them as individuals, as we become ready and willing. When enough of us have changed the paradigms, i.e., primarily the one where we think killing people for *good reasons*, particularly in the name of God, is *okay*, then they might consider going on *Oprah* and schmoozing with us. But right now, it would be akin to a gazelle bounding into a pride of lions and saying, "Let's talk!"

So how do we get to meet them? One may say, "Simple—read this book!" No question, there are eleven steps here that will help you accomplish that goal. But things are not always what they seem. In order to appreciate what you are going to read in this book, you may have to shift some of your cultural beliefs.

You see, on a very deep societal level, most people, especially the well educated and scientifically oriented, are well aware of the materialistic paradigm that currently affects our beliefs. Even if we recognize that we are spiritual beings having a physical experience, we continue to accept that we are in a "scientific" age, ruled by the paradigm that says, "If science doesn't prove it, then it doesn't exist." Never mind that the standards of proof are often determined by the beliefs of the inquirer. We also manage to compartmentalize our spiritual or religious beliefs by confining them to one day a week, where we are allowed to pray and worship. The rest of the week is then devoted to the competitive, materialistic, right-and-wrong, survival mode driving the daily lives of most of us on this planet.

But the ETs convey a very simple message here. If you are open to encounters with them, there are many ways to do so. Some of those ways are non-physical (as most of us would describe it)—for example, meetings in dreams, or in energy-bodies. Even physical contact may involve some phenomena that scientists would label "physically impossible"—such as craft blinking in and out of visibility, bodies moving through solid walls, or telepathic speech and communication.

This extraordinary book will tell you how to have encounters with ETs. It is a choice, but one that is governed by curiosity, not fear. And in my opinion, in the final analysis, it is not the encounter itself that is important. It is what can be *learned* from it, and carried back to others. If we only learn that they are real, that they are our neighbors, that they want to help us—perhaps that is enough. If we can learn more about the universe, about love, about our place in the totality of God, then that is even better.

Robert S. Friedman
Publisher

Part One

Dreaming of Contact

There are two ways to live your life.
One is as though nothing is a miracle.
The other is as though everything is a miracle.

—Albert Einstein

In 1987 while I was a wife and young mother, I unexpectedly began to be contacted by extraterrestrials, although for the first two years, I didn't know what was happening to me. Cones of white light with an electromagnetic charge would burst through my bedroom ceiling and envelop me. Then I would fall asleep, remembering nothing. Shortly after the episodes of light began, I became able to "see" clairvoyantly. Images would frequently appear, helping me solve some problem at work, or to know what I had forgotten to add to my grocery list. I also developed the ability to "hear" in a clairaudient way and I began to hear a voice that spontaneously suggested a course of action, or when to refrain from taking one. For two years I didn't understand that these newfound abilities were made possible as a result of my contact with enlightened extraterrestrials due to my exposure to the higher realms that they inhabit.

After the first night when the lights and sounds came visiting, I began to regularly "hear" people's thoughts as though they were speaking, even when they were not. I could hear the voice of their thoughts even when it contradicted their spoken words.

But rather than feel fortunate and blessed to have somehow developed psychic gifts virtually overnight, I felt traumatized and frightened, because at that time in my life I was squeamish and immature emotionally, psychologically, and spiritually. Instead of seeing the benefits of the experience, I considered that perhaps I was losing my mind. For two years this "chaos" continued as I had been little prepared to suddenly acquire these abilities. Overnight, I was able to see the spirit realm, and some of those departed would visit me. But when an enlightened master appeared before me, replaying scenes from my previous lives, I thought surely that I had lost it. With the encouragement of my then-husband, I checked myself into a psychiatric hospital. While I was there, he filed for divorce, and I lost custody of my son.

During my three-week stay, one of the psychiatrists secretly encouraged me to leave the hospital immediately. He said that he had read through my file and didn't think I was delusional, and that by remaining there, I was further jeopardizing custody of my child. His diagnosis, he stated, was that I had suddenly and inexplicably opened to witnessing paranormal phenomena.

Relieved, I left the hospital and consulted a second therapist who supervised a lengthy clinical evaluation of me by a team of clinicians.

Their professional opinion concluded that I was of sound mind. Four months later, I was able to regain custody of my son.

Two more years passed before my nightly experiences finally produced more than lights and visions, and I awoke to remember a seemingly anesthetized state in which I had a face-to-face encounter with a group of extraterrestrials. I realized that as I gazed in amazement at many gray beings with large black eyes, I had understood what had been happening to me all those years. They told me telepathically that they are anthropologists, and that I, not they, had chosen long ago, as part of my pre-birth agreement, for us to make contact. I understood that it was my destiny to know personally of otherworldly life in order to spread the word of its existence. Like me, millions of other people are also destined to have contact as part of their own blueprints. That blueprint outlined a complete change in my life at that point.

You too may have such a blueprint as part of your own destiny, and by virtue of reading this book, you may be ready to set it in motion.

When I first experienced a face-to-face encounter with these ETs, instead of perceiving of them as "aliens," I remembered them, curiously enough, from long ago, as though they were dear members of my own family whom I had not seen in years. Their very presence touched my deepest memory of the sacred nature of life everywhere. Rather than fear them, I felt deeply humbled, and I was filled with love and peace, as though I were in the presence of a higher authority.

Through many communications since that evening, I have come to know and experience them as spiritually enlightened members of our universal neighborhood. Many years after my initial contact began, Bob Friedman, president of Hampton Roads Publishing Company, encouraged and assisted me in learning how to sit quietly and enter an altered state, "hearing" the ETs' telepathic voice, which I can repeat out loud and capture on a tape recorder. I then transcribe it.

Their message is consistently one of peace, non-judgment, and encouragement to grow spiritually. They say they are unarmed anthropologists and represent many other groups like themselves who have evolved to a status of enlightenment. It's been said that you will know the tree by the fruit that it bears, and their mentoring has had a huge impact on me. They have helped me to grow spiritually, and my life has been wonderfully enhanced as a result of their contact and their communication, which continues to this day. I have asked them many questions about who they are and why they wish to know us, and my questions and their answers make up the content of my first book, *Talking to Extraterrestrials: Communicating with Enlightened Beings* (Larkins 2002).

Soon after that book was released, I began to speak extensively on the radio and in other venues about the process by which

I became mentored by these extraterrestrials. I have received thousands of inquiries, including letters, e-mails, phone calls, and visits to my website at www.talkingtoETs.com from people all over the world, who ask how they too might have their own encounter experiences. Many others who have already been contacted by ETs have thanked me for offering a different perspective from the current "UFO abduction model" that claims that contactees are being victimized.

I believe that the universe, like our planet, is comprised of many diverse groups of beings, rather than having rare groups of friendly "aliens," such as those I met. Those with whom I come into contact, and the nature and quality of those relationships, whether in this world or another, will be determined by my attitude and beliefs. Rather than avoid otherworldly contact, I am actively "calling on extraterrestrials." I invite it because opening to such contact is a spiritual adventure. You too can invite such an adventure.

This is a mystical and curious book. Simply by virtue of reading it completely once or twice, and then deeply contemplating its message, you may start to experience extraordinary things immediately. If you are open, reading and digesting these 11 steps outlined here will generate an inner shift in you. But the steps will ask you to *do* nothing. Instead, if you can deeply consider the assertions and claims that appear here, your own mystical experiences can magically begin overnight.

This book deliberately offers ideas that appear to be made with wild abandon. But then, in 1905 the theory of relativity was considered to have been proposed with wild abandon and wasn't understood until the early 1920s. Almost all major discoveries and ideas are initially considered to be wild and unfounded.

Really, it is our "safe" cultural assumptions that are "wild," not the ideas presented here. Only by abandoning habitual cultural assumptions can you radically change your life. If you desire to know and experience the exhilarating otherworldly opportunities that await you, you must be willing to consider that "unproven" ideas that sound radical and unscientific are often those that hold the most empowering, yet simplest, truths. An inner shift begins with your contemplating the seemingly ridiculous.

Don't be surprised if this inner shift in you begins by some display of seemingly "simple" phenomena. Initially, you may be visited by the spirit of a loved one from the Other Side who brings you a message of great comfort. Or perhaps you will start to see flashes of colored lights, or you will begin to have prophetic dreams. You may be in the middle of a deep quandary with no apparent solution, but after reading this book, your phone will ring and no one will be there. You hang up, but it may ring a second time, and still no one is there. But then, within minutes you realize a most unexpected solution has come to you that assists you in solving your dilemma. Early ET communications arrive gently in order to test your readiness.

This book is like a magic genie in a lamp. Upon embracing its potential by reading and contemplating these 11 steps, your desire for otherworldly experiences can be manifested in a flash, because the extraterrestrials' energy and presence permeate these pages.

Imagine booking a flight to an exotic land where you will be the special guest of an indigenous tribe. Or imagine staying right here in your own neighborhood and being able to activate your ability to know someone who is non-human. Whichever the itinerary, it cannot be booked or coordinated by a travel agent, but rather, by the soul's agenda, one's divine destiny that dictates all that is possible.

This book is about inspiring you to have the courage to embark upon that journey, because it takes moxie to be this kind of trailblazer, the rare pioneer who leads the entire culture by her own example in taking a momentous leap in our evolution to that of a *universal human*: an experiencer who can walk between worlds and seeks to know and relate to the inhabitants of otherworldly realms. Universal humans are able to communicate with other physical beings who reside elsewhere in the universe and be mentored by them for purposes of our spiritual growth.

Such explorers are having a new type of experience, but that new experience will be triggered by an *inner* shift within individual frontiersmen. If this were a guidebook to help you plan a trip overseas, all you'd need would be a map and plane fare. But embarking upon an adventure of this sort requires a different type of preparation because the journey requires that you agree to expand yourself spiritually. This trek begins as a journey *inside*. It is a spiritual process, a deeply profound, yet powerful movement closer to divinity.

Due to otherworldly beings' superior technology, supernatural abilities, and evolved spiritual values, these natives of our universal village remain mostly reticent with tourists and curiosity seekers. They are making themselves available to those who earnestly seek a *relationship* with them. For reasons of spiritual growth, theirs and ours, they invite us to invite them into our daily lives, but only for reasons of our earnest desire to expand our consciousness.

Like the group of ETs whom I know, many different groups of otherworldly beings are not interested in facilitating our exploitation of them, for as highly spiritual beings, they realize that this would only result in more learning required of us. Conversely, they do not seek to exploit us, for they have evolved beyond the need or desire to do so. Unlike the prevailing prejudice against the "grays," they are not super villains. All otherworldly beings cannot be lumped into one category, any more than can one ethnic group. Instead, when we look for *goodness* in others, we will find it. When we reverse our assumptions, instead of presuming manipulative intent by extraterrestrials, we recognize that all beings everywhere are sentient beings. Therefore, their behavior and agenda are as diverse as those of human beings. And since expectations dictate outcome, we can attract more of the enlightened ones by simply making a conscious choice to do so.

Once you've decided that you'd like to know more of your universe and to know the inhabitants who live there, you can turn a key in a golden door that will open onto a world of extraordinary opportunity for you. The journey to their realms will cost you nothing but your intention to trigger your soul plan. You don't need to pay for the flight to their neck of the woods, for they will provide the transportation free of charge, and you won't even need to find a place to park at the airport. They'll pick you up right where you stand, or if you're brave enough, you can venture to different realms from your own living room.

If you're ready, they may also throw in a tour of their world. And unlike the city guide who ends your trip of downtown Manhattan by collecting $19.95, these gentle villagers will require only your willingness as passage, in choosing to play in the universal playground and to be part of the grand production of all time. In fact, these tribes who happen to live off of our planet will even pay *you* for your visit, but that payment is not in the form of dollars and cents, but rather, it is in the legal tender of fellowship.

Does this sound exquisite? Are you one of those people who has always secretly yearned for UFO contact and wondered, "Why don't they choose *me?*"

Heretofore, you erroneously thought that it was up to *them* to decide who gets to go. Now I'm here to tell you that it's actually *your* choice. Would you like to know them and the realms they inhabit?

Opening to contact is not as complex as you think. Why? Because many groups of sentient beings who exist in the universe merely await *our* readiness to know them.

The names and specific identities of these different groups of beings are less important than our understanding that they exist. The details surrounding their identities can be gleaned once you have developed a relationship with them. Generally, they've been known by many names: "extraterrestrials," "ETs," "aliens," inhabitants of UFOs, and the "grays." The group of ETs that I have met say that they have no preference in how we address them, for the label you choose says more about you than it does them, and they're beyond the need to be called anything at all.

Otherworldly beings of the universe are our neighbors, really, although most people don't know them yet. But that's all about to change as our species readies itself to be the New Human who will finally be able to meet more of those who live near us. We will be able to get around the neighborhood more easily on our own steam without the help of NASA, the researchers, our government, or even the airlines.

Instead, we will expand our awareness, which will produce the opportunity to know more beings who exist but whom we have not yet met. This book is the itinerary that will help you navigate your way to their world while you're standing in your own.

But this guide may not be what you expect because these steps will guide you within, which can help you experience a more expanded state of being. From that expanded state, you can come into contact with multidimensional phenomena. You will be asked to learn to change the way that you think, and the way that you view your past, present, and future experiences. You will be asked to expand your world view and to perceive the bigger picture. Recognizing evidence of otherworldly life requires an attitude shift, an adjustment in your ideas, an about-face in your perceptions and assumptions. The reason is that otherworldly contact associated with the higher realms is made possible when you expand your spiritual awareness.

Like most other things of value, to arrive at an expanded state of consciousness will require that you embark on an inner journey, not learn more math or eat grapefruit on Tuesdays. It's not as simplistic as standing on a hilltop with a view of the stars, calling out to extraterrestrials with a megaphone, or zinging them with a satellite dish. But it's not so difficult that no one has met ETs. In fact, millions of experiencers around the world have already had face-to-face meetings with otherworldly beings aboard their crafts and elsewhere, and none of these contactees have needed any technology. I, for one, don't know the difference between a wing nut and a walnut. I'm technologically and scientifically challenged, and I hardly knew a black hole from a gopher hole when I initially had encounter experiences of my own. I didn't have face-to-face contact with extraterrestrials due to my technical prowess. I knew enough to recognize the difference between the inside of my car and the inside of a spacecraft, and I sure as heck knew the difference between a gray extraterrestrial and my great-aunt Yvonne.

This process of opening to contact with those from other realms isn't about technology or ufology. The hard sciences won't get you on board, nor will your clipboard, your pager, your instruments, or your cell phone.

Nope. It's just the regular guy, the girl next door, the long-time "wannabe" who has always dreamed of contact but has never known how to have any. If ever there was an opportunity for the little guy to thumb his nose at the "experts," this is it, because the world's governments have failed at achieving what contactees have already been achieving from the comfort of their own homes and backyards without benefit of any extravagance.

Most of us love the idea of traveling to exotic places and meeting foreign peoples because we yearn to have contact with others who share our planetary home. The differences in all of our lifestyles, appearances, and ethnic propensities are what spark our intrigue. We work hard all year in order to take our annual vacation and travel the globe because we relish the idea of experiencing the diversity of the planet's geography, people, and animals. So imagine your joy at finally discovering that you can actually invite encounters with natives who live off-planet or in other realms. And that contact is glorious, not victimizing. They are healing entities, not victimizing ones. Our innate curiosity about them is fueled by our species' readiness to evolve to our next version of ourselves which will ensure our ability to thrive despite political unrest and environmental degradation. We are being urged onward to our next level of spiritual growth by the ticking of our evolutionary clocks.

Just suppose that now—not next week or in the next decade, but right now—our evolutionary blueprints are primed to take us to the next step. Everything that we have experienced to this point has readied us for it. And that next step involves expanding our spiritual awareness to the degree that allows for us to *finally* meet up with and actually relate to our neighbors off the planet.

It is a challenging path upon which the soul embarks in order to start us on that journey of waking up to who we are as universal humans. We will rarely have the benefit of our soul to help us if its voice is drowned by a barrage of media and cultural noise. If we want to open to contact, we will need to be brave and embrace a perspective shift in practical terms, although at first I thought that to be an oxymoron.

If you're mired in the illusion of our culture, where spiritual values are virtually silenced, opening to this type of paranormal phenomenon can be challenging at best and downright traumatizing at worst. If you adhere to the dogma of the culture that prefers us to feel disempowered, competitive, and fearful, your life experiences—

and your paranormal experiences as well—will take on a quality that matches your state of being.

Instead, if you find the character strength to refuse to buy into the fear paradigm, your whole world, and the whole planet that will become sponsored by you, will change for the better. Perhaps the subject of UFO phenomena, more than any other, is prone to the proclivities that are sponsored by fear and judgment.

When we try to be guided instead by the unused muscles of our higher selves, we will find that we often end up battling it out with our intellect. Our logical minds, from the context of our cultural opinions, often don't have the faintest grasp as to the whys and wherefores of such a leap in spiritual evolution because the rational mind is of the world, not of the spirit. The rational mind, as happily sponsored by the cultural voice, is invested in identifying the enemy and then gathering evidence to find him guilty. That is why this book addresses our often unconscious assumptions and habits and suggests looking at life differently in order to call forth a different kind of life, both individually and culturally. We can't move forward until we stop holding onto the past.

That's why steps 1, 2, and 3 in the following chapters deal with those issues that still bind us, although we haven't realized that they do. They move a person from resentment and a sense of "Why me?" to surrender and forgiveness. They are about how we can "reconcile past, present, and future," the essence of spiritual growth. You can't grow spiritually until you come to some degree of peace about that which has troubled you or continues to haunt you.

As you surrender to all of the circumstances that have made up who you are, you have the foundation for effectively moving from the emotional tumultuousness of grade school to the more mature considerations of college. You have the spiritual base from which you can effectively work on the broader-oriented issues required to "expand your world view" in steps 4, 5, 6, 7, 8, and 9.

This does not mean that you must have mastered steps 1, 2, and 3 prior to moving on to Steps 4 through 9. It means that you've considered the first three steps, and are beginning to internalize them and apply them to your life as made practical by a shift in your thoughts. This shift triggers the sequence involved in expanding ourselves spiritually. The steps will help you manage your growth more effectively because you will have considered what may have once been too taboo to consider, and you will have opened the door for further contemplation.

As a human being who is a *spiritual* being trying to live physically—not the other way around—you still have to relate to the physical world every day. But if you continue to function so fully within the cultural illusion that you forget that your heritage is a spiritual one, you will be choked by doubts and fears relative to the physical world. Understanding how your spiritual ancestry can help you avoid the sand traps of the cultural illusion will help take you out of it.

Steps 10 and 11 are precisely the steps in which you will "see the big picture" and thus facilitate taking you out of it. Your recognition of this creates the final tweak in your decision to realize your soul's destiny of otherworldly mobility and interconnectedness, which will lift you to new heights and to new levels of your personal evolution.

In the chapters that follow, I offer three elements of narrative: my own views, the ET dialogue, and letters from readers. The ratio between these three elements is not equally balanced between chapters since the material is presented in a manner that I believe is most suited to your internalizing them. In the places where I have posed questions to the ETs, my questions are indented and in italic. The ETs' responses are in regular font and indented.

There are some people who doubt that life exists elsewhere. But consider that scientists have already established that there are billions of galaxies out there. Not millions of planets, but billions of *galaxies*. We're hardly alone, and hundreds of thousands of us, probably more like millions of us humans, have already experienced, or are in the process of opening to, some type of phenomenon associated with extraterrestrials or otherworldly beings. And that process of awakening is a profound spiritual trek, lying before us as the uncharted territory that it is. What an opportunity for adventure!

Part Two

Reconciling Past, Present, and Future

Step 1: Call It Forth

In order to begin calling on extraterrestrials, you must desire to have contact. The challenge is that many of us are afraid but don't know that we are. If we're not afraid, we don't believe that contact is up to us to initiate. But every experience begins with a decision. Contact with extraterrestrials is no exception. An integral part of "calling it forth" requires that you choose a "body aspect," which is that physical or non-physical part of you that will first contact extraterrestrials.

Far beyond our sky live natives who have been in contact with millions of normal humans from around the globe. Historically, those of us who have actually met them seldom admit it for fear of shame and ridicule. Although you'd think that as experiencers of phenomena, we would be tickled pink to share what we know, we have kept relatively quiet because our perception of these indigenous tribes from afar does not often jibe with Hollywood's spin, or many ufologists' version, of what contact means to us individually, culturally, or as a species in general.

As a result, in many circles, the public followed along like obedient sheep, adopting the media's version of the "evil alien," not recognizing how we've now managed to project our prejudices into deep space. Rather than adopting spiritual principles as a way to behold life and all of life's events and circumstances, like most everything else in our culture, we often allow our perception of UFO phenomena and the supposed victimizing "aliens," who are part of it, to be shaped by the fear paradigm that attempts to sell us something or to disempower us.

Rather than viewing humans' ability to be contacted as a symptom of our expanding spiritual growth and awareness, we have been taught—brainwashed—into accepting as gospel the "abduction model," which warns of frightening otherworldly entities who hover overhead, ready to swoop down and exploit vulnerable human specimens.

To the contrary, I, and many others worldwide, have discovered to our delight that ET contact is not victimizing, but, rather, part of a profound spiritual journey that can take the initiate on a transformative adventure. And if I can meet them, so can you. But first you have to decide that you want to. When you do decide, state your intention in the same manner that you set your goals in other areas of your life.

ET contact, like the events and experiences that make up the rest of your life, is not random. Neither are the events and experiences of a paranormal nature. Whether we're talking about "regular" life, or your life that's enriched by supernatural miracles, both are shaped by something that is more than mere happenstance. Although it may at times appear to be the case, there are no accidents or "bad luck" but instead, the stuff of our lives has some greater meaning. This includes all of the experiences that make up, or potentially make up, our paranormal experiences. Yet, what we traditionally have named as "paranormal" will become quite normal indeed, as we recognize where we are in our spiritual and evolutionary development. Many humans are in that transitional stage right now, in which our souls are asking us to become more comfortable with the idea that we're multidimensional.

Our lives are part of a universal blueprint, mysteriously unfolding in a way that serves our higher agenda. We choose many of the main themes of our lives prior to birth, and those events that we choose include contact with ETs. When things seem to go well, that blueprint feels familiar, and we marvel at the way things fall together in a synchronous manner. It's as though we sat down at a drafting table long before conception and sketched out the main themes of our life to come. It's not only our individual lives that are guided by this perfect yet mysterious force, but our entire species. It too is being gently guided by the same force, although admittedly, it doesn't always seem that way.

Your interest in a book such as this may portend your own role as a universal being as you prepare to take your place as the universal human that you are. And human beings are not the only entities who have a blueprint for their evolution: so do all beings everywhere, including what we refer to as extraterrestrials. Our mutual blueprints involve knowing each other. Those divine agreements made long ago at the soul level involve our reconciling our differences in appearance, character, spiritual growth, and geography, and remembering that we are all members of the same universal family.

The most important link between all sentient beings everywhere is that we are spiritual beings—not beasts—living out our individual physical lives. This flies in the face of much of what comes out of Hollywood, from our politicians, or from our cultural voice, and that's why it's so hard to maintain a spiritual perspective of life, and particularly of UFO phenomena. There's very little support or encouragement to do so.

Yet, if the grander nature of the universe is spiritual, and the beings who inhabit its realms are too, then the relationships between us have a divine purpose and have been agreed to prior to birth. We can take stock in the greater message and philosophy of every religion, and in every spiritual messenger throughout time who states that we can take ourselves to a more spiritually fulfilling life through our faith, rather than living lives dictated by commercialism and consumerism.

This also means that it is not "human nature" to be victims of each other, but rather, if all beings everywhere have ancestry in divinity, then the inherent desires of all beings everywhere are the same: We want to live in peace with ourselves, our neighbors, and our environment. We do not have to endure lives of pain and struggle. Every wise religious and spiritual teacher throughout history proclaimed a message of love and forgiveness, a recognition that in the final analysis, we are all soul brothers and sisters, all evolving together on a *spiritual* journey. And as spiritual siblings, we're joined together by an invisible thread that ensures our ability to relate to each other if we but choose to. That choice begins with our statement to the universe that we are ready, willing, and able to call forth our awareness of those universal siblings.

But like the dilemma that we face on Earth with each other, we're habituated to perceive others from elsewhere as also separate from ourselves. As the "UFO abduction model" proclaims, "aliens" wish to make victims of us. They're guilty until proven innocent, and few ufologists, or others, have any motivation to perceive of them differently. Forgiveness, tolerance, patience, and kindness are ideas that we are willing to adopt, as long as it's not suggested that we adopt them when we behold those we fear.

Instead, we judge, and get offended by, just about anything or anyone. The more years we live, the more entries get added to our list of annoyances and pet peeves. Throughout the years of our life, we decide who's the "good guy" and who's the "bad guy" based on whatever information we choose to use as our scale.

Our lack of spiritual perspective in life in general flows over to our fearful suspicions about otherworldly beings. So, in life we have our opinions about what is right and wrong, "normal" and "abnormal," and in the case of that which is supernatural, our assumptions may be dead wrong, even when those assumptions we've adopted come from non-spiritual sources. And so, in life with each other and in life with otherworldly beings, we end up being shut out from the magical, mystical, stupendous life of "Heaven on Earth," because we've lost touch with our spiritual natures and have little or no exposure to our potential as powerful beings of the universe. Instead, our life experiences, whether regular or paranormal, prove that we're pre-judging almost everything, and anyone before we've given life—or the "aliens"—a chance to prove otherwise.

Often, the opportunity for contact first presents itself prior to, in the midst of, or just following a personal crisis or significant time of decision making. As we grow spiritually, the soul has a way of ensuring that we work through our difficulties in order to demonstrate our mastery of the course prior to moving on to the next level. Yet we erroneously assume that those events that are unsettling us indicate that we're on the wrong road. In actuality, this choice point on your path is your major opportunity, asking you the biggest question of your life.

Currently, you may be at one of those critical choice points in your own spiritual growth. This is often where we can begin step 1 when we, consciously or unconsciously, call it forth by calling for help. I too faced my own crisis back in 1987, and this is precisely when I began to ask for divine assistance, although I certainly didn't expect that assistance to show up packaged as extraterrestrial contact.

If you sense that you are at a crucial fork in the road and that there are important decisions that await you, or if you're in the midst of some sort of upheaval, take heart. This is good news. This is when we often experience the shift in our path that finally puts us on our road to our destiny.

Our souls have a way of calling to us the perfect vehicle for launching us onto the next magnificent stage of our personal evolution. It is no coincidence that profound life-changing events occur at the same time that we open to otherworldly contact because we're predisposed to do so when we're in the process of shifting. When our world turns upside down, we're a little more open to consider the implausible, the impossible, the unlikely. Often, when we're struggling emotionally and spiritually, this could well be a symptom that we're standing at the threshold of our most profound life change yet. The larva in the cocoon does not foresee the wondrous nature of its next version of itself as a butterfly.

We are about to change wholeheartedly and our ability to call on extraterrestrials for spiritual support is part of the process of changing. Finally, as individuals who are being sponsored by the higher realms, we can spearhead a change in all of humanity. But first we have to get over our past or present upsets that may be holding us back and preventing us from unearthing our grander nature within. When we don't feel good about ourselves, we don't connect to our power base. But still, even those times when we feel the worst can be meaningful opportunities to make drastic changes. And if you haven't noticed, drastic changes will be necessary to change the course of life on Earth.

Those times of our greatest happiness and joy we always remember and appreciate. But what of the difficulties? Does the soul have a reason for them in the context of spiritual growth? What use could our souls have for our darkest hour? These are times when we ask for help.

Many of us recognize, when reflecting back, that years or decades after our worst moments have passed, the trauma, the abuse, and the heartache seem to have produced a change within us, and we wonder just where we'd be today without it, at least within a spiritual context. The wise person starts to notice that almost always, some amount of time after the bad event has passed, there's understanding as to how it was necessary, or how it produced some desirable outcome. We admit that somehow things always turn out for the best.

Many years ago, I too was embroiled in just such heartache. But that very crisis ended up propelling me into the most surprising spiritual awakening of my life. I now understand that my soul had called those experiences to myself in order to propel me to awaken. I discovered that profound life-changing events were occurring simultaneously as I was opening to otherworldly contact. When my world was turning upside down, I was more open to consider the implausible, the impossible, the unlikely, because that was the direction of my prayers and my soul's growth. I was in need of divine help, and so I called it forth, although at the time, I didn't recognize that I had. That is precisely when I began to have encounters with extraterrestrials.

At first blush, it seemed that I was the victim, but now I know better. There are no victims. The soul will use whatever means and whatever heartache to propel spiritual growth.

I remember the events leading up to that first contact like it was yesterday. One "snapshot" stands out in particular. It was a Saturday morning in Los Angeles in 1987, and things had gotten as bad as I thought they could get. At the time, my difficulties were a secret. I was so ashamed of myself, and ashamed of the tumultuousness of my marriage that I said nothing to anyone about it. And on that weekend in the fall of 1987, our seven-month-old baby boy burst into sobs as my husband heaved me roughly onto the bed, straddling me beneath his six-foot-five-inch frame. My arms were pinned above my head as though I were being crucified on the mattress.

He was angry again, ranting, his fist clenched at my face, yet he was no more of an emotional mess than I. Our child cried on the carpet nearby, and from my position as seeming hostage, I wondered how I could get all three of us out of the madness. But I was as lost as he was. And as I shot my child a sidelong glance of regret, tears streamed down my face, puddling in my ears. That eye contact with my infant son symbolized the lowest point in my life. I didn't know with whom I was most disillusioned, my husband, myself, or God: my husband for being the bully, me the weakling, or God, who didn't seem to care that I was seemingly unable or unwilling to walk out or wake up.

But I believed in happy endings. Growing up, I had observed that my mother and father never gave up, and by God, perhaps I had inherited some of their staying power. As English immigrants raising six children, my parents showed stamina, so perhaps I too could make it through. These were my thoughts in the quiet periods between arguments with my husband.

I prayed to the higher power of my understanding, my angels, and anyone or anything who might consider helping me out. For good measure I broke my household budget and bought ten dollars' worth of lottery tickets.

My bank account remained unchanged but my call for help yielded another kind of miracle. White-winged angels didn't respond; extraterrestrials did. And then I had a second dilemma—I wondered, if on top of everything else, I was losing my mind.

To be more precise, I didn't actually know *what* was happening for the first two years. The explosions of light and shards of crackling vibrations could have been my imagination run amok, I soberly considered. I also struggled with low self-esteem; so I considered everything else, including poltergeists, a haunted house, and of course, insanity.

Eventually, I came to understand that extraterrestrials had been contacting me. When I calmed down sufficiently, I awoke on their space craft, rather than "forgetting" that I had. This is when I began my spiritual journey in earnest, which helped me reach the deepest part of myself.

These extraterrestrials sponsored me to embark on an inner journey. And when I peeled back the layers of myself, I was able to heal many of my own character defects and strengthen my attributes until I was reborn.

Perhaps you too suspect that you're already opening to this type of phenomenon, but you're not sure. Well, you're not alone. It's my understanding that worldwide, there are currently millions of otherwise normal people, people just like you and me, who have met or who are about to meet our universal neighbors or beings from other realms. If you think that this is unlikely, or impossible, then you are not in touch with a spiritual surge in which we as a species are going to jump in our evolution, long prophesied by the ancients, and finally awaken to our true heritage as *spiritual* members of the universe. And guess what? We *do* indeed have neighbors, just as you've always suspected. And a whole bunch of us have met them, or are about to. Because it's in our blueprint, individually and culturally. It's our destiny. It's time to wake up, and we planned this awakening long ago.

In these pages, I do not specifically address the issues of skepticism, debunking, or even "proof" regarding the existence of otherworldly life. I know what I know and what I've experienced. I accept my own understanding of my life experiences and don't worry about what anyone else thinks about them. And I suspect that your soul may be deeply moved by the idea of otherworldly life and what it may mean to you.

This book isn't written for the debunker. I have no need to prove anything to anyone, and so I don't even try to. The timing is just right and you, my readers, are already poised to receive it, for many of you have already had some type of contact of your own and are relieved to hear of others who have too. Or, the idea of having contact with extraterrestrials has long excited and mesmerized you. Do you think that this is a coincidence? Do you think that it's an "accident" that more people on this planet seek information through the internet on UFOs and extraterrestrials on any other topic but sex? The reason for this is that our souls are being stirred awake. The idea captivates us. Our imaginations are beckoning us home.

And like all experiences that the soul has determined to call to itself, if it's in your blueprint for this lifetime, you *will* have contact with UFOs: sightings of crafts, or face-to-face contact with extraterrestrials or otherworldly beings themselves, *provided you invite that very contact through a shift in your world view.* The first step in this shift begins with your explicit request to expand your awareness by agreeing to call forth phenomena.

But you may object to this statement. Perhaps you protest, stating, "I've seen a UFO, but I didn't *invite* it. It just happened."

I beg to differ. You *did* invite it, on some level, and were open to the event, whether you remember it consciously or not. The intellect, despite what the authorities tell us, is not the boss of us after all. So things happen, and events take place, and although we believe that we're powerless, we're not. We're multidimensional beings, awaiting our memory of who we really are.

Once invited by calling it forth, this process of opening to knowing our universal brethren is no more difficult than riding a bicycle. But there are a few tips, a few reminders that, although seemingly simplistic, set your destiny in motion. But those reminders are not techniques or exercises, but rather seeds of reflection that once implanted in your ideology, will change you forever. Because part of *my* destiny has been to remind you of yours, and so we have long ago agreed to meet this way, you and I. I have wanted to remind you that you may have chosen contact too, long ago, and now it's time to begin, if you still choose to. And if you do, fasten your seatbelt, because once awakened, you will never be the same.

But you don't have to choose contact. We all have the gift of free will. You can ignore whatever plans your soul made "earlier" and our species will still evolve, but you will simply deny your role as one of the first humans to pioneer our shift.

Soul blueprint or not, some of us will drag our heels, and

that's okay. Some of us prefer to follow the pack once things are underway and a belief system established. It is indeed a tremendous role to spearhead any change in a culture's paradigm. But others of us want an overhaul. We want to be restored to our shiniest, fullest potential. And if we can muster the courage and resolve to make this leap, then we can show the rest of the world how it's done. Great ideas, when first presented, are ridiculed until eventually they're accepted as part of everyday life. Contact with our extraterrestrial neighbors will one day soon be considered "normal" and a common occurrence.

But there is no requirement whatsoever to "serve" the original plans of your destiny, which itself serves to pioneer the shift of our species. You don't have to be the first one out of the gate. The choice is yours to agree or refuse to call forth contact in the first place. If you agree, you will know that something within has been touched awake.

So the first step—Call It Forth—simply asks you to bring to your consciousness the desire to make contact with enlightened members of our universal neighborhood. You need simply to bring your desire front and center and add it to your intentions.

Once you've decided that it's your goal, it won't be difficult. For the process leading up to your own contact with extraterrestrials is the most natural thing in the world, as natural as walking across the street to meet your new neighbor.

According to the mail that I've received and the response to my first book, *Talking to Extraterrestrials: Communicating with Enlightened Beings,* many, many of you are longing to call it forth, but don't know that doing so begins with your intention. One man put it this way when he wrote to me:

> Dear Lisette, for so very long I've had this deep feeling that I am more than I appear to be; more powerful, more knowing. And I have a feeling that I'm not really from here. In your conversations with your otherworldly friends, they say to "invite" them. Well, I have long dreamed of having positive face-to-face encounter experiences as you have, Lisette.

It's funny, you describe initially being traumatized by those encounters with aliens when they first began because you don't feel you'd ever consciously considered such things. But a person like myself, who actively wishes for it, has nothing happen, at least as far as I know. So my question is, what can I do to have those experiences; to be able to sit there with them and converse with them as you are doing? I too would like to be shown other worlds with them. I've dreamed of doing such things since I was young. Other than simply meditating, how can I make it happen? Perhaps since you are able to speak to them telepathically, you could ask them what I can do to have them contact me or take me for a ride.

When you call forth contact, you must deeply believe that phenomena will begin to appear around you, which may not, at first glance, appear to be extraterrestrial in nature. Initially, phenomena of all kinds begin to show up in your daily activities. This book will address some of those possibilities. The new initiate often expects a knock on the front door, but otherworldly entities use their own means and mechanics for contact and communication. They exist in the higher realms and so the "touch" of their contact has a different quality and characteristic than what we are accustomed to or what we anticipate.

Because of hundreds of similar conversations and letters, I knew that it was time to provide this next book, in which I identify the ideas that help bring about an inner shift that will produce contact. It is this inner shift that makes calling it forth produce tangible results.

Although many of you have never had any encounters, some have. But maybe the "phenomena" stopped, and you're now considering that you'd like to expand on those earlier contacts. Perhaps you weren't quite ready to go to the next step, but now you are. Often, many have never told anyone about their contacts, or if they have, they've mentioned them only to a few trusted friends. After the publication of *Talking to Extraterrestrials*, I was pleasantly inundated with letters from all over the world, from people sharing with me their own amazing encounters, such as this one:

> Dear Lisette, people think of me as a level-headed 65-year-old woman. This experience happened 25 to 30 years ago but I will never forget it. I wasn't asleep when it happened. In fact, I was running away from an abusive husband because he was about to beat me again. I was running through a crowd of people by a bus station, when this little man just held out his hand to me, and I went with him. He wasn't gray or anything like that, but he was only about 3 or 4 feet tall. His hands only had about four fingers and they were all wedged together, sort of like a bird's. He drove me out to Fontana, California, and it seemed to be high on a hill somewhere. I remembered a lot of other little people came running out of what I thought was a large building with lots of lights.
>
> I was startled at first, but the little man told me not to be afraid. Just as you said in your book, he didn't speak with his voice, but rather through telepathy. He was wondering why I would stay with a husband who beat me every day. Then, he asked me to look over toward the trees and to tell him what I saw. Amazingly, I saw the pyramids and a long string of camels with people riding on them. It seemed so real that I would have sworn I was actually there! Many other mysterious things happened and, when I returned, I had thought that I had only been with him for a few hours; but when I got home, I discovered I had been gone for five days. Interestingly, that week in the newspaper it was reported that many people in Fontana had spotted UFOs.

Granted, after hearing this type of story, many clinicians in the psychiatric profession would automatically bellow "mental impairment!" And certainly, there are those who *are* impaired who have some wild stories to tell. Yet, there are also many high-functioning people around the world who have had experiences that cannot be explained within the standards of "normal" experience. Those people are not necessarily delusional. (For a full narrative on this, please refer to the appendix of *Talking to*

Extraterrrestrials, and read the contribution of clinician Alan Ludington, M.Div., M.S., M.F.T.)

What I have come to know is that, once the door opens to otherworldly phenomena, all bets are off. The world as we know it stretches, and causes our minds to stretch along with it. Certainly, these mysterious encounters are not for the squeamish, but for the pioneers among you who long to know yourselves as the universal humans you are.

Some of you have had contact, but those encounters stopped occurring and now you long to open the door again. Perhaps you're ready now to take it to another level. Consider this letter I received from a woman in Virginia:

> Dear Lisette, I know about the existence of beings beyond Earth. It was 1978 when I had my first experiences with them. Up until I read *Talking to Extraterrestrials* I had never felt inclined to read books about the subject, perhaps because I think that there are a lot of misconceptions and manipulations toward the understanding of these beings and the true spiritual nature of these encounters.
>
> I was living in Caracas, Venezuela, when I had my first encounter. I was working as an architect and raising my children, doing nothing particularly special or out of the ordinary. I met a person who changed my life in many ways. At the time, I didn't recognize this person as an actual ET who had taken the appearance of a human, but today I have no doubts that this person was one of them. "She" knew everything about me and told me that our meeting was not accidental. She said that we were "family" and that our connections began long ago: many eons ago. It was then, just after I met her, that I started having sightings of spacecraft. For a period of time, one ship was often poised over my house, as I was living on the outskirts of the city in a very isolated area.
>
> Soon after the sightings began, I started having many paranormal experiences. Big explosions of energy accompanied by a sound would burst suddenly in the middle of my living room. My sensitivity increased to the point that I

began to know things before they happened. Suddenly I could read people's intentions. All of this was totally new to me, and before the sightings began, I had never previously had these abilities.

Before long I began to have telepathic communication with these extraterrestrials. They provided me with spiritual information and explained ideas about different energy frequencies, and such. Then one day, they asked me if I would like to visit their craft, every night for a period of one week. But I was told that I would not remember the details of those evenings because it would affect my normal living experiences on Earth. Nonetheless, I accepted, and during that week, I found myself "awakening" at 6:00 A.M. in the most absurd places while doing mundane activities such as opening the refrigerator or walking up the stairs to my bedroom. Then, when I reached my bed to lie down, the sheets were cold as though I hadn't been sleeping there.

In the beginning, I could not remember anything, but later, I began to have memory flashes and remembered being beamed out of my bed and aboard their craft. The strangest thing was that I remember observing a huge park inside one of their ships complete with plants, and I questioned this memory as absurd until I read in your book that such things are possible.

I have other memory flashes: I remember being nude during some type of energetic "cleaning." I'm not certain about this but this is my intuition of this experience. I was then received by several very tall beings, olive skinned and human in appearance, and then I was taken to another place on the ship. Sadly, this is all I remember.

Many times, I have had doubts about my memories, wondering if they are accurate or not. I continued the telepathic communications with the beings for about three years, but it was very difficult for me, because I kept wondering if I was insane. In any case, I wondered if I was even hearing the communications accurately. The degree of self-doubt was enormous and so I just decided that I could not continue with the contact any more. The beings tried to help me build my self-confidence, but I could not. I was just too unsure of myself. In addition, I could never reconcile why they had chosen to contact me.

I am writing you to tell you that my experiences corroborate that there are many of us who, in one way or another, have had some kind of encounter. We're normal people, not crazy or fanatic. Like others, I am just trying to live a normal life. I think we as a species need to open our awareness, not only to the existence of other beings, but also to our own Divine ancestry, and to know that there is really no separation between all of us—that everything is just One. Most of all, there's nothing to be afraid of.

To the UFO debunker, or the therapist grounded in textbook theory, this is madness. But for the rest of us, how does one actually "call it forth"?

In a similar process (outlined in *Talking to Extraterrestrials*), I asked this same question of the extraterrestrials of my own contact (my question follows in italics and the ETs' response is in regular font):

I don't know if these steps will be helpful to people. I think we all expect a more practical, tangible list. If you told us to throw salt to a full moon, that we can wrap our heads around. We want technique. But this? It seems to me that we're offering about as much practical advice as I could get from a stick of incense.

And yet, this is precisely the resonance that your soul seeks. We are addressing now your *soul*, not your cultural mind. This is the nuance that will make all the difference in your experience. Now take another look at the steps, but this time, read them gently, allowing your judgment to soften. Suspend what you deem to be "helpful" or "not helpful." If you're so certain that you know what works and what doesn't, why are you now seeking an alternate path? What has your result been thus far? Just for these next few hundred pages, drop your assumptions about what you think you know about creating or inviting a change in your life, particularly as that change relates to "paranormal" experiences.

31

Okay, but shouldn't we come up with a formula of steps that can be studied and memorized and then put into practice?

You think that what you are needing are concrete steps, those from the "world," but we encourage you to be in your world, but not of it. We encourage you to blossom to an *unfamiliar* state of expanded awareness by expanding the way that you think. You cannot bridge your present state of awareness to your next evolution from the same path that you are presently on. If you want to transcend your present level of awareness, adopt a willingness to embark upon an alternate route. That route has a different feel to it, a different feel that you are not accustomed to, because it's not heralded by your world. We can help take you out of your world, figuratively and literally.

But how do I know that these steps will work for anyone? Shouldn't I first have a dozen of my closest friends and family try this before I publish it? Even Betty Crocker tried out her recipes on family before they made it into a book.

This is not a recipe to make a cake, but rather, a recipe to help you understand that you need *make nothing.* You need merely to call the cake forth from thin air—instantly—not having to make it at all. Do you see the nuance? They are two vastly different paradigms, and that is what we are offering: *the perspective shift that can lead you to another paradigm.* In essence, none of your readers even need this book.

Then why are you encouraging me to write it?

Because all that's needed is to give oneself permission to jump into your next evolution, now. It's about making a *decision.* And that doesn't take a book, or a recipe. The decision to expand one's awareness then leads to all things in the universe. But, there are many steps to achieving an expanded awareness, and you can offer one helpful roadmap. But it's not required, nor is it necessary. For those who are called to it, it will be helpful.

But how do I know it really works? Shouldn't I first come up with testimonials before I publish it so that I can include them here?

How many testimonials would you like?

This feels like one of your trick questions.

How many people would have to be helped by this book and to provide you with testimonials for you to feel justified in publishing it?

It would be nice if we helped a million people to experience encounters.

So if one person short of one million people are helped by these steps then you wouldn't want to bother with it?

Of course not. But many people should be helped by it.

Okay, define many.

Oh, for heavens sake, many more than just my sister-in-law.

So if your sister-in-law is the *only* person you help through this material to open to contact with otherworldly beings that, by the way, immeasurably enhances her life, you don't think it would be worth it?

Well, yes, of course it would be worth it, but it wouldn't be practical. The publisher wouldn't even publish it under those circumstances.

Are you sure about that? Hampton Roads has published many wonderful books that haven't necessarily been embraced by mainstream America.

There is no way to predict which souls, or how many souls will benefit from this book since they are all considering options every day, including these steps. This should not be your motivation. You are offering these steps as part of your own soul's path. It is something that you have said that you'd like to do: If you go to work to volunteer for the Red Cross to help the impoverished, is that path something that you are choosing for yourself or are you choosing it for another?

Well, it's both. I want to help others, and I want to experience myself as being helpful.

You are acting upon that which your own soul is calling you to do and when you are in touch and act upon the knowledge of your soul's desire, you always step into the synchronicity of other souls' desires. And so you have begun to dance the dance at last: the dance of synchronous agendas of many souls. Do not worry about how many are in the dance. Simply enjoy the dance itself.

For this reason, you should offer the material, for it is your own soul's gift, to whoever would like to receive it. It is the experience of creating this gift that is your path. You are stuck worrying about the outcome of others' paths.

Yes, but it's natural when I'm offering a "how-to" book. I want to know if the "how-to" part will work. If the material sucks, then I'm a laughingstock.

It will work for those for whom it works, no more and no less. It is a subjective judgment in any case. Decide if you are writing this with concerns for your "reputation," or if you are offering it as the gift that it is. Then, whichever souls can benefit will benefit, and you will be happy to simply have offered it.

By the same token, the reader would like some guarantee that they're not wasting their time working steps that lead to nothing. Their hopes would be dashed, not to mention wasting $15.95.

Steps never lead to nothing. All steps taken by the soul lead somewhere. It is defining the somewhere that the reader's soul will be choosing. That's their own soul's agenda, not yours. Their "somewhere" will be answered by their life experience. Are you now thinking that you're responsible for their life experience?

No, but a simple reassurance that it will work for someone would help.

You cannot be reassured to the degree that you will find satisfaction because there is no agreed-upon method to measure the outcome of these steps.

But if people can "call it forth" by calling forth a cake out of thin air, then this recipe works, wouldn't you say?

The dilemma is in our differing ideas of what a cake is. You do not know which one thing leads to another thing. So even when it looks as though the steps have failed, they have not, because only from the hindsight of "time" can you answer that question.

Find pleasure in the offering of an idea. That idea may help another to sprout wings to fly. The knowing of us does not look just one way or another, so even you will have a hard time measuring its benefits, for some outcomes cannot be measured by any of your instruments, or even by your present level of awareness.

But they can be measured by people's accounts of emerging contact or experiences. That is the cake after all.

Yes, but even that is a *process*—an evolutionary process—and can be very subjective. So stop looking for guarantees and simply offer your ideas. These steps can evoke a change in path, once the soul causes the being to choose contact. Really, that is all that is needed, permission of self to open to contact.

Then why these steps? Why the whole book?

Because sometimes giving permission to oneself is being blocked by the mind. That is what you are up to here. You are attempting to help people circumvent the mind in order to touch upon and ignite the memory of the soul and its very nature as a universal being. These steps do that quite effectively. The resulting change in this perspective shift is that one begins down a different path.

Okay, I'll resist the impulse to reject the steps out of hand, but at the very least, you'd think you'd have to learn something scientific or tangible to achieve contact, like studying up on quantum physics. Hey, perhaps this is where we'll all finally use our high school algebra. . . . Somehow I just figure there has to be some left-brained schooling yet to be mastered. Or at least we should all have to move to New Mexico or Machu Picchu to place ourselves in a vortex more suitable to spacecraft.

Yet you first encountered us in the middle of Los Angeles.

Well, that's true. You found me, traffic and all. Okay, so I'm willing to relax my preconceived ideas that people expect and need practical steps. Because what you've given me is a list of ideas that people must contemplate. At first glance they do seem like fluff, intangible musings: tofu to a steak-and-potatoes mentality. You've given me fairy dust.

We have provided you with a source, a solid platform from which to originate your contact experiences. True, these do not seem "practical" tasks that you can check off like a laundry list, but keep in mind that steps towards any outcome only elevate you if you glean the spiritual undertones that undergird those steps. These ideas will *drive* your experience. You seem to be expecting a new set of rules such as to eat potatoes on Friday night or to bow to the East before retiring. Those will not change your Monday morning. We are suggesting through these steps that you can begin to adjust to a different *perspective*. That perspective shift will make all the difference in your experience. You will be practicing an emerging context shift as you transition towards that of a universal human.

The mind, the ego, demands practicality and scientific verification. Yet the mind-numbing assignments from your schooling, of which you are well familiar, ask you to memorize and regurgitate. Such assignments seldom elevate your spiritual expansiveness. That is why, out of habit, you keep deferring to a model that you are familiar with from your formal education. Drop that model. You don't need to memorize anything. All that is required is your readiness and willingness, coupled with your imagination.

And so here is the dilemma: that which the mind approves of will not create an encounter experience. The mind can only come along for the ride. You, at the seat of your soul, will create an encounter experience, if you so desire. And so, to appease the mind, you can include practical suggestions, but we emphasize that without addressing the spiritual concepts that underlie contact, you will remain immersed in matters of logic. And you are now moving away from the idea that the logical mind is all-knowing. So now, consider the first step: Call It Forth.

What do you mean by that?

There are many different ways in which you can meet us. Encounters are experienced by the soul via myriad different expressions. Some of you will experience us face to face while in the physical body, whether in your realm or in ours. And even those experiences may be initially detected by just one of your physical senses. You may feel us but not see us. Then there are those of you who choose to have those experiences through the dream state, or as a result of a contact while meeting us via an out-of-body experience. When we say, "choose a body aspect," we mean choose the body aspect from which you would like to encounter us. Choose a body to use to meet us. It is your choice.

The soul knows no containment but your present consciousness does. But even that is an illusion, for in your present embodiment, you think that what you can see, touch, and smell is all that there is. As you are growing in your spiritual understanding, you are experiencing more. You are understanding that simply because you do not see it or smell it does not mean that it is not there, but rather, your senses are temporarily limited.

You understand that your dog can smell things that you cannot. You take it for granted that the hawk can see movement in the prairie below from great distances that you might not be able to detect. You are beginning to understand that there is much more that you have not yet seen, heard, or felt in this embodiment. And so when we say, "choose a body aspect," it is a matter of your soul's purpose. It is a matter of your soul's agenda and your desires regarding the relationship between us. Certainly, much decision-making is going on already on several different levels, but now we are challenging you to bring the decision to interact with us and others like us to the forefront of your consciousness. This way, it also helps you to understand that should you choose a different type of communication or contact, it is something that you can begin to understand as being created by you.

Encounter experiences are subject to the same universal laws as are other experiences. That is to say that you are not a passive participant; you are very much an active participant. So too are your "paranormal" experiences. Begin now to understand that the manner and degree to which you know us and remember us is set up by you in conjunction with us. So although it seems like a simplistic first step, it underlies the fact that you are in fact choosing or not choosing this contact in the first place, whether or not you have been aware of this choosing, or lack of choosing.

The manner of that contact is part of your creative ability. When you think that it isn't, you are only asleep to the greater workings of life. As determined by your many layers of consciousness—superconscious, conscious, subconscious, and unconscious—the manner upon which your contact is both pulled to you by you and delivered to you by us, you can change these aspects throughout your life.

On Tuesday evening, you may have an out-of-body experience in which you visit the desert and marvel at the beauty of the cactus flower there. The next weekend you may visit the desert again, but this time you drive there in your automobile and visit while in your physical form.

And again, you may experience the desert one more time the next week through a dream. Six months later, you might visit the desert in your imagination while you contemplate your afternoon there. Such imagination may inspire you to create poetry or screenplays, music or conversation, all having been evoked by that very experience of the desert, but this time, through the images that it induced. The experience of the desert can be known via myriad aspects of your body as determined by your soul. Now you are simply noticing that even this is your choice, although it does not seem that it is. You have believed that the events and the relationships of your life are outside of your control. But now you are beginning to comprehend that the creation of your life experiences and therefore creation of all of your *relationships*—including the knowing of us—can be created and therefore experienced at a more conscious level.

Should you choose to embark upon a path in which you

move towards that of a universal human, then you will become aware of more experiences that are part and parcel to that of a universal being. The complexity of that which is available for you to experience can now expand dramatically. That which you have thus far experienced is a minor piece of all that is possible to experience, this limited experience you say you are now choosing to expand. And we are here for you, whenever it is that you decide to make this choice.

But isn't it obvious that anyone reading this book would want to choose physical contact, not just have a nightmare about you?

We are speaking of the different aspects of your "body," constituting varying degrees of denseness of energy, which experience reality, whether physical or non-physical. That reality can be experienced physically from your plane, or non-physically, as perceived from your plane, but is actually quite real. For instance, many of you believe that a dream is just that: simply a dream. But the dream state allows for certain soul mechanisms to occur that continue your growth and clarification in a certain other realm. And so, as you dismiss dreaming as not really "real," it is very real, from one perspective. As such, your spiritual growth can be impacted by different aspects of your soul experience. If you have a very significant dream, you may actually make life decisions based on that dream. Perhaps, sometime in your life you have found this to be the case. Perhaps you had recognized that there was very profound guidance coming through your dream and it so impacted you that you made a decision in your physical reality to do something different or take a different path because of it.

So too imagination is considered to be almost suspect in your culture because the rational mind disallows what the imagination comes up with. However, the imagination is tantamount to creating all things wondrous, but is often beyond the rational mind's understanding. Therefore, those areas can be accessed through your imagination or your dreams that once seemed impossible or seemingly "unreal," but are actually quite real. The reason for this is that the imagination gives rise to physical reality. If you clearly understood this you would pay more attention to what you are imagining and how you are imagining it. In fact, there is no other way for reality to be created. Thoughts are the bringers of your dawn. Thoughts are birthing your next event, and so why not understand this from the outset? Do yourself a favor and recognize that to the degree that you imagine, to the degree that you can abandon what the mind understands, can you take yourself to your next evolutionary stage. That is why you might not so readily dismiss imagining us or dreaming about us as merely whimsical. Imagining us, imagining contact with us is the very real step towards knowing us. Thus, imagining anything *else* is a real step towards experiencing *it*. Conversely, it would cause you great comfort were you to recognize that changing your life is rarely as difficult as you "imagine" it to be. Just change your idea about it. All the great written works that you love remind you of this, and it brings hope to you on a very deep level. But why stop there? Bring that idea into the understanding that *all* of your relationships are created by you at some level. And if this is so, then the imagining of us or the dreaming about us are steps towards actual contact.

Similarly, being in a state of readiness, as has been prepared by your imagination or dream state, is no small undertaking. Imagination brings you to that readiness. So, imagine what such contact would be like for you, what it would mean to you, and how things might unfold differently for you, were you to get a glimpse of such expansion.

There is also physical contact, of course, and although you might think that most will readily choose this option, there are those of you who do not recognize that you still hold some fear about meeting us face-to-face. To the degree that you recognize if this is true for you, you will best utilize the introduction through imagination and the dream state, for physical contact is the end result of both imagining and dreaming. A preparation of sorts goes on in both those states. The physical expression of that will find you in union with us, but you don't always recognize that allowing for imagination and dreaming can better set you up for the type of encounter that you'd like.

Further, your astral body, that part of "you" that travels without your physical body, can also meet us and know us. This does not minimize at all any possible physical contact. In fact, where we are, and from the spiritual realms, that very experience is as "real" to us as is physical contact to you. And so, do not readily dismiss out-of-body, or any other, contact in which your physical body remains in your home. For this is as "real" as other physical experiences.

After contemplating the ideas behind this first step, I had to agree that my own encounters that span more than 16 years have changed and transformed over time. But in those early days, I hadn't really accepted the fact that I was the one co-creating those very changes and transformations. When I first opened to this type of contact in 1987, I was confused and frightened by the electrical zapping sensations that pierced my skin. Blinding lights would fill my bedroom, but my eyes couldn't make any sense of what I saw.

It would take me five years before I became ready to take more into my conscious awareness. It was then that I suddenly "awoke" during an encounter to see extraterrestrials before me. But the transition from flashback to full-blown awareness was slow in coming. It would be years before I transitioned to a type of contact that involved my ability to receive telepathic communication from them from the comfort of my own home. Now that I am more comfortable and confident with this type of contact, I will be considering what other style and type of relationship I would like to establish with these and other beings in the universe.

Looking back, I now understand that, along with the ETs, my soul had orchestrated the steps of each of the stages of contact that best suited my growth and development at the time. It's a very personal journey and the manner and details of the many stages and types of contact will vary from person to person. No one particular type of contact is "better" than another. The style and manner of your contact will vary depending on what suits the agenda of your soul, at any particular stage of your life.

Step 2: Remember Soul Connections

When exposed to paranormal phenomena, we often become frightened or even traumatized and then assume erroneously that our upset is proof that something bad or negative has happened to us. Instead, when we "remember soul connections" to sentient beings everywhere and the otherworldly realms which they inhabit, we can become more comfortable returning our awareness to the fact that we are not physical beings, but rather spiritual beings living in a physical world. Activating our soul memory helps us re-unite with family members (whom we already know, but have forgotten that we know) who make up our greater universal family.

Most of us assume that we are aware of the significant experiences and events that have made up our life thus far. Therefore, we grow up believing that what we remember is real, has occurred, and is part of the stored bank of information that makes up our memory. Conversely, it seems reasonable to assert that what we don't remember hasn't happened, right?

Not necessarily.

Suppose you are raised in a culture whose ideology is reinforced overtly and covertly, and you are taught that certain experiences are impossible, except within the context of insanity or psychopathology. Then, if you are confronted with that very experience, what would your mind do? It may forget the experience altogether. Traumatic amnesia becomes a useful tool of the mind as a way of processing events, not to reduce suffering, but to ensure survival.

There is nothing quite as terrifying as questioning one's own sanity when you experience something that's not supposed to be possible. If you are raising children, the upset is quadrupled. As a parent, you not only worry about your own mental health, but you wonder how your impending mental impairment, as well as the "evil spirits," may impact your offspring. Such emotional conflict and turmoil can become a trauma on its own.

Many contactees suspect that they have already experienced some type of encounter phenomena and recognize that they might have forgotten it. Within the context of our cultural standards, many still suffer from the aftereffect of unremembered trauma through partially remembered dreams, flashbacks, and subtle fragmented memories. But still, experiencers reasonably question how it could be that they'd fully forget something so significant as having contact with extraterrestrials.

Clinicians who study the differences in how memory is stored have found that ordinary memory is very different than traumatic memory. In his book *Memory and Abuse: Remembering and Healing the Effects of Trauma* (Whitfield 1995), author Charles L. Whitfield, M.D., explains:

> In ordinary memory there may be no prominent blocks to remembering an experience. But in traumatic memory, blocks are common and they tend to occur most frequently in the area of *rehearsal* (thinking, talking, or writing) and in retrieval. An important part of the genesis of traumatic forgetting is that the person is somehow inhibited or prohibited from completely processing and expressing their experience.

Although Dr. Whitfield specializes in the results of traumatic forgetting in relation to childhood victims of sexual abuse, I believe that his work shows that there are some startling parallels between both experiences, in that recognition of both childhood sexual abuse and encounter phenomena is vehemently resisted by public, professional, familial, and cultural groups. For this reason, it is interesting to note that studies in traumatic forgetting can apply to both.

If it does not feel safe to remember all or part of an experience in our conscious awareness, a common coping mechanism is to simply forget it. In this comparison, the social and cultural stigma against remembering is significant, and therefore similarly shelved within conscious awareness.

But unlike sexual trauma, trauma linked to encounters does not necessarily point to abuse, although we have often assumed that it does.

Simply experiencing an event within the context of our cultural norms often produces confusion, upset, repression, or denial, *even when the experience itself has not produced harm.* Hence, the real trauma then is having something happen that everyone says is impossible. As a result, we can no longer assume that the symptoms of trauma, denial, or repression are present as a result of experiencing harm. Essentially, this idea blows away many of the precepts of the "abduction" model, which states that fear, denial, or repression "proves" abuse at the hands of the aliens.

To emphasize my point, consider the famous story of the Portuguese sea captain Ferdinand Magellan. In October 1520, he set sail from Portugal with 241 men aboard five ships to navigate the world. Eventually they came ashore at the southern part of South America at what is now called the Strait of Magellan. Specifically, they anchored at the rocky, barren land at Cape Horn, at a place they called Tierra del Fuego. This was home to indigenous people Magellan's men called the "Fuegans."

The "phenomena" behind this incredible story begin as Magellan's ships anchored offshore, and while in full view to the natives, *were actually imperceptible to them.* The Fuegans, then, could not see Magellan's ships, because they were not able to even imagine, as they had never heard about, such things in their reality. The natives did not see the ships, or if they initially saw them, they immediately forgot they had. This "traumatic forgetting" did not occur because there was any intrinsic harm done to them by the ships; rather, from the perspective of their world view the existence of the ships was to some degree traumatic to the intellect.

Unlike the soul, which knows no boundaries and holds no restrictions, the rational intellect desperately needs to be right about what it deems as right and wrong, good and bad, and possible and impossible. The following is an account taken from Magellan's logbook and illustrates the "stressors" placed on the rational minds of the Fuegans:

> When Magellan's expedition first landed at Tierra del Fuego, the Fuegans, who for centuries had been isolated from the rest of the world and only knew about canoes, were unable to see the ships anchored in the bay. The big ships were so far beyond their experience that despite the ships' bulk, they perceived the horizon as unbroken: the ships were invisible. This was learned on later expeditions to the area when the Fuegans described how, according to one account, the shaman had first brought to the villagers' attention that the strangers had arrived in something, which although preposterous beyond belief, could actually be seen if one looked carefully.

This may very well explain how it is that some contactees witness UFO crafts and their occupants while others nearby see nothing.

Either we can't see it at all, or if we *do* see what we're not supposed to see, it creates a mighty stir within us, sometimes processed as "trauma." Given public opinion about encounter phenomena, the emotional impact of actually meeting extraterrestrials can be painful, even when there is profound joy inherent in meeting other members of our universal family. Tremendous conflict often develops within the contactee's conscious and unconscious mind. Partially or fully forgetting the event altogether is one way to cope with this conflict. If everyone important to you in your world—parents, teachers, friends, helping professionals, society, and even your government—states privately and publicly that meeting physical extraterrestrials is impossible, then there are few avenues available for coping with this conflict. Inhibiting and blocking a memory becomes one way out of the dilemma.

Until our cultural understanding shifts to an awareness that validates one's encounter experiences by providing a safe environment in which to be honest, many close encounter witnesses will continue to forget their encounters or to be considerably upset by them. Often, it's simply too emotionally dangerous to remember encounters because society prefers not to deal with this phenomenon. Within this context, then, how "useful" would it be for the mind to remember contact?

There are some who claim that certain memories that surface decades later, such as childhood sexual abuse memories, are actually induced or imagined. The most publicized argument is presented by the False Memory Syndrome Foundation, which, at closer scrutiny, appears to be spearheaded by a group of accused abusers. For a fascinating, in-depth analysis on this subject, refer to Dr. Charles Whitfield's extensive research in which he and his colleagues refute this false memory syndrome through time-tested clinical experience and studies.

Dr. Whitfield and others in his field build a very impressive and strong case for understanding that advocates of false memory syndrome tend to rely on results of studies of *ordinary* memory— not *traumatic* memory. In essence, the conclusions that support the false memory syndrome may result from simply studying the wrong data! Dr. Whitfield makes a crucial distinction between the two:

> Important ordinary memory tends to be easier to remember and understand than traumatic memory. This characteristic is illustrated in part by the findings in seven studies showing that from 16 to 64 percent of traumatized people could not remember their traumatic experience for a long time after it happened.

Hence, when we apply this to UFO phenomena, there is significant clinical research indicating that traumatic forgetting and how it relates to later flashbacks and lingering memories should not be readily dismissed as ridiculous or imagination. This "curve of forgetting" explains why often contactees only retain partial memories or begin having memory flashbacks years, and often decades, after the initial contact occurred. Over and over again, experiencers struggle with their emerging memories, often long after the contact occurred.

A woman from Ohio wrote me the perfect anecdote that describes her version of the "Magellan's ships" story:

> Dear Lisette, I am a 53-year-old female who was raised as a "hell-fire Baptist," but my beliefs have greatly changed as a result of my experiences. It was a fall evening, and the sun was just setting in 1975 or 1976, when my three children were small. We had just finished eating supper when my mother, who lived across town, phoned me. In an excited voice she said, "Tammy, something really strange just flew over the pond. It's not an airplane but I don't know what it was. Anyway, it's headed in your direction. Keep an eye out and phone me back if you see it."
>
> We hung up and the kids and I ran to the living room window, propped ourselves on our knees and waited, peering outside. No more than a couple of minutes went by when this gigantic saucer came into view over the neighbor's house. It hovered above a maple tree in their backyard, causing the branches to sway. The saucer emitted rotating, flashing lights of red, amber, and white. The kids and I stared at it in amazement, and it felt as though someone was looking back at us at the same time. Oddly, my thoughts were centered on my concern that there was going to be a big pile-up as the cars passed our house and saw that thing! After all, we were living right on Main Street, and there was a busy gas station right across the street. I kept looking from the saucer to the traffic, and then towards the gas station to see how others were reacting, but no one even seemed to notice. People continued to pump gas, and traffic flowed normally up and down the street. For the life of me, I could not understand their lack of response to such a huge object with such

brightly flashing lights, but apparently it was only visible to us. The last thing I remember is that the saucer slowly lifted and hovered over our house as though it would continue traveling in a northern direction.

When my husband came home from work that night, I didn't mention it to him. In fact, oddly, I can't recall whether weeks, months, or even a year went by before I realized what I had seen. I seemed to only remember bits and pieces until the whole thing came back to my memory. I also never mentioned the incident to any of my friends. I believe that it took a full year until I suddenly remembered it. Many years later, after I had remarried, I mentioned it to my new husband and he started asking me questions, which seemed to trigger my awareness that perhaps, at the time, I had experienced "missing time." For example, he asked me if the kids had been frightened. I don't remember any of our reactions! I don't remember calming them down or even reassuring them that everything was all right. And the more I thought about it, the more I realized that I can't remember anything at all after looking at the craft through the window. It's all blank!

So now, all these years later, I'm questioning my sanity. Had we actually seen the craft or was it my imagination? Then it hit me. Call Mom! After all, it was her phone call that started the whole thing. So I phoned my mother and asked her if she had ever called me two and a half decades before, in the mid-1970s regarding seeing a craft. She confirmed that she had, but since I had never phoned her back, she assumed I hadn't seen anything. So after all these years I filled her in—twenty-five years after the fact!

Notice the extraordinary manner in which the soul will call to itself the opportunity for some type of closure. Some avenue of further contemplation will open to us, but not until we're ready for it. As the adage goes, "When the student is ready, the teacher will appear," and in the same vein, when we're ready and willing to know more, when we can finally cope with knowing more, another layer of the onion will be peeled back.

Certainly, there are numerous definitions of a traumatic experience. What was traumatic to me fifteen years ago may not be traumatic to you today. My trauma associated with my early encounter experiences was due in large part to my emotional, spiritual, and psychological immaturity at the time. So not only did I have contact within a cultural paradigm that made me feel unsafe, I was also immature in my spiritual and emotional development. In those days, I was afraid of my own shadow, uncomfortable with establishing boundaries and even unsure of what healthy boundaries were. I was already attempting to process traumatic stress as a result of abusive relationships, both professional and personal. In addition, I had no support structure in place, which doubled my dilemma when the encounter phenomena began.

This context, then, was fertile ground for my soul's agenda of catapulting me awake, for emotional pain is a potent platform from which to be motivated to change. In other words, I feel that it's important to not judge myself as "wrong" or "bad"—or to judge anyone else who was interacting with me to a similar degree of dysfunction as "wrong" or "bad" either. It is simply a gift to grant oneself permission to finally stand outside one's experience and unemotionally and objectively comprehend that, "Yes, now I see the perfection of everything. I do understand how there seems to be a greater universal rhythm in place to all experience."

This understanding can set us all free, and also, can help us finally forgive anyone whom we have deemed to have hurt us. For there can be no accidents of the soul. All experience we call to ourselves, both individually as well as collectively, in order to continue the process of nudging ourselves awake.

When we better understand the studies that are being conducted on the leading edge of memory research, we begin to approach our cultural "habit" of traumatically forgetting important, often historical, encounters and experiences with a more patient and gentle demeanor. We contactees can begin to establish our own theories, rather than inheriting and adopting the fear-ridden standards of the UFO literature. Since so many UFO "experts" teach that such encounters are actually "abductions," the close encounter witness might now begin to feel empowered to define for herself if the contact is a spiritual process or not. And if you feel that these encounters are actually part of a grand spiritual adventure, you're in good company. Whitley Strieber, the best-selling author who also hosts the popular *Dreamland* radio show, has observed that of the over 500,000 letters and e-mails that he has received from contactees, only about 20 of those claim victimization.

The abduction model has permeated the UFO field, and other opinions about the nature of contact often have a hard time being heard. So not only must a contactee cope with the stress of a life experience that isn't supposed to be happening at all, but the mind is simultaneously aware of the standard party line, coupled with the barrage of Hollywood media noise, which states that contactees should view their encounters as victimizing kidnappings only. If you describe another perspective, based on your encounter, then you're often dismissed as being brainwashed by the ETs themselves. No wonder experiencers' memories are impaired! For further information on the discussion of supposed "brainwashing by aliens," refer to UFO investigator Joe Nyman's appendix 2 in *Talking to Extraterrestrials: Communicating with Enlightened Beings*.

Fear of shame and ridicule are not limited to the contactee specifically. Even those who are related in some manner to an experiencer can feel vulnerable. One of my readers suggested that I send her therapist a copy of *Talking to Extraterrestrials*. The therapist in question was in the process of helping this reader to resolve issues of her encounters while in a therapeutic setting. I agreed that the book might be helpful to her, so I typed a note and mailed it to the clinician, stating that I'd be most interested in her feedback. Soon after, I received an urgent e-mail from the clinician, asking me to please refrain from mentioning her name in association with encounter phenomena. Despite the fact that she was helping her clients to deal with their own issues surrounding encounters, she was not yet ready to "come out of the closet" with her own professional peer group.

In other words, even this psychiatrist who "believes" in UFO encounter phenomena and supports her clients in working through the emotions of their contact, is not ready to admit to such a livelihood. She was happy to help as long as she could remain "underground." After I promised to respect her anonymity, she admitted to hoping that one day soon she too would be able to risk the professional criticism of her clinical peers.

Certainly, this therapist, and the public in general, is well versed in the content of the clinician's reference book, their bible, the *Diagnostic Statistical Manual* (*DSM*). Psychologist Dr. Whitfield notes that in its definition of "Post Traumatic Stress Disorder and Memory," *DSM-III* defined trauma as a "recognizable stressor that would evoke symptoms of significant distress in almost everyone." Certainly, if you've had an encounter that conflicts with your whole cultural and scientific understanding of what's possible, trauma would be a common reaction.

Therefore, even this reference book allows that trauma can be induced as a result of recognizable stressors. I can assure you that a recognizable stressor is to find yourself on a spacecraft in the midst of little gray beings, *even when no particular victimizing has taken place.* As you can imagine, traumatic response is "natural" when the contactee later attempts to make sense of the details of an encounter.

Dr. Whitfield indicates that seven years after this initial definition of trauma the *DSM-IV* definition was narrowed down to any event that was "outside the range of usual human experience and that would be markedly distressing to almost anyone." This, then, still qualifies as a classic definition of the encounter experience and hence of trauma.

Obviously, no matter the definition, "approved" causes of trauma or post traumatic stress disorder do not yet specifically recognize the opening to paranormal phenomena as a legitimate potential cause. But eventually, as more and more of us speak out about our contacts, even the *DSM* definition will be revised. This is just one example of how individuals' experiences, not the textbooks, are shaping the future. Fortunately, war veterans, survivors of childhood sexual abuse, and others now benefit from clinicians' and society's recognition of the emotionally charged issues surrounding their experiences, at least to some small degree. But even those gains are hard won.

Contactees still remain in the closet, often unable to feel safe in seeking professional help since clinicians' professional manuals do not acknowledge the emotional and psychological fallout of encounters. In fact, if anything, clinical standards often presume the opposite: encounter reports are symptoms of marked psychopathology. Imagine how conflicted an individual becomes when an excruciatingly upsetting event, as beheld by the conscious mind, finds no outside support whatsoever, given the cultural context in which those experiences occur.

Still, the tide is turning. Individual contactees with brave, wise clinicians and investigators are at the forefront of this movement, provided they can refrain from the habit of perceiving of the world and all its events within the context of our cultural illusion. True leaders—the masters of the ages—have always reminded us of the grand nature of humanity and the universe. As I reported in my previous book, the ETs reminded me that we humans "are not beasts waiting to awaken. We're divine beings, merely asleep." Reminding each other of this and refraining from spreading negativity and fear is what will most quickly heal us and our planet. What a powerful legacy indeed to impart to our children and to anyone who will listen that it's time that we refrain from furthering the myth of the intellect, which doesn't recognize that humans are first and foremost *spiritual beings living in a physical world.* As we begin calling on extraterrestrials for spiritual support and mentoring, we demonstrate our understanding that humans and ETs working together can solve the dilemmas that face our species.

The stigma and prejudice inherent in speaking out about encounter phenomena run deep, but you don't have to be a contactee or even a therapist treating a contactee to experience ridicule. One of my readers from Wisconsin told me of how potentially embarrassing it was to *hold* my book:

> It's been one of the first times that I've read a book where people see the cover and title, and then smile and say "yeah, uh-huh" and not comment on it. I actually feel a little self-conscious when certain people see it. They make that immediate judgment on this subject matter. Others want to read it, but only after hearing my enthusiasm about it. That's

just one element about this book. It showed me my own limitations and prejudices about the subject as well.

Perhaps I should consider wrapping the next book I write in a brown paper cover! I suppose it's not surprising that, like sex books, my books are often purchased on the Internet, where you don't have to ask a clerk to help you locate that weird book about "talking to extraterrestrials."

Not everyone struggles with how society responds to encounter phenomena. Unlike my own early days of encounters, some people, already armed with strength of character and a solid spiritual base, are not only free from trauma, they actually feel painful emotions when the encounter ends. One writer put it this way:

> Dear Lisette, I know too well what happens when you "share" your experiences. My first encounter that I remember was a sighting only, at the age of 13. I cried when they didn't come back and take me home. I felt like I had been abandoned here. I will be 50 years old in August and my birthday wish is to make conscious visual contact. Oh, I know they've been around in my dreams and meditations, but I want to be able to sit down and have a good old gum-flapping session. Your books suggest that all we have to do is call, so ETs, I'm phoning home to you! We are not alone, we never were, and anyone who thinks otherwise is only fooling himself.

Considering this, I began my dialogue with the ETs with this question:

> *As you said in the last book, many people have already had contact, have actually met you, or others like you, but they don't remember?*

Yes, and for many of the reasons just mentioned, this suggestion alone can feel threatening to the unconscious. But as we suggest it, and to the degree that you allow yourself to consider it, you can soften your resistance to remembering what you already know. That remembering can start you on a different path, as you conceive of what is possible for you personally. Suddenly, you are no longer relying on another's account of what is possible, for you will allow yourself to remember your own experiences, events that have the potential to pull you into your next evolution—during *this* lifetime, we emphasize.

So, many more of us can begin relating to ETs and other-worldly beings, during this lifetime. That is really an exciting possibility, a stupendous idea to ponder, since we so often assume that such a future is one hundred years away.

How can it be one hundred years away when millions of you have already met us? So, now we are speaking about this present moment in "time." The stories of your science fiction suddenly become real, with the exception of violence and abuse. You do not have to bring your habits of war into your future, nor is it necessary to project your own habits onto other beings in the universe. Most of us, by far, are evolved, enlightened, and peaceful. Allowing yourself to remember that you've already met us suggests just how far you are along the path of expanding your awareness. This is a solid indication that you're evolving. As you begin to know yourself, to recognize your true nature as a member of the universal species, you can then help spearhead a shift in your collective experience.

This seems to be quite a responsibility, from the perspective of our species' evolution. I can just imagine that as our culture looks back at this time in our history, we'll realize that the close encounter witness will be credited with shouldering this whole movement towards awakening to our universal neighborhood. But I guess like anything that precedes a leap in our awareness and consciousness, our souls are inviting us to stand proud against the tide of shame and ridicule in presenting seemingly ridiculous ideas that will soon be accepted as commonplace.

Yes, this is the definition of a pioneer and a leader extraordinaire. All of you become pioneers of your global experience as you are ready to take your place and know yourselves as our brothers and sisters. And family reunions do not have to be traumatic. All the wonders of the universe await those of you who simply raise your hands and say, "I'm ready for more."

But I've noticed that some people doubt that inviting contact is really this easy.

All experience is born from a thought, an imagination. This has long since been proven by your quantum physics. As such, the application is no different here. But the recognizing of this is what we are offering. It is as simple as you believe that it is.

Some of my readers have forwarded me compelling letters along these lines, telling how they have personally experimented with harnessing their thoughts as a way of inviting contact. Jan Kregers from San Diego, California, sent me this letter:

Dear Lisette, After hearing you speak on the "Art Bell Show," I decided that I needed to write to you. Last year, after listening to the witnesses at the Disclosure Project press conference in Washington D.C., I decided that I wanted to personally talk to sky people. Dr. Steven Greer's presentation was a really strong motivation, and since I have prior experience with meditation techniques and such, I decided that I would see if I could contact them using my thoughts. Since I like to sky watch, I decided that I would go outside on clear nights and send a mental message that I was ready to communicate. It wasn't long before I started to see these star-like dots of light that did odd maneuvers, like making sudden right-angle turns. I even saw two of them fly a swift zigzag pattern the entire length of the constellation Cygnus, as if they were playing tag with each other, and I *knew* at that moment that I was looking at sky-person technology. Sometimes, when I would carefully make myself think the word "hello" at them, they would brighten or change color, or make an odd-angled turn, as if they had somehow heard me. I decided that I needed to have some sort of call sign that was easier to visualize than the word "hello," and since I decided I wanted them to know that I was a friend, I chose the shape of a heart. Each night, then, I would go outside and begin my evenings by visualizing an image of a heart in the sky overhead, and when I would observe one of the flying dots, I would also visualize a heart shape around it.

Eventually, I decided that I wanted to ask the sky people for a more concrete response, and since it is my belief that sky people are responsible for the crop circle phenomenon, I asked them to send me a sign that they had heard me via a crop circle, and to include a heart motif as part of their next crop formation. I also told them that I wanted to communicate so badly with them that it was okay with me if they shared my consciousness and looked at my world through my eyes, so that they would understand the mess that was going on down here. As I was thinking all these things, I saw several dots do the brightening or sudden turn thing, and I just kept thinking, "Please, please send me a heart." That was the evening of July 15, 2001, and I phoned a close friend of mine to discuss what I was doing and for what I was hoping.

To my delight, on July 18, 2001, the web site in the UK, *The Crop Circle Connector,* published a picture of a perfect heart-shaped glyph that appeared at Newton St. Loe in the United Kingdom. I was completely beside myself with joy, because not only was the heart a simple one, exactly like the one I drew with my mind's eye, it was placed in the landscape in such a way as to mimic my view up into the night sky from my backyard. In my yard, there is a huge pine tree which obscures the view to the southern sky from where I sit at night and so from my view, I'd draw the heart in the sky just to the left of a dark mass of pine tree branches. The formation at Newton S. Loe duplicated this by placing the heart right next to some trees, whose outward bend towards the heart mimicked precisely the position of the branches of the tree in my yard. The sky people had literally "looked through my eyes!" I wrote a letter to both the *Crop Circle Connector* and to *Swirled News,* an online newsletter in the UK, regarding my experience, and *Swirled News* was nice enough to print part of my letter on their website to document the event.

As it turns out, in "the olden days" it never occurred to us that the experimenter herself affects the experimental results, not only in psychological experiments but also in physical ones as well, which physicists have now proven. The concept of field theory explains how forces in the universe interact with each other. Barbara Ann Brennan, in her book *Hands of Light: A Guide to Healing through the Human Energy Field* (Brennan 1998), describes field theory this way:

> A field was defined as a condition in space which has the potential of producing a force. The old Newtonian mechanics interpreted the interaction between positively and negatively charged particles like protons and electrons simply by saying the two particles attract each other like two masses. However, Michael Faraday and James Clerk Maxwell found it more appropriate to use a field concept and say that each charge creates a "disturbance" or a "condition" in the space around it, so that the other charge, when it is present, feels a force. Thus, the concept of a universe filled with fields that create forces that interact with each other was born. Finally, there was a scientific framework with which we could begin to explain our ability to affect each other at a distance through means other than speech and sight. We all have had the experience of picking up the phone and knowing who it is before any words are spoken. Mothers often know when their children are in trouble, no matter where they are. This can be explained in terms of field theory.

As Barbara Ann Brennan concludes so astutely, it has taken most of us well over one hundred years after these theories were proven to begin to use such concepts in describing our personal interactions. Some of those personal interactions can be with otherworldly beings and that which arises from multidimensional phenomena, such as crop circles.

I posed the following question to the extraterrestrials:

> *We discuss the idea of crop circles in more depth in my previous book. This phenomenon then seems to be one*

manifestation of personal communion between the species. It must have all begun with a thought, with an imagination that this could take place.

Precisely. Consider the crop circle phenomena from our viewpoint and how it is that many beings unite, physically and energetically, from our realm and yours, in producing this symphony in your plants. And so, we are not outside of that which we are suggesting to you, we are a living example of how thoughts can create magnificently. One of us had to consider the idea in the first place. Imagine one of our species stepping forward, proclaiming, "Hey, who wants to visit Earth and do some artwork, play some music; heck, let's create a symphony with the souls of the crops. We'll invite the plants themselves and see if they have any other plans for the evening. And any otherworldly beings who care to join us, can do so. Let's all get together and make music, the likes of which the Earth people have never seen. And this way, it will not only assist us in generating the choir of phenomena, but it will also stir certain souls awake, those souls who have longed for a sign from us."

Very funny. It didn't happen like that. Now you're making fun of us.

How do you suppose any idea is played out? It begins with a thought, an idea. It is no different in our realm. The sooner you embrace this concept, the quicker you will catapult into a change in your individual and cultural experience. As such, watch your thoughts. Observe them and notice what they are and how they are producing your tomorrows. So simple, isn't it? Yet so difficult for you to embrace. Allow this simple tenet to change your life and to change your experience.

There's a story about a yogi who, every morning, decided to make a mark on the ceiling with a black charcoal every time he had a negative thought. By the end of the day, the ceiling was darkened. Do you suppose that the majority of our thoughts and ideas are fearful, negative, judgmental?

What do you think? Just take a look at your world.

But there's not a lot of support to "think happy." We're supposed to be frightened and feel unsafe in an unsafe world. Personally, my wish for my own life is to get better and better, refraining from thoughts and words that uphold the illusion of the intellect.

Then simply practice this. Begin to observe your every comment, your every thought, and notice how your life is beginning to change. This is the ultimate journal entry, when you begin to keep track of what you are saying and what you are thinking.

You're suggesting that we walk around daily, jotting down our every thought and word?

Why not? You said it was one of the greatest wishes for your life, to transform the majority of your thoughts and words to those sponsored by the divine.

It doesn't seem very practical.

We dare say that if so motivated, you wouldn't have to practice this for very long before seeing an improvement. Yet many of you demonstrate this level of vigilance for years at a time, and even for decades, when you carefully keep track and monitor your calorie intake, football scores, and stock market values. But when we suggest that you track your *thoughts* for the purpose of taking yourself to the life of your dreams, this seems impractical?

Like many people, I would like to completely transform my world and myself. And you're saying that this is how we can do it, by believing in our thoughts and imaginations as the magic potion that they are?

Yes, and by the way, if you haven't already figured this out, the knowing of us is the gateway to your universe.

Gee, you don't sound egocentric or anything. Talk about megalomania.

We are your brethren who, as the fable goes, refrain from merely giving you a fish to help you change your experience, but rather, can show you how to fish. And so as you hang out with us, you may remember who you really are.

Remembering who you really are will change your paradigm and bring you to your next evolution as spiritual, universal beings that is your birthright. You have said that you long to live in peace and in joy, and this is how you can create that life of your dreams.

So you will be our mentor?

Yes, if you would like to be mentored.

One of my readers wrote me a letter asking me this question about the subject of your mentoring us:

Dear Lisette, I heard you speak on the *Dreamland* radio show hosted by Whitley Strieber the other day. I really enjoyed it. I've read all of the *Conversations with God* books, so you and I are definitely on the same page. I'm pretty confident that we "create our own reality" or choose one that is out there already, something like that. And it's . . . of my own explorations and experiences in creating my own reality that brings me to ask this question of you: I'm open to the idea of "mentoring" civilizations, but doesn't the idea of "mentoring" automatically put one in a subordinate position? Maybe this is my ego talking (or maybe not), but by bringing in a mentor, don't you disempower yourself to a certain extent?

So I too am posing this question to the ETs. Can you answer this please?

At any given time in the history of your planet, certain souls arrived there to serve as a beacon, a reminder of your fullest capabilities. To this degree, Jesus, Buddha, or even the Dalai Lama has "mentored," and does "mentor" you, as an example of what is possible. Just as your professional athletes or others "mentor" underprivileged children from impoverished backgrounds in holding themselves up as an example of rising up from poverty and finding one's life work, so too can we show you how to rise up from your quandary. It is not about disempowering you, but rather about empowering you. A great mentor is one who ignites your memory of who you are, just as Jesus said, "All this and more ye shall do." He didn't say, "You'll never do this yourself, but you can watch me and admire me." Jesus didn't disempower those who looked to his capability, but rather acted as a reminder of what is possible for *them*. We also do that, although we are not suggesting that we should be worshiped.

We, like other masters before on your planet at various times, are deeply in touch with the kernel of our being and connection to the I AM presence, the one heartbeat of all life. That heartbeat runs through all of us, even you. So if we can evolve and develop certain inherent capabilities, then you can too. We are placing ourselves as your example, because in actuality, we are you—evolved. So there is, in essence, no difference between us. We are of the same spirit, you and we, and so you can "use" us to inspire you if it serves you, because we too are children of the universe who have evolved from individual and cultural despair. And if we were able to do it, so will you be able to. This reminder should inspire you and empower you, not strip you of power. And look what is possible, for we are all God's family members. We simply recognize that we are and therefore, that we are inheritors of that which is Godlike, whereas you have not yet remembered this. And that is what we might provide you, a mentoring in the form of a reminder.

Just as Jesus reminded the villagers over and over of what was possible if one believed, so too do we remind all of you of what is possible if you only believe. Masters—mentors— are not there to save the world, they're there to remind you of what the world can become. And so, if you'd like a relationship with another who is good at reminding you, then you can establish such relationships at will.

So this step is asking us to believe that our connection with you runs deep, so deep that we may already know you at the soul level, or even at the physical level, but we don't remember?

Yes, and imagine that you actually met us before you took on your human form. Prior to your birth, you resided in a spiritual dimension, and there, many of you knew us, for no soul is relegated to only one single existence at one moment of time. Although we are physical beings, living many thousands of your Earth years, we are not limited to this form, and have connected with you often, while you are between lives. That is why it would be good for you to remember this, or to at least consider it, as you contemplate your higher relationship with us.

And to think that the UFO literature often writes off the connection between us as merely a kidnapping, or "abduction."

It is the wise soul who can comprehend that there is more, much more, than you are presently comprehending. And this consideration and willingness to suspend your disbelief can cause you to unearth latent images, dreams, or fragments of memories that may have already occurred. This is helpful for those of you who suspect that you have already had encounters of some type, but still feel doubtful. You may be surprised to know how many of you have actually already seen, heard, or have met us and yet are not consciously aware of those contacts or communications. By the very act of reading this chapter, something deep within can be stirred awake. In this way, you have brought yourself to a state of readiness and are now prepared to know the extent of what you know, but have forgotten that you know it.

It's amazing to me how many letters I've received from others who, although they're not necessarily aware of having had any physical contact, wonder if they have, and indicate that they continue to have dreams about contact with extraterrestrials, such as this letter:

Dear Lisette, I'm a 47-year-old engineer at a nuclear power plant in the United States. I never thought that I might be an experiencer until I read the first page of your last book where you describe your experiences and how they began. It hit me like a ton of bricks. I too had the very same experience and it was the most profound moment of my life. I always considered it as a supremely spiritual experience, but never thought to connect it to ETs. I'm still not sure.

One night, when I was in college, I was very frustrated and unhappy and was fervently praying to God for a long time. I then fell asleep. Several hours later I awoke and saw an intense beam of white light, like the one that hit Richard Dreyfuss in the movie *Close Encounters*. It started at my feet and slowly moved up my body. There was incredible sound with it like a hum and a symphony all at once. As it moved toward my head, it increased in volume and pitch and beauty. As it neared my head, I didn't think that sounds could achieve such a high pitch, yet it still climbed higher and higher. When it finally reached my head, I was instantly out of my body and in a beautiful inner dimension, and I walked into a mystical experience that quickly faded in memory.

I have always cherished this experience but it never happened again, although I have had other out-of-body experiences and past-life memories and the like. Now I wonder about many things in my life and wonder if they are connected to ETs. For example, I had a very vivid dream as a young child of five or six of a spaceship landing in my backyard. I was scared, and I ran and hid in the basement and the little green alien man came for me, and I was terrified because I thought I saw a ray gun in his hand.

Just the other night, I had a dream of being a child with other kids around on the street and then a strange white-faced monkey came across the street to talk to me. I was so terrified of that monkey. I would have done anything to get away. Now I wonder if it is symbolic of the ETs and some inner repressed fear that I have.

And one item of note: Once, five or six years ago, I woke up in the middle of the night and my arm was really hurting. When I looked at it, there was a strange geometric figure etched into my arm. I have searched to try and get an interpretation of what it means but no real luck so far.

After reading this letter and as I am typing it at my computer, the ETs' telltale electrical zapping is filling my body, indicating that they wish to communicate. Their response is for the author of this letter, and perhaps for the authors of many other letters that I've received like it:

> Yes, we have encountered you many times, for many of you have indeed chosen these snippets, these moments in time to connect with us. We, and others like us, have come to many, many of you, in this manner and others, in which you are left with a fleeting memory, a snapshot of something glorious having happened, but upon closer scrutiny, the event fades and recedes like a wave rolling back out to the ocean. The harder you try to catch it, the more illusive the memory is. But as you decide and choose if you'd like to continue these interludes with us, more contact will be available to you, of this you can be certain. You do not need to fear us, nor does your mind need to hold the memory of us at bay. As we all begin to relate to each other more expansively, we stage these reunions and come together again as the universal family members that we are.

You're saying then that even our dreams can hint at our grander life blueprints, our deeper connection with you, either now or between lives? I don't know about anyone else, but it's very comforting to me to recognize that we're part of a greater consortium of souls in the universe, and some of those evolved souls such as yourselves would like to get to know us on a more conscious level.

Yes, for spiritual beings are part of a spiritual "network" and therefore are part of the fabric of experience available to limitless, spiritual beings. In many ways, this is the theme throughout these books, that you're not limited, nor are you relegated, to one-dimensional experience, although you think that you are.

Be willing to consider that we have come to you for a specific purpose. That purpose runs along a broad spectrum, beginning with whatever agenda your soul has determined that it's up to. You may not be consciously aware of what you have agreed to long ago, but you can expand that awareness even still, so that you do become aware of your soul's desire.

As with all of your other relationships, those do not have to leave us out of your memory. Welcome home to your universal neighborhood. You are also being asked to tap into that ancestral memory that remembers a life possible without that which you call heartache, subjugation, oppression, illness, fatigue, and even smog. You are moving towards creating a planetary home that better suits your survival. Be willing to know us. Be willing to remember that you may have already met us. Be willing to consider what more you have forgotten. This is the magic of this step, for it invites you to consider that perhaps there is much more that you have experienced, but you have not allowed yourself to remember. Now you will throw open the doors, for you will consciously give yourself permission to unlock those memories now and begin to know more and remember more.

When you are willing to suspend your disbelief and allow that all things are possible, you recall that all things were possible even before you believed that they were. This means that you may have seen things, heard things; you know things although you have not allowed yourself to remember what you know. So now, give yourself permission to remember. You may already have met us. You may already know us. You may have lineage to us that you are not aware of. There are no accidents in the universe. In the highest sense, there is no thing that is imperfect, for all is unfolding in a grand way towards all of our highest idea, even those who follow a path that you call unenlightened. They too will eventually find the light, for they will become more motivated to seek it when being surrounded by the dark. So, do not fear that things will never change.

When you give yourself permission to bring into full consciousness all of the memories that you have, then you grant yourself the gift of full knowing. When you become a lobbyist for your own experiences, then you no longer automatically defer to anyone else as to the meaning of what your experiences have meant to you. Now, you are seeking your own counsel, for you are the one who has had the experience, not another. Why, then, would you defer for meaning to that other who has not? This is not to deny others' professions; it is only to suggest that now you as experiencers are studying the paradigm for yourself. Now you are articulating what these experiences have meant to you. No longer will you continually defer to others for the meaning of your spiritual path. Enlightenment comes one day at a time, or all at once, in a moment.

This day, can you know yourself, your true self, your higher self, more fully when you embrace the memory that you are part of a grand unfolding of human experience. There is a grand awakening going on, where all of humankind will begin to interact with others who live elsewhere. Those of you who are asking yourselves to begin this path simply lead the rest of you. You may now be forthright and delineate where you choose to seek your own counsel and those areas in which you choose to receive professional help. Sometimes, outside help comes in the form of simply having someone with whom to speak about your feelings associated with encounter experiences.

Begin then by preferring a mindset that welcomes new memories to unearth themselves. Limit yourself no longer and come to the picnic of our unfolding relationship. You not only owe it to yourself, but you owe it to the rest of those who come after you. Do you now see the perfection of your mission? Do you see how important it is that you wake up to your experiences? For who will be the voice for those coming behind you? Be brave and grow into your broadening understanding of all that you are capable of and all that you have experienced.

Blessings on your journey for we come to you and those others who say that they are willing and ready to know us. Who else will lead the way, if not you? Who else will brave the ridicule, if not you? Who else will shine the light on the rocky road?

Step 3: Forgive the Pain

The survival of our species requires us to proceed gently with love, no matter how much pain and suffering have been part of our past. Forgiving the pain of our past helps us move forward with our spiritual expansion, which in turn makes it possible to be aware of the higher realms and our universal family, of which it is part. Once aware of our role as part of that family, we will be mentored by extraterrestrials who will sponsor us home.

One of the most difficult challenges for the emerging universal human will be to adopt a loving countenance as we proceed on our journey, despite the pain of our past. This universal human will be able to come and go throughout the universe and will enjoy interplanetary relationships with its inhabitants. And we won't need our governments or NASA to orchestrate this for us. Contactees are already demonstrating to themselves what is possible, and now we are learning to expand on our potential through the mechanics of our expanded spiritual awareness. But we cannot know our divine self, or know the divinity in extraterrestrials, unless and until we're willing to leave the fearful paradigm of our cultural illusion behind. And that illusion requires that we stay angry and wounded. Instead we can let it all go.

This is not merely a suggestion. It may very well be a requirement in starting us on this path of expanded awareness, since the quality of our attitude and demeanor will attract more of the same. Quite simply, if you want to know the higher realms of which enlightened extraterrestrials are part, you must actively be moving towards enlightenment yourself. And the expanded awareness (enlightenment) is no longer invested in judging, making others wrong, or finding a reason to hate anyone.

The state of an emerging expansion in awareness allows one to ponder the perfection of everything and to recognize that what once seemed bad, evil, or wrong, may actually serve a mysterious, yet synchronous purpose towards the evolving perfection of our species. So, we no longer assume that death is bad; we no longer insist that the enemy must be punished; we no longer assume that illness and disease serve no higher purpose; and we don't insist that difficulties are an accident, or that "accidents" need be difficult. We do not assume that one event is horrible and the other event is okay, based merely on the manner in which our intellects process them, because we understand that the intellect isn't the highest authority after all. We don't have all the answers, but we trust that the answers are there, and that things always work out for the best.

This new perspective doesn't indicate that we're satisfied with the state of our world—just the opposite! It does reflect our recognition that change, healing, and transformation occur through the vehicle of love, not anger, and it is not to say that only evolved humans can have encounter experiences. But it does mean that the quality of our relationships with all other beings, including otherworldly beings, is dictated by the quality of our vibrational demeanor. Just as it is possible to "invite" abusive and unpleasant relationships with each other, we can also "invite" that same degree of abuse and unpleasantness with other beings elsewhere. Conversely, we can also know and experience divinity in its highest expression, as demonstrated by evolved beings from elsewhere.

I have received some mail that denounces my claim that extraterrestrials can be enlightened. This response entirely misses the point. For of course, on Earth, as well as elsewhere in the universe, there is the "all" of it. Along the spectrum of experience, everything is possible. My emphasis is on noticing that the majority of humans, and the majority of all other life-forms in the universe, are overwhelmingly peaceful and positive. I'm not arguing that every extraterrestrial is enlightened or that every contact experience is uplifting. It's possible to be enmeshed, embroiled in dysfunction, or "victimized" by anyone, here or elsewhere. The point is that we are individually at cause in the matter, calling to ourselves that very dysfunction by what we are putting out, and thus calling forth, from the platform of our emitting frequencies, the events and relationships that make up our life.

In part, the magnet of our present demeanor determines what we will experience next because we will attract more of what we are, since like energy attracts like energy. This law works in tandem with the biblical teaching that what we reap we will sow; what we put out will return to us in kind, either in this life or in the hereafter.

Those who most vehemently argue against or deny this spiritual tenet are often the very ones who are the most asleep. That's why the contactee takes on the role of pioneer and leader, for we recognize that we can no longer hold ourselves as blameless if we find that we're experiencing victimization and dysfunction in our interpersonal and cultural relationships—or in our relationships with otherworldly beings. We are beginning to apply some of these spiritual axioms to ourselves, our cultural experience, and especially, our otherworldly relationships. "As ye sow, so shall ye reap" (Gal.6:7). We recognize that it doesn't work to condemn another for exhibiting behaviors and characteristics that we don't approve of, for if that other is part of our experience, then we have, at some level, attracted it to ourselves, and must look at that in order to change it. "With what measure ye mete, it will be measured to thee again" (Matthew 7:12).

You better believe that this is a very unpopular stance in the more well-established UFO literature since often, spiritual principles haven't yet been applied to ufology. That is why this very chapter may infuriate you if you're invested in seeing life and your interpersonal and cultural relationships, whether in this realm or another, as having nothing whatsoever to do with the perfection of the soul and the all-knowing wonder of an evolving universe.

When I state that the extraterrestrials are spreading a message of love, forgiveness, and understanding, I'm often met with some of the most heated denouncements, for many of us are extremely invested in the paradigm that furthers ideas of fear. This is the reason, historically, why so many of our most peaceful ambassadors, such as Jesus or Gandhi, have been crucified, murdered, snuffed out. When you encourage fear and hate, you get better approval and a cultural nod. When you suggest that there's something grand going on behind the scenes of our individual and cultural experiences, you're told that you're in denial, brainwashed, or just plain ignorant and uneducated.

To illustrate my point, I'd like to share a letter with you that I received recently from a man who heard me on the radio. The reason that I'm including it here is that his response symbolizes what many contactees face when they come out of the closet. I'm calling on you to be brave and to stand strong with me against the tide of shame and ridicule that you can expect to receive when you start openly speaking up about the divine nature of contact. Keep in mind that I'm not suggesting that you now make this person, or others like him, the new enemy. But I want us to objectively observe how much hate, backlash, and ridicule is stirred up when we merely hold firm to the ideas of peaceful non-judgment, suggestions of loving our universal, and other, neighbors, and above all, the "blasphemous" idea that until we love our enemies, we will not evolve.

Here's the letter that I received, although it's original font was all in capital letters, to communicate the writer's fury.

> Dear Lisette, I listened to you on Art Bell recently. I have been a field investigator, assistant state director, and state director for the state of———MUFON. I have never heard more bullshit in my life. You continually made up crap as you went along. You also are a pseudo-intellectual, using words in the wrong context. Some advice, don't forget your medication the next time you are abducted. Of course, you will

respond by saying that I don't know you, or don't understand. I do understand. You are clearly delusional and need psychological counseling.

Even this letter to me was a gift, for it helps me to clearly define just what I am up to. What I am up to is what all experiencers are up to. We're heralding a new potential for our species and communicating what that path has been like for us. As such, dissent and criticism can be expected when contactees begin to discuss new ideas and offer new perspectives based on their emerging contact with extraterrestrials. If it were easy to speak up, everyone would do it, and frankly, I'm prayerful that more and more of us will. Despite my imperfections and the potential pitfalls of public speaking, I hope to hold myself as an example that you can proceed anyway on this path, understanding that the quality of the message and the manner of the contact may appear to be far from perfect. The communications you receive from the ETs, and your repeating of those messages to the public, may be unpolished. We will stumble and struggle, and make our way as best as we can, but we won't be silenced any longer.

Now, if you happen to have listened to the Art Bell show that this writer was referring to, I consistently reiterated the ETs' message of acceptance, non-judgment, and a suggestion that the universe is safe and so are we. Events surrounding ET contact are admittedly often shrouded in mystery, intrigue, and confusion. Strange things happen when we witness unfathomable scenes during UFO contact, yet it is not a requirement to regard these through the angry, suspicious eyes of our cultural mindset. Yet, ironically, if contactees regard their ET contact through a negative filter, and feel indignant, frightened, and suspicious, this type of response is well received by the media and the "experts." Messages of peace, love, and acceptance often receive the most vehement, hateful response.

Yet individuals who consider themselves to be "on the path" to awakening respond strongly also, but their responses are overwhelmingly ones of congratulations. In fact, after this show aired, my website (www.talkingtoETs.com) received 50,000 visits; 90

percent of the response was "thanks" and "it's about time some-one said it." It looks as though there are quite a few of us who are "uneducated" because we're seemingly deaf, dumb, and blind to our cultural assumptions about such things.

If you've emerged from painful and dysfunctional relation-ships and difficult life experiences, as I have, you may notice that what catapulted you into a higher level of experience was not more fury but, rather, compassion, forgiveness, and understand-ing. Once I deeply recognize that I am a creative participant in every single experience of my life, I am able to place myself more at cause in the matter in changing every experience to one that better "works" for me. When we soften our angry judgments about just about everything, our very lives soften too.

Suppose that you now recognize that you may have latent memories submerged in your subconscious like a splinter. You're ready to consider that perhaps you've already opened to encounter phenomena, but you also recognize that you may be traumatically forgetting the details. As I have discussed, even though the encounter may be generally positive, there may still be some traumatic amnesia surrounding the memory.

Or perhaps you feel that you have indeed been "abducted"—kidnapped—and you don't appreciate me or anyone minimizing or glossing over the pain that you have endured. If you have had vivid encounters and they have not been pleasant, you may be struggling with my suggestion that extraterrestrials can be enlight-ened. In your case, you feel you have been victimized, and your active memories of horrific encounters at the hands of uncaring aliens do not feel part of a "spiritual adventure."

I readily admit that this may not be the book for you if you are invested in upholding our current cultural and world view. This book is about causing certain experiencers to notice that they are spearheading a change in our world view. And the most diffi-cult job at hand is not only to apply these ideas to our relation-ships with extraterrestrials, but also to pause for a moment, back up, and remember that we must also apply these ideas to the events, experiences, and particularly the relationships that make up our "regular" life—the relationships of our childhood, adolescence, and adulthood, for we can't only address one relationship without addressing the others. They're all magnificently interwoven with each other.

So, you may feel that I've stepped on your toes if you're invested in staying pissed off at your parents, your ex-husband, your government, the Iraqis, or the "aliens," because I won't collude with you in finding an enemy in any one of them. That philosophy simply doesn't work in changing anything. Just look at our culture, and our planet, as we get ready to bomb someone else, as we get ready to kill someone else for killing us.

It's not my intention to minimize anyone's past anguish or to be insensitive to those experiences that have been difficult for you. But when we begin to adopt a perspective shift, we are able to grow spiritually, and this is what I am addressing. And you are here reading this, so come with me a bit further. For it is in the process of seeking peace that you will have to come up against the issues of our cultural illusion. And it is an illusion of the first degree to believe that we are "justified" in having enemies in anyone, in this world or another. Of course, you can hate whomever you'd like, and continue to feel that you're justified in doing so. But my point is that this perspective will get you nowhere, fast.

Many of our fellow human beings do not even think encounter phenomena are possible, but for those of us who have traveled that road, or for those of you who would like to, it's time to recognize the unique role that contactees are playing at this time in history, whether or not you feel your encounter experiences have been "good" or "bad," or whether or not you have even had an encounter. If not, there's a good chance you're about to.

I found that I could not progress in my spiritual growth until I forthrightly began to apply certain spiritual principles to the areas of my paranormal experiences—UFO encounters—as well as to my "normal" life.

What I have discovered is that the worst experience that I have lived through, the most heart-wrenching, mind-numbing, burdensome, tortured experience can be flipped over, turned inside out, and be perceived from the viewpoint of a universal being. I am willing to consider that there is perfection to the unfolding of our life's events. Even the worst experiences imaginable bring a gift. As Napoleon Hill said, "Every adversity, every failure, and every heartache carries with it the seed of an equivalent or a greater benefit."

To best illustrate this idea, let's discuss another experience that society would rather not talk about and that could be surprisingly analogous to ET contact, but not for the reasons that you may assume: childhood sexual abuse. Recent studies indicate that a whopping 25 percent of the world's population have been sexually abused as children. And these are only the cases that we know about, so the actual percentage is probably much higher, given the cultural and familial secrecy surrounding it.

One of the reasons that UFO-encounter phenomena, whether "positive" or "negative," and childhood sexual abuse can be analogous, at a very deep level, is that traditionally neither has been recognized as being called to the individual as part of the soul's agenda. From the perspective of our cultural illusion, both sexual abuse and the "alien abduction" version of encounters can be considered victimizing. But if there can be no accidents or random experiences in a spiritual universe, then how can we reconcile those events that we call bad? I believe that all encounter experiences can be spiritual epiphanies. But even the types of experiences that we often view as victimizing, such as encounters referred to as "alien abductions" or even childhood abuse, can also be transformative if we allow them to be. From the perspective of the soul's grander destiny, perhaps even experiences considered to be painful serve some grander purpose.

Although I'm not suggesting that sexual, or other, abuse is a prerequisite for ET contact, I am noticing that many of us who have had contact have also known emotional pain as children. Perhaps that very pain has motivated us to seek deeper answers, and thus, we have set in motion the expansion of our ability towards experiencing more of the universe.

I too experienced sexual trauma as a child, and within the context of childhood trauma, I learned how to access other dimensions in order to escape my inner life—the abuse. Of course, traditional clinicians define this as maladaptive and a possible indication of the presence of a learned dissociative disorder. In other words, depending upon the degree and manner of that dissociation, it is often evidence of an unsound mind.

Despite traditional theories, I'm suggesting that if you've opened to significant paranormal or otherworldly phenomena and experiences (whether or not you label the experience as "positive" or "negative"), it is very possible that you first "discovered" otherworldly realms in the context of significant trauma, abuse, or victimization. But the early childhood trauma is not necessarily "bad" in the long term since it may have served the greater destiny of the soul, individually and as a species. In this light, "learning" how to access other realms is not necessarily an indication of mental impairment, but, rather, it's part of an evolutionary code, ensuring our arrival as an evolved status of beings. When we can access otherworldly dimensions and their inhabitants, we can be mentored by them and finally return to our power base as fully realized spiritual beings.

UFO encounters do not require a pre-existing condition of sexual or other trauma. But when that trauma has existed, the trauma has induced an ability to know and relate more readily to otherworldly life. As a result, sometimes abuse overcomers are not less spiritually aware, but more so. This expanded spiritual awareness paves the way and prepares the initiate for a grander role still, that of a spiritual pioneer who will help our species find its way to the New Land of otherworldly experience.

I am not denying that childhood trauma is terrible at the moment it occurs, and creates hell for the individuals every moment of their lives until they can transcend the experience. But if we choose all of our experiences, then we have also chosen traumatic ones. And why have we chosen them? I contend that these types of traumatic experiences will enable certain initiates to transcend and transform not only the experience, but the world as we know it. The individual who can access the higher realms is more capable, not less capable, of leading us all out of our collective illusion.

One of the tools that will help initiates accomplish this is the learned behavior of dissociation. Psychologist and author

Dr. Martha Stout, in her book *The Myth of Sanity, Divided Consciousness and the Promise of Awareness*, suggests that most of us are dissociating on a regular basis, to some degree:

> Dissociation is a perfectly normal function of the mind . . . which is the universal human reaction to extreme fear or pain. In traumatic situations, dissociation mercifully allows us to disconnect emotional content—the feeling part of our "selves"—from our conscious awareness. Disconnected from our feelings in this way, we stand a better chance of surviving the ordeal, of doing what we have to do, of getting through a critical moment in which our emotions would only be in the way. Dissociation causes a person to view an ongoing traumatic event almost as if she were a spectator, and this separation of emotion from thought and action, the spectator's perspective, may well prevent her from being utterly overwhelmed on the spot.
>
> A moderate dissociative reaction—after a car crash, for example—is typically expressed as, "I felt as if I were just watching myself go through it. I wasn't even scared."

From the perspective of the soul's agenda, how then is all this dissociation serving our species? How might we reconcile the presence of dissociation within the context of the universal law that states that there are no such things as accidents or coincidences?

Suppose that my ability to access another dimension in order to meet extraterrestrials was originally learned as a result of trauma, through the "skill" of dissociation. This would mean that, in the grandest sense, my learned dissociation is not an accident, nor did the emergence of the dissociation simply happen "accidentally" as a coping mechanism that I learned in order to deal with abuse.

Rather, suppose that it's the other way around. I didn't accidentally happen upon the abuse that caused my ability to access other realms; I chose to participate in the "abuse"—from the standpoint of the soul who is all-knowing—so that I could be certain that I'd learn how to access multidimensional phenomena and hence, meet my universal neighbors! And then I could tell all of you about it. Suppose that this is the small role that I have chosen to play in the healing of the world.

Certainly, we can understand this pattern only if we step away from our cultural assumption that we are victims within the nightmare of our cultural experience. Rather, no matter the degree of our protest, we are participants, co-conspirators, and co-creators within the grand thing we're calling a "nightmare," so that we might awaken from the illusion. For this is what evolution is about, and we are all individually and collectively evolving.

But it's very easy to see ourselves as powerless when we've had difficult experiences. In fact, you'll get a lot more cultural support by not confronting the illusion. But if we accept and champion the cultural voice, the general ideas about what's right and wrong, it keeps us stuck in a judgmental stance, which cannot accept the understanding that you and I and all of us have made up the events of our lives for the grandest of reasons. We're habituated to perceive life as a struggle to be survived, and often we don't want to consider that anything else is going on besides the minutiae of the drama and pain of everyday life.

Dissociation may be a key that can unlock the door to paranormal experience, although admittedly, the manner and degree of that dissociation determine if we are functioning well or not. Many people have had to address their exaggerated need to dissociate, wherein that ability has become problematic. If I dissociate during a tender sexual moment with my lover, then my habit of "switching" to "elsewhere"—or perhaps other dimensions—is not serving the moment, but thwarting me. Although my ability to access other dimensions can be a gift in the long run, like anything, if it's turned up too high, it impacts my ability to function.

I believe our lives are about to change forever and what we are all going through right now will bring us to our next evolution. It is because of our turmoil that we will finally emerge from our cultural illusion, because we won't be able to stand the pain any more. As all-knowing, sentient beings, our souls recognize that suffering is precisely one of the tools that we can use to cause the awakening. Calling on extraterrestrials is another way to cause our awakening because their influence helps us to hear the voice of our soul. The soul reminds us that there is a natural order to all things, and when we forgive, we demonstrate our understanding of this.

There can be a secret to suffering: it can propel us to our own healing, but that healing is a greater, more global healing than what we would have achieved without that suffering. Although evolving does not require that we suffer, when we do, we can indeed use it for our soul's purpose. Those of us who know great suffering have something powerful fueling us that will not be extinguished. We have gone through too much, and have come too far, to give up now.

Despite the difficulty in my adult years in sexual experiences as a result of my childhood sexual experiences, my soul has called upon me to heal from these wounds, just as my soul had participated in my calling it to myself in the first place. The transition to understanding and accepting this has not been so easy. I grew up in a paradigm that labels each of us as the good guy or bad guy, victim or victimizer. This is not to buy in to the voice of perpetrators and others who claim that it's the victim's "fault"; rather, it's time to soften the whole idea of "fault" in the first place. For me at least, it's empowering, rather than disempowering, to objectively observe how all of the events and circumstances of my life have led me to this moment.

After I did some preliminary "work" in which I began to find a way to internalize that all men are not abusive, any more than all aliens are, my soul then asked me to consider the impossible: even those others I have deemed "bad" or abusive have served an important role in relation to my soul; further, they have been invited by my soul to do so.

There can be no accidents of the soul. There can be no coincidences either. Either you believe that the universe and all that comprises it is chaotic, disordered, and haphazard, or you believe that there's order, meaning, and synchrony, despite the fact that we may not, on this level, understand the reasons for things.

If I receive a raise or get promoted, if I win the lottery or heal from a disease, then I like to accept that my soul has "created" this, or called it to me. I might even take credit that, on some level, it was my doing. In those cases, I'm proud of my result, confident that I've played some part in bringing the outcome to me.

But what if I experience something that I determine to be "bad"? Then I disown it and reject it out of hand as being no part of my creation. Or, worse, I beat myself up, blaming myself for being a victim of abuse and chastising myself for not avoiding it. Neither extreme is healthy, or even accurate. Notice how inconsistent we are when we change our minds about the nature of how events have shown up in our reality, depending on whether or not we label the event as "bad" or "good."

Childhood trauma then becomes a symbol of that type of experience that most everyone agrees is "awful," in the same way that so many experts in the UFO community agree that alien abduction is "awful."

But suppose that all of what we experience, in the way and the manner that it is experienced, is part of the totality of our soul's blueprint and destiny, the likes of which we may not understand, but we are being caused to heal so that we can grow. And if we decide that we'd like to change those experiences, we may do so, but not because we're the victim of them, but because our free will ensures that we get to decide what it is that we're up to and what we want to do with our "time."

But it will be mighty difficult to change anything, or to choose differently, if you are still operating from within the illusion that believes that you can't. That belief is demonstrated by your judgment of how horrible life can be as evidenced by "wrongful death," "accidents," or the like. How can a death be wrongful when each of our souls is contributing to the orchestration of all of the details of our lives and we're choosing when we arrive here and when we leave? How can abuse be "imperfect" if it propels my soul to know something of the universe and I turn around and help you to know it as well? Suppose, then, we as a group change the world?

From our hurtful experiences, individuals change the course of our societal agenda. A mother who grieves for her child who was killed by a drunk driver single-handedly initiates national legislation addressing drunk driving. Are you of the belief that the child who died and the drunk driver have nothing to do with this? If suffering causes us to enact legislation, to address ways to make changes in the way that our culture conducts its affairs—and eventually helps to heal it from our collective experience once and for all—then who is the "bad guy" or the "good guy"?

We, as a culture, are being asked to take a leap in our evolution by embracing the idea of knowing each other as beloved members of the One Soul. We are not separate physical bodies having nothing whatsoever to do with each other. Instead, we are individual parts of the greater divinity that makes up a divine universe. Like drops of water that originated from the ocean, we still share characteristics with our divine origin even though it may look as if we're separate from it. As such, many of us will have to deal with our negative perception of the "enemy," whether or not the enemy is our sexual abuser, the Taliban, or the "aliens." Before we will be able to grow in spirit, we will have to face the traumas of our past in order for us to grow into our future as evolved beings. Evolving means leaving our present cultural assumptions behind like so much old clothing that no longer fits.

And one of our craziest cultural assumptions that hasn't served us at all is the idea that anger, revenge, and killing each other are leading us out of our mess. And so, we're going to have to stop doing that. We're going to have to start thinking differently of each other and who we are to each other.

Let's let go of our tendency to perceive our life's events myopically. When we are unable to perceive the big picture, we stay fearful and timid because we can't understand the "senseless" acts of violence, upset, and struggle around us. From that stance, we grow careful and cautious, less able to break out of the box and venture forth. Then, year after year, event after painful event, we become so justified in perceiving everything as potentially harmful that we're not experiencing much of anything that's not. Our narrow-minded focus becomes the birthplace of our opinions about everything and we hardly notice anymore that the pace of our spiritual growth has slowed considerably.

Our ability to bond with each other, and our ability to bond with enlightened others who are off-planet, will be the key to our paradigm shift.

If you have already been frightened by what you would deem as negative experiences with otherworldly beings, you too will not be able to broaden your role to that of a universal participant unless you find a way to heal those wounds as well. And in the same way that I must learn to recognize that not all men are potentially abusive or evil, we must also learn to recognize that not all "aliens" are evil, just because there may have been frightening or confusing experiences in our past.

In this context, then, we begin to understand why our species has not yet benefited by more direct worldwide ET contact. We are collectively terrified by what we understand "strangers" to represent, whether those strangers are our fellow humans or extraterrestrials.

Eventually, I chose and "created" relationships with men in which there was no abuse. In fact it felt emotionally healthy, and I was left to dig to the heart of my lingering pain in the context of a "safe" relationship. Once I recognized that my perceptions were driving my choice of men, then I began to have different types of relationships show up in my reality because I ceased subconsciously pushing healthy relationships away. The same can be said of the manners and types of otherworldly relationships that you call to yourself.

Taking it one step further, as a culture, we cannot get on with our collective healthy experiences with extraterrestrials until we unconsciously cease pushing them away from our collective experience.

It is interesting how many people have commented to me that they would love to have more direct contact with ETs, yet almost in the same sentence, they acknowledge that they're frightened of what might happen if they do. This lingering sense of caution is what stands between us and our family reunion with ETs because we're sending mixed messages about what we really want for ourselves.

The only way out of this cautious perspective, which has been continually limiting our spiritual expansion, is to once and for all adopt a mindset that forgives and trusts the process of life itself. As author Wayne Dyer reminds us, despite the wake produced behind the speeding boat, it does not determine the state of the water up ahead. In the end, we are able to reconcile past abuses, trauma, and upset because we begin to trust that there is a lot more "healing" going on behind the scenes than we're aware of.

If each of us has chosen and set up a particular blueprint for our life that is in concert with the blueprint of the universe, then we can relax and enjoy the ride, trusting that we need not fear anything. No matter the bumps and detours, we are right on course.

We are all members of a universal "management team" of souls, arranging a miraculous adventure while we're on the other side, before being born. The biggest illusion of our lifetimes is that we don't believe that we're part of the management team. We think that we've been left out of those decisions. But that's simply not true. It is prior to birth that we choose the main course of our life, and the details and nuances can be addressed, once we're in the physical, from our ability to use our free will. At any time, that course can be altered by the permission we grant through the use of our intention and our will. We are actively co-conspiring the creation of our experiences to help us to progress in our spiritual growth.

The key is to find a way that will help us to let go of our emotional pain through our intention to do so. This way, we will be able to play a larger role as we take this momentous leap in our evolution.

We don't have to have suffered extreme abuse in order to require healing. In addition, we don't even have to have suffered extreme abuse in order to have tasted some degree of dissociative tendencies. Dr. Stout suggests that *most* of us—not just *some* of us—have become well versed in the mechanics of dissociation. Therefore, this raises some interesting questions about what we are all up to, if there's truly no such thing as an "accident." She states:

> We are a thoroughly shell-shocked species. Though we have not all suffered abuse as children, we have all endured experiences that we perceived as terrifying, and that utterly exhausted our tender attempts to comprehend and cope.

From a troubled world that often seems to menace, many of us have absorbed repeated, toxic doses of secondary trauma as well, from people we care about, and even from an impersonal media. And as a result of our histories, and of our inborn disposition to become dissociative when our minds need protection, moderately dissociated awareness is the *normal mental status* of all adult human beings.

The reason I have so much discussion here about dissociation and other "symptoms" that are supposed to be evidential of an unsound mind is that experiencers need not be defensive because they "learned" how to access other realms as a result of childhood dissociation. We are pioneering a new frontier, of which dissociation is often a part. Contactees are pioneers extraordinaire. As such, pioneers end up coming up against entrenched theories of the culture, science, and medicine and those of us who are doing so will be beset with criticism and labels, until the current model is replaced with a more expanded one.

In the meantime, if there is perfection and synchrony to *all* events of the universe, then dissociation may be accomplishing something on an evolutionary scale, despite its controversy and being much maligned by traditional mental health experts.

Dissociation, then, rather than being dismissed as a symptom of trauma or evidence of a mental impairment, might also be viewed as a psychological condition pre-selected by a soul to help find the way to become a more evolved spiritual being. A lot of us may have chosen that doorway.

Who is to say what "strategy" my soul enacted for me as a means for me to meet more of the very spiritual mentors who would one day lead me home? And if I can find my way home, I can return to show you the way too. And you might lead the whole world. Who is to say that you won't?

Consequently, it is not necessary to collude with psychiatry's assumption that, simply because we may have first learned how to meet and know ETs through the mechanics of dissociation, there is something wrong with our minds or we are vulnerable to confusing imagination and reality.

If my emerging awareness recognizes that trauma once happened, that dissociation happened, and that the dissociation that resulted produced more expanded awareness, then I'm advancing in my spiritual growth, not closing down or becoming dysfunctional. Leaps in our spiritual growth are seldom graceful or pretty. So then, on an evolutionary scale, who is to say which symptom is unhealthy and which is sound? Dissociation serves the purpose of helping us to remember our connection to divinity and then return to it.

Now we can get some closure as to perhaps why all that trauma and dysfunction happened to us in the first place. God works in mysterious ways. So do the ETs.

As Dr. Stout suggests, most people on the planet today are functioning in a state of "moderately dissociated awareness." This portends our expanding ability to more easily and readily access multi-dimensional phenomena, and we will eventually not require this "tool" to teach it to us. Essentially, we are moving towards the ability to not need trauma at all to induce the experience. Once mass consciousness shifts and we understand all that we're capable of as spiritual beings, we will no longer need to call upon trauma, for its use will have been served. What we once learned through the experience of trauma, will, on an evolutionary scale, have become unnecessary, and so we can move into a paradigm where it is no longer useful to our species. We will no longer need trauma to teach us how to become multi-dimensional beings.

As a result, who, then, is the bad guy in our culture? Now we begin to understand that each of us is playing the role of a lifetime. The terrorist and even the pedophile become my very teachers, as my soul calls forth those events and experiences that will serve my individual, and our global, mission.

Thus, the paradox is that often, our dissociative abilities have helped us to know otherworldly beings in the first place, and so, ironically, in some strange twist of fate, we have been assisted in our very own evolution by all this upset. In the short term, the intellect uses dissociation to cause us to "forget" what we know. Ironically, this dissociative "tool" that is developed to induce the forgetting actually becomes our long term insurance policy that ensures our ultimate awareness of extraterrestrials. In the long term, the memories bubble up until we're ready to acknowledge them and to integrate the experiences as part of our spiritual growth.

As children or young people, we have utilized this learned ability to actually expand our awareness, although at the time of our trauma, it actually looked as if we were attempting to find a coping mechanism to *contract* our awareness. So what appears to be one thing is actually turning out—on an evolutionary level—to be another.

The challenge now becomes to learn to keep that ability to easily dissociate from expanding to the degree that it no longer serves us. We can use this ability to dissociate as a means to access other dimensions, and then once recognized and comprehended, we can reach these realms and meet the beings who reside there, without having to dissociate at all.

This is why there is always perfection to our every experience. That is why we would do well to cease judging what seems "bad" and to pause with gratitude that we can be trusted to evolve. Each of us can be trusted to find and enjoy the lives of our bliss, and thus to help awaken our paradigm to a spiritually evolved status.

We're recognizing that our dissociative abilities as children or adults may have helped us to know extraterrestrials or other-worldly beings. Our new challenge has become to find a way to stay emotionally and physically connected with other *humans* on this planet, and also with other beings from far-off star systems. Awareness is everything. We are now ready to consider that the dissociative skill which once served us can be viewed as evidence that perhaps we have been preparing ourselves for something stupendous. Perhaps the soul is up to something after all.

Now I am ready to consider the seemingly impossible: before I was born, I knew that I would be placing myself into a neighborhood during my youth where I would be "close" to a pedophile. I chose my family, my extended family, and my neighbors. I knew who they would be before I was born. I know this because during a very moving transcendent experience, I saw a vision of myself within my mother's womb where the unborn child who was me told the "me" of my forties that I was well aware of what I was about to experience. I knew of what those nearby were capable, and the details of what I would endure. I also understood my soon-to-be perpetrator's own traumatic past. And from the perspective of a mature, wise soul (who just happened to look like an unborn child waiting to be born), I was able to forgive the future perpetrators, for, as I would soon be, they too had once been children victimized by another.

We are playing furiously important roles. You are playing one of those roles. At some point, while somewhere on the Other Side prior to conception into this human form, you and I raised our hands when someone asked, "Okay, now who wants to play the role of such and such?" A few of us shot up our hands because for reasons of our own soul's evolution, that role jibed nicely with our soul's goals. Then we had to decide to which parents we would be born. We had a few choices to go over, but based on the agenda of our blueprint, we made certain preferences, for very special, "saintly" reasons. And keep in mind that from the perspective of the higher realms on the "other side," where there is no time, no judgment, and no fear, the events of our lives on the Earth do not seem anywhere near as "traumatic" as they do to us while we are "living" them.

The child born into a family of abuse; the young girl or boy being sexually molested by her father or mother; the unspeakable horrors of the child undergoing severe mistreatment, or maltreatment; the malnourished and suffering; the innocent lives leading a tortuous existence—all cannot be explained away as coincidence or accident. But then conversely, how can any of this possibly be explained away as "perfect"?

Many of us have raised our hands to lead the rest of us out of our quagmire. In order to play our roles with zeal, we first have to remember that we have all chosen the darkness of our pain in order to experience the joy of awakening. We have chosen our slumber so that we can then emerge from our chaos, victorious. For this is what evolution is all about. We have planned our unconsciousness so that we can escape from it. This is part of the plan. It is of what all sentient beings choose to partake. For this is life, that which evolves and changes, and we are now ready to progress to a life that has more of the joyous stuff and less of the drama. All of us will be emerging from our cultural sadness to that of joyous, peaceful beings.

Those of us who have made this choice to be one of the first to emerge from the darkness had to find a way to ensure that we could play the role required of us at this significant time on the planet. Some of us chose trauma so that we would strengthen in order to survive it, and experience more of the universe because of it, and then, when older, we could name it—and then forgive it. We would then model to others how we had done it. In so naming and then forgiving, we are all on the road to being healed.

We are poised to become universal participants. This means that we will be leapfrogging into a future that is hard for many of us to imagine when we're busy paying bills and scrubbing the bathroom. And some of us are doing more than that. We're coping with a job and a family, while at the same time, keeping at bay tremendously painful memories that have been held in the tissues of our cell memory. Many of you have barely survived your own childhoods in this lifetime, and you agonize over your relationships with everyone from your spouse to your plumber, particularly if you've been struggling with issues of childhood abuse.

But that abuse is our insurance policy. While on the other side, we have recognized that shortly we would be entering the world of illusion and loss of awareness of our true spiritual heritage. And so we have wanted a way to ensure that we will evolve, both individually and collectively. Survivors of abuse know better than anyone how to access more of the universe.

When we start to announce that these experiences are possible, we begin to believe that we may really *be* members of the universal neighborhood that we are.

We have called to ourselves an opportunity to learn the skill of dissociation or the ability to access other dimensions, in order to survive, *both in the short term, but also in the long term,* for we experiencers of paranormal phenomena will lead the way home, because we will know how to; we will have had lots of practice accessing otherworldly dimensions and experiences and that very ability will ensure our relationships with enlightened otherworldly beings. Those relationships then, become a source for us to heal ourselves and our planet, for by their very status as enlightened, they will mentor us home to God.

Since there are no accidents or coincidences, it cannot be an accident or coincidence that we have experienced untold emotional and physical pain. And one of the reasons for this choice is to be able, when it's time, to model the role to the rest of the planet as to how to become in touch with our true abilities, while at the same time, forgiving all that didn't meet with our approval.

I would venture to suggest that you have wanted to be one of the humans who would first understand and be able to access other dimensions and otherworldly phenomena. But not just because you're bored, but because you have understood what it means to be a human at this point in history. You have brought yourself to this moment, and have chosen your past so that you'd be sure to get here with all your universal abilities. Through the experiences of your trauma, you have been an unwitting recipient of an amazing ability to participate as a universal being. And once this idea spreads a bit—that there's more to life than what meets the eye—then we can all go to the *next* step in our evolution and begin creating the world of our dreams, with the help of our other enlightened, universal neighbors who have been doing it even longer than we have.

You ask, but isn't there an *easier* way?

Well, yes and no. First you have to define "easy." It's a relative term, isn't it? But yes, some people are leading the way within a different "specialty." Perhaps this time around they're not "doing" sexual abuse, because they did that last time. I know someone who's doing "handicapped" right now. There's dignity and honor in each of our choices. Conversely, there's even dignity in our most unhealed states because through these roles, we can play the role of the "bad guy" and be practiced upon by those we've abused to help others learn to be compassionate and learn to forgive. So yes, even my perpetrator's role has been part of the "recovery"—my own and my species' recovery. And, no, there isn't an "easier" way since each of our souls has a different agenda, and differing ideas about what constitutes "easy" or difficult when it comes to our personal path of growth.

One day we will all look back, recognizing that we *each* had unhealed aspects of self. So you see, every single drunkard and pedophile is an angel in disguise. Even society's most hated is playing a role of the ages. Our enemies are there to be healed. Saddam Hussein exists to be healed. Who will help me model that we are the ones to help heal our own perpetrators and thus, the world?

For reasons of our own destiny, each soul has outlined a different blueprint and each has had to deal with its own issues related to those blueprints. And everyone has an important role to play, not just the Mother Theresas, but also the pedophile, for his actions will ultimately assist me in remembering who I am in the scheme of things, and then I will remind *you*. And then, more of us will more passionately recognize that pedophiles and others are themselves survivors of sexual abuse or other horrors. So why do we want to punish the victim who grew up to be the perpetrator? We must find another way. We cannot bomb the Osama bin Ladens and execute the murderer or abuser if we ever want to heal them and ourselves.

Some have raised their hands when they volunteered to be part of the masses, virtually asleep to spiritual ideas. Some have even become sucked further into their darkness, since they too have free will, and we as individuals who are part of the culture can help awaken the idea that we ourselves once played that "unpopular" role at one time or another. So what would be the best way to help awaken our brethren? With this perspective, we begin to lose our self-righteous indignation. Heck, we might even stop bombing each other.

For the great transition is upon us. Many of us will help lead and others will help us by following. But how can those of us lead who have chosen leadership as part of a soul blueprint, if there's no one to lead? Someone had to volunteer to be the bad guy or the sleeping, working stiff who thinks that an altered state is the next addition to the union after Hawaii and Alaska. Some poor sucker got stuck with the role of the least prestige, at least in the eyes of the world. But behind the scenes it's a different story. We each are playing a role, all orchestrating the grandest awakening in the history of the planet. Why do you think all those UFOs are out there watching us? They've lined up and have the best seats in the house, for they too have a role to play as we begin to recognize *them*.

But we *can't* recognize them until we have begun to recognize *ourselves* as the multifaceted, multi-dimensional spiritual beings that we are. And no matter how politically incorrect it is to suggest it, trauma, particularly childhood trauma and victimization, offers a surefire way to come to that knowing. And while we're at it, we get to deal with other issues of the soul having to do with accumulated karma, and so we have an opportunity to be on the fast track to enlightenment.

But when I speak of karma, I'm not speaking of calling punishment to the soul. It's simply about the choices the soul has made for itself, no matter how unthinkable those choices seem to be. Most of us have such a hard time imagining that we would actually call heartache to ourselves for purposes of evolving our own soul. But some of us have decided that we want to do a lot in one life at this particular time in history, because we want to be part of the transition to that of the New Human, during the time of the Second Generation.

I am not trivializing the effects of childhood trauma or any other abuse or victimization. It is from my experiences that I can dare to offer these ideas, for I have lived them too, and have come out the other side. Has it been easy? No. Was it worth it? You bet. That is my point.

I do feel that there's an appropriate time to be angry and to grieve our painful experiences. Denying emotional pain never healed anything. But there's also time to move to healing, rather than staying stuck in the after-affects of abuse and trauma. At some point we have to insist that we get over it, and move beyond it. But you don't have to if your pain is serving you. In fact, knock yourself out and stay downright furious, or perhaps emotionally numb, for a few decades. But when you're finished with that and you want something else, consider this: there's more still for you to do, and your role is so grand that you won't be able to do it unless you're mostly healed—until you can forgive your past in order to get on with your future. Last time I checked, by example, our spiritual masters weren't furious.

Here's a conversation I had with the extraterrestrials about this subject:

> *So how can I transcend all this emotional pain, if it affects my every waking moment, my relationships, my ability to connect with anyone and everyone? How can I lead anyone out of anything, if I can't even lead myself out of my own dysfunction?*

You will do it through love, since love transcends all pain. That is why this step is so important for you. In these days, the days just prior to your spiritual transformation, you have called on yourself to be here for your world. Does this seem too grand for you? It is not our idea, but yours. You have just asked us to remind you of this, at this particular time in your evolution.

There's a mighty task ahead of you, ahead of all of you. Your entire species is on the verge of awakening to a life that suits your heritage. When you come to these pages, recognize that you have even agreed to be part of reading *this*. You volunteered when someone asked, "Raise your hand if you want to awaken in this way, with a reminder like this."

There are many more inhabitants in the universe than us. Who will meet them as ambassadors for you to herald to the world that we're all out here? This is a team effort, a team adventure. This is one part of the plan; this is but one piece of the solution, and this may be yours, to be part of the ambassadorship of the coming age.

But you will have to address the condition of your heart before you proceed any further. Not the heart muscle as determined by the EEG, but the heart place. Leaders best model to their comrades what they too have achieved and have overcome. There is palpable mistrust and pain among your fellows, but you will be needed to offer a way home. There are many other paths leading to the homeward journey, and others are playing those roles.

This role, though, will require that you model how to overcome the events of your traumatic past—either individually or culturally—in order to continue moving towards your glorious future, having been cleansed of your own grief. And so, your individual ability to transcend grief and trauma becomes a symbol for how you can do this culturally and globally.

This is how you will become more effective at your stated role. If love heals all, then love can heal you, and love can heal your enemy and then your whole world. For you are part of the all.

Down under the blanket of denial runs a river of grief so despairing, that your pain is but a thread compared to the suffering in some areas of the world. So begin to recognize just how mighty this plan is. It involves the coordination of your very galactic neighbors. The angels from on high smile at your readiness. Love your way through this journey. Find what ways you can be healed; find by what means you can heal your wounds, and then get on with it, for there is much to be done, and you are needed with an ability to demonstrate how to love those who are coming behind you. And the masses, billions of your fellows, are coming behind you and are looking to you as an example. Are you ready to show them how it can be done?

You are up to this, for you have volunteered from long ago. Do not be afraid; you can change your mind at a moment's notice, and no harm will befall you. Your path is up to you and each soul takes the twists and turns of its own journey.

But you can do this if you have courage; you can love your way out of your pain by contemplating that love for your world has gotten you this far in the first place.

Love the emerging potential of your whole species, for many of you will model what it means to become alive after years in dormancy. But this dormancy has also been part of the plan as you have rested for your next cue. And here it is, for we too are right on time. Now, with your heart filled with compassion, you can begin to face the demons of your yesterday, whatever demons those are. For even the demons of your path have been demonized by others, for how else have they become wounded? The victimizers have been themselves victimized.

Is this why it's so crucial to learn to heal the most hated among us?

Yes, it's "easier" to love the enlightened. That is why every message of love that's been handed down from the ages has been a reminder to love your *enemy*. Was it your belief that this "enemy" didn't include your pedophiles, or your suicide bombers?

Ironically, many in our culture refer to this "philosophy" as denial.

You have asked for help. And we are helping in the form of this suggestion in that it can change your experience, simply by adopting this perspective. For once you begin to emanate a loving demeanor towards all of your comrades, you will call more experience of a loving nature to yourself. And this same paradigm will be going on with your neighbor, until finally there's more love and compassion being spread among you than there is anger.

Now you are motivated to get on with it, for you have a much broader role to play. You have not wanted to be stuck in mediocrity, but rather, in pushing the envelope of your next experience. That experience will catapult your species beyond your Earth into the waiting hearts of other beings in the universe.

When you adopt the demeanor of love, you emanate an aura that can be felt from light years away and beyond. We can feel that loving aura and we, and others, will be drawn to you for we will know you are now ready for the next step—that of a universal participant.

Bring an open heart to all of the experiences of your life, for love begets love, and a loving nature sets up your next loving encounter. Negativity draws to itself similar energy through the matrix of the universe.

Passionate, energetic feelings of excitement will bring the same. Feelings of victimization, depression, a sense of isolation, bring the same. It is one of the teachings throughout these books, that you are the creator of your experience, including what you call "paranormal" experiences and so recognize from the outset that just like friends that you meet in your neighborhood, the friends that you meet in your universal neighborhood will be drawn to you in resonance of like kind.

But I thought we just established that experiences of trauma have often been called to the self by the soul. So which is it: like attracts like, or the experiencing of trauma and abuse is part of the perfection of the soul's plan?

As difficult as this will be for you to behold, it is both at the same time. Like does attract like through the matrix of the universe, and simultaneously, the soul calls to itself what it will to evolve. It is not your job to dissect this idea, for you are not fully able to analyze this from your status within the illusion. And even though you are discussing these concepts, you are still very much a participant within the illusion. And so, some concepts you can consider, but the intellect will not be satisfied at the explanation, for the area is outside of that which the intellect accepts as "real." Hence, historically, new ideas receive the most attack.

Exactly. Just as Galileo was deemed to have an erroneous belief, by a culture that believed that the sun rotated around the Earth, until it became widely accepted. But even that cultural acceptance came long after well-documented evidence to the contrary had been published. In 1600, the scholar Giordano Bruno publicly disagreed with the culture's dogma, was convicted of heresy, and burnt at the stake.

Yes, and the public shaming and ridicule you and other contactees receive are your culture's version of being burnt at the stake.

That's not encouraging to continue speaking up.

But it's a small price to pay for setting the example, and leading others on the road to recovery.

Being burned at the stake is a small price to pay? What, are you kidding?

Do you realize that when you once raised your hand to "volunteer" to be a child who would experience sexual molestation at the hands of another, other souls cringed at the very idea?

Are you suggesting that childhood abuse is our modern-day version of being burned at the stake?

Not the experience itself, but the backlash of public scorn, shame, and ridicule that is engendered as a result of your raising your hand and stating that you've experienced something that's not supposed to be happening. For that matter, offering any idea that's different from the norm can feel threatening. Coming out in the open from any given closet and agreeing to succumb to the onslaught of public criticism, judgment, scrutiny, and scorn is your version of being burned at the stake.

Well, it doesn't feel that great while it's happening, although it's not that bad, I guess. I can handle shame and ridicule, but I'd rather not be burned at the stake. As it turns out, I can see how the more powerful the message, the more it actually elicits ridicule by "society." Historically, why are they both so intrinsically linked?

Because the mind is extremely invested in its beliefs. When you drop the investment in a cultural belief, you no longer feel offended, affronted, triggered, or bothered simply by hearing of another viewpoint. You would simply shrug your shoulders and say, "Okay, that's a crazy idea, and it's not for me." Instead, the degree of your reaction will indicate the degree of the mind's investment in the illusion. That's precisely when the guillotine is set up, and the hate letters are generated.

Gulp.

No need to be afraid. Remember, all of the experience called to you by your soul is serving the grander plan.

Why doesn't that comfort me?

Experiencing the ravages of childhood sexual trauma, or other challenges, takes fortitude to heal and transcend. You'd be surprised to hear how many of you who have experienced childhood abuses were also burned at the stake or tortured for your beliefs in other lives and who are now, or will be, contactees. For what do you think you have been preparing yourselves?

The connection between all of these experiences is about strengthening your understanding of who you are. Any "experience" called to the soul by the soul is not an accident or a coincidence.

Eventually, you understand that you cannot be harmed. There is nothing that anyone can do to hurt you, for your body is only a transient article of clothing.

And thus, at this time in your evolution, you are prepared to confront the ultimate cultural voice that states that either: (a) other life-forms don't exist in the universe or (b) if other life-forms do exist, they're evil and not to be trusted.

You have gained much experience through all of your lives by calling experiences to yourself in which your "reputations" have been scandalized and ridiculed. You have learned to readily allow your message to be assaulted, for the soul has no need or requirement for "reputation." The souls of you are leading the way to a different paradigm, not your reputations.

Allow love to calm the ripples and settle over the waterfront of your life. Here, the boat glides freely along the glassy surface. You no longer need the turbulence of your sadness or angst to propel you forward. You need only the gust of your intention to blow the sails of your experience to a new tomorrow. This way, you can transform your normal, or your paranormal, experiences. There is no distinction between how your worldly relationships or your other-worldly relationships are created and maintained. Feel free to mold the future of your desires.

You are not a stray leaf upon the river. You are the river itself. Bring the leaf to where it best suits you now.

Part Three

Expand Your World View

Step 4: Celebrate Family Reunions

Despite physical and other differences, extraterrestrials and humans share a bond as family members despite our doubts because we appear so different. Encounter experiences serve to help us "celebrate family reunions." Encounters return us to our universal connection, but first we must notice our tendency to mistrust and be frightened by those who appear different from us in appearance, manner, and custom. Extraterrestrials stand to be humanity's greatest purveyor of spiritual mentoring, if we can refrain from being suspicious and fearful of those who seem different from us, whether human or extraterrestrial. Ultimately, there is little difference between any of us.

For one and a half years, I had the exquisite opportunity to work as personal assistant to Neale Donald Walsch, best-selling author of the *Conversations with God* books. Neale and his wife Nancy, and the staff of his organization (The Conversations with God Foundation) quickly became family to me. Yet as it turned out, I couldn't stay long since I decided to move to the Boston area, so that I could enroll my son in a wonderful private school. Later, when I was offered a position as sales director at Hampton Roads Publishing Company, I faced the daunting challenge of relocating my teenage son again, but this time, from Massachusetts to Virginia.

But after exploring schools, we settled upon one that was located in another state altogether. It was the first time as a parent where I would not mother my son on a day-to-day basis. But since his new school offered a unique educational setting, one that wasn't duplicated in many areas of the world, we were both willing to figure out a way to make it work. As a result, he now lives with a host family, something like the arrangements made for foreign exchange students. Periodically, he catches a train home to see me.

When he came to visit last month, I hadn't seen him for a while. Since I had been a single mom most of his life, our new living arrangements were still a bit strange to me. Although we were both delighted with how happy he was at his new school, it felt a bit weird to be suddenly divested of my daily responsibilities as a mom. It was as though I was dealing with the sudden departure of a young man going off to college, but in his case, he was only sixteen. I hadn't yet gotten used to the idea of us living apart, nor that literally overnight, I was no longer grocery shopping for a finicky teenager, acting as soccer mom, or operating mom's taxi service. In essence, I am no longer part of my son's everyday life, although we speak regularly by phone. Now, our time together during our monthly visits is far more emotionally potent than it would be if I saw him every morning and evening.

I stood on the platform as his inbound train rolled into the station. My eyes filled with tears at the prospect of giving him a great big hug. As he stepped from the train, he bounded towards me in his tall, lanky form, with his trademark skateboard and helmet dangling from his backpack. As he swung around to give me a hug, he clumsily just barely missed sideswiping an elderly woman with his skateboard. But the woman—and I—instead was curiously examining his freshly dyed, neon blue hair. After our hug, I nonchalantly scanned him for body piercings or tattoos.

As many parents of a teenager can probably understand, I'm now getting used to the idea of my son's expressing and exploring his independence. And sometimes, his interests—or his very appearance—may start diverging from my own. My son is wonderfully confident and exhibits a mature, kind strength of character far exceeding his age, and he has demonstrated that he's capable of my trust, and of handling the responsibility required of a young man who is not under my watchful eye every day. I could only pray that the blue hair thing was just a phase.

Despite his azure mop top, he is still my kin, and no matter our differing hair tones, eye color, or other evidence of our differences, I was caused to notice that we still share a deep bond, the kind that families share. No matter how much time passes between our visits, our family reunions are joyous.

Reminiscent of the bond that we share with our human family members, our relationship with certain of our *universal* family members can and does have the same feeling of connection to it. Rather than holding at bay other beings who may look and act very different from us, in essence, our UFO contacts and experiences actually function as *family reunions.* In this context, then, *we're beholding our own kin,* loved ones whom we haven't seen for a while, but those with whom our souls recognize a deep connection.

Yet, when we react as the UFO literature says that we should—when we habitually think of these other beings in our galaxy as weird-looking "strangers" that we have not yet met—we perpetuate our cultural illusion that we're all separate from each other. Indeed, we may very well have forgotten our connection to ETs, or we may sense there is one, but when we begin to recognize that otherworldly beings are very deeply connected to us individually—no matter what they look like—the nature of our encounters will expand in scope.

In actuality, not only are extraterrestrials kin, but in most cases, they also function as our beloved spiritual mentors. Not only are we deeply connected through a mysterious tie that goes beyond "blood," but our souls recognize that our willingness to open to contact with evolved beings ensures our own evolution. As a result, we would be well served to recognize that we have outgrown the old paradigm of perceiving "sky people" as "strangers" or potential victimizers.

The word "stranger" no longer fits this changing paradigm. We're beginning to suspect that we may not remember all that we know. Consequently, if we are stirred by the thought of contact with ETs, then we may already have met them, but don't remember doing so. If the word "stranger" no longer describes other-worldly beings, then let's stop using the word "alien" and other synonyms to describe them. It would serve us to drop the idea that they *are* strangers, and instead consider them to be the kin they are. Consider the *Random House Webster's College Dictionary* definition of the word:

> **Stranger:** 1. a person with whom one has had no personal acquaintance. 2. a newcomer in a place: a stranger in town. 3. a person who does not belong to the family, group, or community; an outcast.

If extraterrestrials, and our relationship with them, serve the highest agenda of our souls, then they are hardly strangers. If there is an important soul connection with these enlightened beings for the purpose of our individual and group evolution, then we had best drop the notion that we need to "learn" to develop the tools to feel close to them, and instead recognize that our souls already do. It is our *intellects* that object. We have a situation in which the soul waits patiently for the mind to "catch up" in its understanding that we're all part of a universal family.

The fact you are intrigued with this book and others like it suggests that your soul knows something that your mind may not comprehend.

Here is a letter I received from a young man who, like many others I have heard from, recognizes that something deep is stirring within him, but can't quite put his finger on what, or why.

> Dear Lisette, I am eighteen years old, and since I was a little boy I have had recurring feelings of "something isn't right" itching at the back of my head. I remember seeing my first UFO in broad daylight when I was seven years old. I have bits and pieces of memories of seeing them earlier than

that, however. When I was about ten years old, I was walking through the public library and I saw a book on the shelf turned spine out, entitled, *Communion*. As I read the title, I thought to myself, "What's a book about religion doing here?" and I picked it up. As I did so, the moment I saw the face of the ET on the cover, my breath literally flew right out of my chest. My heart seemed to stop beating, and I dropped the book in fright.

For the next three days I could not sleep, during which time I was extremely paranoid, especially at night, even though I had not read the book, nor did I intellectually understand what the ET's face had triggered in me.

Throughout my life, I have had vivid dreams about seeing gigantic UFOs or of seeing aliens in my house, and I've had many episodes of sleep paralysis—at least that's what I think it is, since I'm in a state in which I'm not really awake, but not fully asleep either. But even though I have grown up with *The X Files* on television and all the familiarity with the face of the gray alien, my strange memories and reactions don't add up to me, since I was raised by parents who were devoutly Christian and sheltered me from "scary" shows.

What I'm trying to say is that it seems to me that there's no rational reason to be afraid of that alien face on that book cover on that fateful day in the library as a small child, nor do I have any reason to think I had really witnessed UFOs. I have tried to talk to my parents about this, and my mom has always seemed terrified of the subject. When I was very young, I remember my sister and I saw a UFO one night while we were outside on the steps of our house. When my sister cried "Look, Mommy, a spaceship!" my mother began to panic and started fumbling with her house keys. My dad tells a story from his own youth about a "frog man" who came into his bedroom when he was very small and sat on the edge of his bed poking repeatedly at his feet. So my question is what does this all mean, if anything? I would appreciate any reply you can offer.

As this young man describes, opening to contact—returning to the family reunion of our universal connection—has significant challenges. But the emotional and physical challenges of opening to contact are what step 4 suggests, part of a grand family reunion. One of the biggest hurdles to overcome is that we usually don't recognize that reunion for what it is or that we're even opening to contact in the first place. One of the surest indications that we have is our reaction as our memories are triggered. Those memories can be from this life, or from our soul agreements made long ago.

But despite the self-doubt and self-questioning that it induces as we notice our strange reactions, it is a vital process heralded by the bravest among us. This young man, then, although he doesn't yet recognize it, may be one of many who are blazing the trail for the rest of our species. If he is brave enough, and continues to grow at the behest of his soul, rather than shirking from expansion at the behest of the fearful intellect, he will be justly rewarded. For those who are given a lot have a lot to give.

Each generation, starting with younger and younger souls, is less willing to adopt the cultural fears and assumptions of it's predecessors. This spark of curiosity within them and others is the insurance policy of our species, as individuals like him dare to lead us down a different path which involves a different experience. This is why our futures need look nothing like our present. Our present cultural experience where children die of starvation and we kill others who disagree with us can change overnight, because we humans are changing overnight.

We are so much more than we think that we are. Relationships with enlightened beings can take us further than we've ever dreamed possible, if we will but let ourselves spread wings and fly. For this reason, step 4 is offered as a stepping-stone along the way towards the evolving perception of our universal neighbors because the quality and quantity of any experience are birthed from our thoughts, from our imagination, and from our prevailing ideas about a thing. Conceiving of ETs as universal siblings sets up the type of encounter that we will invite. When we choose to celebrate family reunions, our soul and the souls of the ETs orchestrate a way to bring us together again.

This change in context will, in effect, change everything. It did for me years ago, when I first came face-to-face with extra-terrestrials. Initially, I was frightened as I beheld otherworldly beings before me. But soon, fright gave way to an inexplicable sense of love and connection, a bond that broke all the rules—"rules" that are so frequently published in the UFO literature, and promulgated by Hollywood. Not only do I *not* feel that I have been "abducted," but in fact, I feel that I have stumbled upon my very *family*—albeit, my long-lost family whom I had not seen in years—and that reunion has been extraordinary. The emotional punch behind our meetings has been both surprising and wonderful, all at the same time.

This very unmistakable sense of *family* with these beings is what is so intriguing about opening to contact. Once my mind overcame its upset, my *feelings* told me something about my connection to them. No one had given me a script telling me who to love, or why. I just felt it, strongly. As my initial surprise dropped away, a sense of a deep connection between us emerged, one that could not be broken, despite others' criticism or concerns for my safety or sanity.

And no matter the "time" between our visits, these extraterrestrials, like the heartfelt connection to my son, remain with me in my heart. All of these "reunions" become charged with the same stuff of love that I feel towards other souls who are dear to me and to whom I refer as "family." In the end, I have let go of my knee-jerk reaction to extraterrestrials' appearances, as I've done with the knee-jerk reaction to my son's blue hair. I now recognize that physical differences need not perturb me. In addition, we can let go of our knee-jerk agreement with the UFO culture, or the reaction of our own intellects, that insists that aliens are our next enemy.

This tendency to be offended by others at the drop of a hat, whether those others are from this world or another, is nothing more than a cultural habit.

Most of us don't recognize our habit of criticizing each other on a regular basis, although this is not the natural state of things. Since we are spiritual beings living in a spiritual universe, experiencing a profound sense of connection to otherworldly beings is a symptom of a spiritual expansion, not brainwashing, naïveté, or stupidity. It is the natural state of things when we love one another. When we leave our cultural illusion, we recognize the deep connection between souls everywhere, no matter our differing neighborhoods. We are tied by a kinship of universal brotherhood that becomes palpable when experienced.

This, then, is a telltale symptom of knowing one's universal connection, for the trials of our earthly concerns and shallow judgments fall away with our clothing, even if we have to wade through initial discomfort to get there. Suddenly, we sense that we are all beings of the One Source, all sharing a connection to the cosmos.

But initially, when faced with the encounter experience, our rational minds are strongly confronted and the "critics' committee" attempts to step in and supervise. It often mimics the greater cultural voice which tells us that we mustn't trust those who are different from us; we mustn't love too deeply; and most importantly, if we've been hurt or betrayed before, we ought to be very careful this time around, particularly when that "other" bears very little physical resemblance to us. But these objections can be quickly overcome as the agenda of the soul steps in, leading our minds beyond its resistances.

So how can I expand my circle of relationships to my universal brethren when I'm still struggling to connect and bond with my human brothers and sisters?

Many of us don't trust love or the intimacies of family ties in *this* world, let alone another. The answer is to recognize that a bond already exists between all of us, whether or not we remember those ties.

We're all capable of projecting our unhealed stuff onto someone else, whether or not that someone is our lover or an extraterrestrial. If you don't think humans tend to project their fear-based mentality onto otherworldly species, just visit a UFO convention. Rarely do we recognize that, by habitually conceiving of ETs as evil, manipulative, or victimizing, we're often merely projecting our own exploitative qualities on to them. And the more individual, unhealed issues we each have, the greater the tendency to perceive of another as the new "bad" guy of the moment. "Aliens," in case you haven't noticed, have become the latest target of prejudice and subconscious projection.

This suggests that our unhealed issues will definitely impact the way that we conceive of our otherworldly encounters. It is why, if you are motivated to expand your spiritual base to know other dimensions and the beings who inhabit them, the context of your experiences will be greatly influenced by whatever colored glasses you are looking through. For this reason, it will be difficult to consider ETs as your extended family until you address those issues that might prevent you from doing so.

Whatever the circumstance that set up our mistrust, we must commit to learning to love and trust again if we are to grow spiritually, and to expand our lives beyond suspicion and fear. We're not only learning to love and bond with those of our same species, we're also being encouraged by this step to go one step further and, while we're at it, throw into the mix otherworldly beings by calling on extraterrestrials.

As a result, step 4—Celebrating Family Reunions—is more challenging than it first appears, since so many of us are still struggling with how to feel this way towards humans, let alone extraterrestrials. But when we recognize that there is a divine plan to all experience, despite our present individual and global dysfunction, then we are able to feel centered, trusting that we are right on course, no matter what has happened in the past.

One of the most difficult divine dichotomies to hold in one's consciousness is that we are contributing to all of our life's events, yet at the same time, there is no personal "blame" for having contributed to those events. So there is a mental challenge that I will need to reconcile before I can get on with my life—or even with this step. As such, I will need to pass this mental struggle through the sieve of my new perceptions in order to come out the other side.

Heretofore, my struggle has been this: how can I have been deeply affected by having been a child of sexual molestation, while at the same time, not have bought into guilt that suggests I should blame myself for having been victimized?

Children of childhood trauma—and all of us who have been emotionally damaged by terrorist activities, an increase in crime, or just plain lack of joy—are sometimes tormented by an unstated assumption that we're at fault, somehow being responsible for all of our tortured pasts, even our own parents' divorces. So how can we reconcile our new understanding that we knew about, and therefore didn't stop, childhood or adult difficulties, if I'm suggesting that we chose our soul's destiny before birth? I posed this very question to the extraterrestrials:

If I recognize that I've selected all of the experiences of my life, how can I address my tendency to feel that I'm to blame for my dysfunctions resulting from those choices?

You don't consider that the "abuse" itself can be part of your healing.

Many might feel that this is an outrageous statement. It implies that our perpetrators and/or co-perpetrators are right, that our abuse is "good" for us.

What has brought you to your torment, and more importantly, that which will bring you through to the other side of that torment, will be the very characteristic that you are developing that will heal both you and your world. This is not to say that surviving abuse is the only way to enlightenment, nor is it a requirement for growth. It is just one of the ways, and many of you have chosen that way, for the reasons previously mentioned.

We recognize the stigma in suggesting that "atrocities" such as childhood sexual abuse or terrorism should be perceived as serving some higher purpose.

Yes, it almost sounds like you're suggesting that our criminals are actually our heroes.

When you recognize that nothing is by accident, then you will be compelled to consider the greater meaning and purpose behind all that you consider to be "accidental," abusive, or victimizing. If there are no coincidences or accidents, then what has been served by abuse, pain, and suffering? Suppose that, one day, from your status as enlightened beings yourselves, you reflect upon your cultural past to see that your suffering was that which actually woke you up?

But our species has had plenty of suffering since the beginning of time. What's different now?

Collectively, the *timing* of your evolutionary jump is what is different, and what is now upon you. Although you don't recognize it, everything up to this point has readied you for this moment. Your readiness to emerge into your expansion is what is being addressed here. You will then lead the rest of you, as you are doing.

All of your suffering has not been in vain, but will propel you to the point where suffering is no longer part of your daily experience. Yet we understand that within the context of your cultural understanding and assumptions, this mindset seems impossible.

Most people will have a hard time accepting why an innocent young child would choose torture, or any derivative thereof, whether or not there are "long-term" benefits.

Jesus chose the path that he did. In his own way, from the perspective of his own soul's agenda, he created a life that inspired others to, among other things, recognize that he was more than his body, and by implication, so are you.

So then it's his own fault that he was crucified?

Suppose you decide to become a volunteer for the Peace Corps and you travel to the far regions of Africa, working with the impoverished and diseased. While there, during your tenure as a Peace Corps volunteer, you contract a disease yourself; suffer some horrendous abuse; are raped, or you're murdered or die while in the midst of a local military skirmish. Is it your "fault" for having suffered and died? Are you to "blame" for causing these events to yourself? As your family and your hometown newspaper account the story of the events surrounding your death, imprisonment, or suffering, does anyone suggest that you "deserved" the pain or torment that you suffered because you originally volunteered for the mission in the first place? No. In fact, usually the opposite is the case. The "victim" is heralded as the brave and courageous angel that she or he is, having risked life and limb to serve a greater purpose.

Others of you also select "horrendous" events, the experiencing of which catapults your spiritual growth for having endured them and then transforming despite them. As such, you are some of the more hearty volunteers. There is no other way to describe this.

But studies show that society's criminals are usually children who have suffered the most abuse. So their abuse hardly "helped" their spiritual growth or society's, if they're wreaking havoc on the rest of us.

Considering the numbers of you who have experienced extreme suffering and trauma as children, those who lash out at society still represent a minor segment of your total population who have also suffered trauma.

But those "few" do so much damage.

This may seem to be the case in the short term, but they will provide you with unforgettable examples of how your society is delaying transformation by the manner in which you are addressing them through your laws and attitudes.

These abusers, whether pedophile or terrorist, represent the group on which the rest of you can direct your spiritual practices. How can the rest of you learn to forgive and learn to heal others, if there is no one on whom to practice?

Yes, because they're society's most hated. People see them as causing all our problems.

The state of your world simply suggests that you've decided collectively to up the stakes.

What do you mean? Are you suggesting that even the present chaotic state of our world is somehow part of a grand orchestration? It's hard to believe that our souls are choosing all this.

Now, more than ever, there are more of you to model forgiveness because more and more of you have been "harmed." You are the ones who stand to make the most impact by your own example.

My eyes filled with tears as you said that.

Potentially, millions of you can have the impact that Jesus did, when he modeled the way of the peaceful, spiritual being, no matter what is going on around you, or happening to you. If you stay in your peace, the world will heal faster than if you react and respond with the opposite. Of course, you don't believe this, but it is the case.

Who then becomes the most potent candidate to teach love and forgiveness? Those of you who are victimized but still model "forgive them for they know not what they do" will teach a new paradigm by your own example. The story of how Jesus taught this even as he was being crucified is still being told among you, even after thousands of years. At some level, you suspect that this demeanor will save you. It is an illusion that you can only be safe if you create safety through violence.

But do you agree that not all victims of abuse and trauma evolve beyond it? Some stay messed up their entire lives, often becoming violent themselves.

Your soul recognizes that certain pre-birth selections carry more inherent "risks" than others. But that recognition does not stop the soul from offering the opportunity for growth anyway. Certain events and circumstances do hold more "risk" than others, and those of you who choose those events and circumstances choose them for a reason. So the "risk," then, is that you will disconnect and learn to hate as a result of your trauma, rather than transcending those experiences, at least in the short term. Even so, the criminal's status does not prove that the most challenging opportunities for growth have been in vain. In fact, even in that "failure," there now exists a new opportunity for others to forgive and heal *him*.

There is often emotional, spiritual, and psychological fall-out inherent in participating in certain missions, just as when you first decided and embarked upon the journey to Africa as that Peace Corps volunteer. Yet your simply volunteering does not make your mission less noble, nor does it suggest that the event was for naught if you suffer because of it, or even turn to violence as a result of having experienced it. For there is more to your soul's experience than simply suffering.

You have chosen that expedition to the far reaches of that foreign continent for a reason. The details of that reason are very personal and pertinent to the soul, and are always interwoven within a broader, global movement towards your evolution, personally and culturally.

Each small role we play imbues the greater good, for we all are evolving home. Simply becoming aware of your volunteer status before birth does not mean that there is cause for self-blame or self-loathing or, for that matter, that somehow the road that you have struggled through has been less virtuous. All of your roles are virtuous, for you are all participating in the grand plan.

Some roles, at one time or another, are more fraught with land mines, discomfort, and physical pain at least until you change your paradigm completely. But this does not mean that somehow it is a self-punishment. Such circumstances have not been chosen by the soul for reasons of self-punishment. It is a volunteer mission, whereby you take on a role that you feel you are ready to handle, and that role can produce all manner of threads that eventually will make up the finished fabric of your, and your species', next jump ahead to spiritual enlightenment.

Reconciling the idea of suffering is difficult for you, particularly when we suggest that those who experience great suffering and trauma, have, at some level, chosen these events. You have a difficult time reconciling the words "victim" and "volunteer." But there is no difference; there needn't be a difference, for all of us are volunteering on these paths, and in these roles, even the victim of the most horrendous outcomes.

The reasons are complex, but if you stop, look, listen, and feel, you will find indeed that suffering is not in vain, but is leading you towards your next step in which there can finally be less suffering. For your own experiences are making it so and making this possible.

So-called "victims" of terrorism or abuse, are not "at fault" because they may be aware before birth of that event that is to come. That knowing does not make them "at fault" for their pain and suffering, any more than a Peace Corps volunteer is "at fault" for the outcomes of volunteering in the first place.

Many such volunteers have staggering levels of bravery and courage, and sometimes they *loan the experiences of their own life to your culture in order to bring about an eventual paradigm shift.* Eventually, through the volunteer missions of such "masters," society will be caused to notice something about itself. From this noticing laws change, paradigms shift, and enlightenment achieved. How then has this volunteer's life been in vain? How then can this life be said to have been wasted? There is perfection, even in the seeming imperfect.

But suppose I'm adversely affected as a result of those very experiences for which I volunteered? Some of us can't seem to live as full lives as we'd like to because we've suffered trauma. How then is it virtuous to be miserable?

Many of you are indeed holding on to the vestiges of trauma, and it's time now to let it go. And then you will be poised to kneel upon the rocky road to help your younger sister find her way home. What nobler path is there than that? You who have suffered, more than others, grasp just what it will take to lead your civilization out of its quagmire for good.

Are you suggesting that survivors of trauma are our next spiritual leaders?

Yes, if you can reconcile your past suffering, let go of your anger, and become ready to play your next role, which is to lead the way to healing by your own example, and then to transform.

That's a strange idea, especially in light of what clinicians have historically said about what trauma produces. Survivors of abuse are supposed to be weakened emotionally and psychologically. We're almost clinically suspect. We're hardly viewed as sages in the raw but, rather, as basket cases in the raw, having latent symptoms of post traumatic stress disorder.

And yet being in a state of "raw," as you call it, places you at your most vulnerable. The state of vulnerability is from where you will expand your spiritual growth, for your walls of Jericho have come tumbling down, and the rational mind is momentarily quieted. It is no coincidence that your society applauds just the opposite: your most hardened and powerful political and business leaders are most admired by the cultural voice, whereas the most sensitive and compassionate among you are considered the most insignificant and weak.

To arrive at a state of vulnerability and sensitivity often produces a willingness to see life differently. It enables you to know who you are, for you may come to recognize that all of you share one soul. This knowing will ensure your next leap in evolution.

The psychologist and author Dr. Martha Stout suggests that her most traumatized and victimized patients seem to emanate an unmistakable light. She says of her interest in working with them therapeutically:

> I believe I was drawn to them for their fire. The honest, purposeful self-examination of a traumatized life creates a heat so exquisite that it burns away the usual appeasements, self-deceptions, and defenses. "What is the meaning of this life?" becomes a very personal question, and demands an answer. Some of the people I have known have burned so fiercely that they have gone all-stop, have quit their jobs, even endured temporary poverty, because answering the question consumed more energy than can reasonably be generated by a solitary individual. . . .

Perhaps when adults survivors of trauma attempt to answer this question, all of society benefits. Dr. Stout continues:

> . . . As I listen to the telling of a personal history, more often than overt "symptoms" it is just such Faulkneresque understatement of the sometimes macabre, along with the burning light in the eyes, and the cunning humor, that makes me begin to suspect extreme trauma in the individual's history.

As a psychologist, and as a human being, I am impressed with the irony that these severely traumatized patients, people who have been through living nightmares, people who might blamelessly choose death, often emerge from successful treatment by constructing lives for themselves that are freer than most ordinary lives from what Sigmund Freud, a century ago, labels as "everyday misery." They become true keepers of the faith and are the most passionately alive people I know.

So I asked the ETs:

I suppose all this is suggesting that it is this degree of passion that is necessary to make changes. If trauma and suffering have somehow readied all of us unwittingly for yet a grander role to come, then we have been preparing to take our next huge evolutionary leap. Still, we will have to get over our issues before we can evolve. How are we to do this? Some of us are still pretty affected.

Your job is to become willing to recognize that if you are connected to your experiences and if you have been part of their orchestration, then you are also capable of their resolution.

I've never really thought about it that way.

Every one of you has the strength and ability to transcend the fallout from traumatic experiences in order to bring yourself to your next evolution, although granted, this is where many of you become stuck. You have simply given up, staying in your individual and culturally dissociated conditions. You do not need to, any more than you need to stay in Africa as a Peace Corps worker. Having once volunteered and participated, there is a time for recognizing that one's mission is over, and another mission is beginning.

I think we've gotten sidetracked. This whole discussion started because of this particular step 4, in which you're suggesting that we recognize our contacts as the family reunions that they are. Discussing this launched me into recognizing that most of us don't even consider our own relatives as dear family, let alone extraterrestrials.

How better to arrive at a state of connection with us, than to practice feeling a state of connection with each other? And conversely, how can you better practice honoring those who are different from you, than by leaping ahead and practicing relating to others and loving those who appear to be drastically different from you? Of course, as you move into this knowing through these relationships, you recognize that there is no difference at all between us.

Your relationship with us will help you to do just that, for if you can reconcile who we are to you, then you can reconcile who every other being is to you. Getting to know us, then, represents the ultimate training in your remembering that all beings, all souls, are interconnected. You are not being asked to simply work on knowing *us* as family, but to step onto the path that will assist you in recognizing that each one of us is family. Only here, your knowing us as family will trigger your soul memory that there is a grand orchestration of which we are part, and you are part, and your every neighbor is part. Knowing us as family instantly expands your understanding and triggers your soul memory of all that you are engaged in, within the context of your evolutionary blueprint. If you can know *us* as family, you will surely know another as family, for you will have finally seen the forest instead of the trees. You will have seen your very planet from the perspective of the universe. Now you understand why your own astronauts are forever changed by having this new context.

Okay, but what of those of us who are still messed up?

In the example of the Peace Corps volunteer, when you return to camp, or to your homeland, exhausted and weary, perhaps even injured or damaged, it is necessary to tend to your physical, emotional, and spiritual needs. This means that it is your responsibility to identify and pursue all of the modalities of healing that might fit your personal soul's characteristics. Simply because you embody symptoms of trauma does not mean that you must remain shell-shocked.

Instead, transform. You do not need to remain weary and affected, holding your baggage of emotional distress. There are avenues of healing available that can help you to let them go. It is not a requirement to remain unhealed, even if you have volunteered for a great mission. It is not a requirement that you remain distressed and triggered by every event in your life.

In fact, just the opposite is the case. It is your responsibility to rise in inspiration and find and locate that way and manner, those other people, healers, modalities, other sources, or differing paths that enable you to fully heal so that you can model to others that you have done it.

And more importantly, once this has occurred, then you can forgive. You can forgive all of it. You can forgive Africa for being a part of your distress. You can forgive Africa for being impoverished in the first place and requiring your help. You can forgive anyone and anything that you feel is responsible for impoverishing you. You can forgive yourself for taking yourself there in the first place. And then, those who are still spiritually impoverished and are acting as such will benefit from your sainthood for you are tending finally to the wounds of your unhealed aspects, individually and globally, and you are thus tending to theirs.

This way, the last will become the first, for you are now leading the rest of you.

Step 5: Be the Expert

Experiencers of extraterrestrial contact are the new experts of encounter phenomena, not the academicians, researchers, and scientists. The contact itself serves as contactees' "credentials," even though our insight may diverge from currently accepted scientific assumptions. Those who personally experience ET contact are best suited to "be the expert," in determining what that contact has meant to the growth of their own soul.

The media, the press, and all of society tend to defer to what the experts have to say about something when they're looking for the "truth" about anything. Interestingly enough, that "expert" does not usually have firsthand experience in the subject at hand, but instead, is considered credible based on research, education, publications, and credentials. Despite the claims and experiences that are reported by tens of thousands, and even millions, of individuals, "new" ideas and concepts will not receive academic or societal acceptance until the scientists approve. Ironically, rather than being the harbingers of new ideas, scientists and researchers have tended to discount that which challenges accepted theories. Science should be about pursuing knowledge that is unknown, rather than corroborating beliefs that are already held, which seems to be the tendency.

Further, society and the media have been "trained" to accept this paradigm, and when new and controversial ideas are posed, there is a knee-jerk reaction to first check with the academicians and researchers for validity, although they have shown historically that they tend to resist that which confronts their own beliefs and standards.

When we begin to discuss an emerging phenomenon such as contact with otherworldly beings, about which there is plenty of public opinion and controversy, and little scientific verification, the "experts" typically demonstrate a characteristic delay in even considering new thought. Their hesitancy stems from the fact that, in part, scientific proof is lacking and the evidence does not support the proposed theory. Yet, what may be more often the case is that the researchers' very instruments, techniques, and methods cannot be used on new theory, and so there is not yet a way to evaluate it. In fact, that's why it's considered "new" in the first place. There is no "approved" manner in which to measure or quantify it—yet.

In addition, the claims of tens of thousands or even millions of otherwise normal people whose own lives have been changed, touched, or impacted by contact phenomenon are not usually taken into consideration as part of the evidence. And so, the common person, the one in the trenches, the softest voice in the crowd who usually can offer the most insight through the evidence of their own experience, is the least likely to be consulted about what the phenomenon means to the experiencer or society as a whole.

Experiencers represent millions of silenced witnesses, shut down by the culture, the experts, and the scientists who don't want to hear from them. Instead, scientists, researchers, and others with secondhand knowledge, and no personal experience, are queried. The media want to know what the evidence shows and the experts are well versed in measuring the evidence, but only as a result of concepts with which they are trained or familiar. The mistake of science is that it so deeply focuses on the veins of the leaves in the trees that it has no way to grasp the wonder and the nature of the forest as a whole. Contactees speak of that forest.

But what if there is no "evidence" that is acceptable to investigators and scientists, but there is plenty of evidence when approached from a different stance? Suppose there is no scientific data, no hard facts or double-blind studies to analyze, measure, or quantify that fit the *familiar and acceptable standards?* Then why are we still deferring to those whose best contribution is to read and interpret such analyses? If the phenomenon under scrutiny "looks" different from what scientists are expecting, then perhaps we should consider that what is suspect is the outmoded scientific protocol, not the theory that cannot be proven.

As journalist Neal Grossman postulates in the September–November 2002 issue of *IONS,* the *Noetic Sciences Review,* this "materialist paradigm" is inherently faulty. He states, ". . . materialism has been shown to be empirically false; and hence, what does need to be explained is the academic establishment's collective refusal to examine the evidence and to see it for what it is."

Although Grossman's article is addressing NDEs (near-death experiences), not UFO phenomena, there are some parallels between the ways that both are approached from a scientific standpoint, particularly how researchers and scientists often love to hate, or to refute, both the near-death experience and the UFO encounter.

Consistent with what Grossman concludes about the study of NDEs, UFO phenomena often do indeed provide evidence; and so it *is* available, but it may come packaged differently from what a scientist is comfortable receiving. As Grossman suggests of those who study the NDE, "The academic establishment is in the same position today as the bishop who refused to look through Galileo's telescope."

Grossman goes on to state that researchers' assumptions are killing the research:

> When researchers ask the question, "How can the near-death experience be explained?" they tend to make the usual assumption that an acceptable explanation will be in terms of concepts—biological, neurological, psychological—with which they are already familiar. The near-death

experience (NDE) would then be explained, for example, if it could be shown what brain state, which drugs, or what beliefs on the part of the experiencer correlate with the NDE. Those who have concluded that the NDE cannot be explained mean that it cannot be, or has not yet been, correlated with any physical or psychological condition of the experiencer.

I wish to suggest that this approach to explaining the NDE is fundamentally misguided. To my knowledge, no one who has had an NDE feels any need for an explanation in the reductionist sense that researchers are seeking. For the experiencer, the NDE does not need to be explained because it is exactly what it purports to be, which is, at a minimum, the direct experience of consciousness—or minds, or selves, or personal identity—existing independently of the physical body. It is only with respect to our deeply entrenched materialist paradigm that the NDE needs to be explained, or more accurately, explained away.

As a result, what is needed is not more pressure exerted upon contactees to "prove" what they're claiming, but rather, a shift within experiencers themselves. We might begin to move from the need to have our contacts, sightings, and experiences validated or corroborated by investigators and researchers, and instead, hold firm that what we know is the truth for us, period.

Soon after my first book was published, I mailed a signed copy to author John Mack, M.D., and one to his assistant, with whom I had had some communication, since I deeply respect Dr. Mack's work. After receiving the books, a "thank you" was communicated back to me from his office, with the acknowledgment that Dr. Mack enjoyed seeing this next evolution of books, which mine represented, in which contact experiences were addressed matter-of-factly, with no attempt to prove anything.

Refusing to be placed in a defensive posture, many contactees, like myself, are simply proceeding from the position that it's real and is happening, and we discuss the way those contacts have impacted us. As step 5 suggests, experiencers are choosing to be their own experts, looking within for the answers and reasons that we've chosen contact. No emotional energy or effort is expended in defending a thesis. I simply offer ideas and if anyone would like to read about them, great. The same can be said for the dozens of radio shows on which I've been interviewed. Even the hosts and disk jockeys are dropping that old format, in which the one being interviewed is grilled with questions and is asked to prove what he or she offers.

Instead, I have no expectation to be taken seriously by the researcher, most investigators or scientists, and certainly not the academic world, and so I would no more spend my time attempting to convince them of something than I would bother to convince them of how I feel love towards my own son. What is true for me is what is true for me. If a radio show would like to invite me to discuss some of my ideas, that's fine. But I have no need or interest whatsoever to be believed or validated by the academic world, which is often the very group who historically shy away from new thought. I recognize that many of my ideas and others' ideas will, in the long term, prove to be far ahead of their time, so I'm satisfied, in the present moment, to have none of their support.

In this context, can you see how empowering it is to begin to move in a direction of becoming your own expert in regards to what you are experiencing? Contactees then become the "experts" of our own lives, and are becoming more confident, within ourselves, as to the nature of our experiences and what those have meant to us. This way, contactees no longer require acceptance at all, for there no longer is a need to be believed. It is enough to have had firsthand contact. Everything else becomes unimportant.

What is called for is a willingness to become the expert—your own expert—and when we do, we cease waiting for anyone else to accept us, or our claims. Instead, we understand that we're ahead of the game from what the academicians know from their experiences, and *we* are leading *them*, although they don't know it yet, and in many cases, neither do we. Experiencers are part of a phenomenon that hasn't yet been labeled, categorized, measured, and quantified. That's why contactees are leading the researchers and the rest of the world with respect to what encounter phenomena are, and not the other way around. We know about it first, prior to the scientific and academic community's stamp of approval. We must cease looking for the acceptance of the left-brained community who wouldn't know an ET from a BLT if one fell from the sky at their feet.

As time goes by and we experience and know more, we recognize just how much our culture and the experts who dictate the norms really don't know. And ironically, even academicians themselves are beginning to suspect this about their own colleagues! For example, at the University of Virginia, Ian Stevenson, M.D., established the Division of Personality Studies, primarily to further his research on reincarnation. Dr. Stevenson says that he set out to show that he could apply his classical scientific training to study phenomena largely ignored in the last century by mainstream scientists—although considered fact among millions of Buddhists, Hindus, and many people of other cultures. Most surprising is UVa's mission statement. According to its web site, the main purpose of UVa's division is "the scientific investigation of phenomena that suggest that currently accepted scientific assumptions and theories about the nature of mind or consciousness, and its relationship to matter, may be erroneous."

Imagine a *university* that hosts a program that actually studies the *erroneous* nature of "currently accepted scientific assumptions!" And UVa is not a school operating on the fringes. It is a bastion of repute within the mainstream, having been ranked consistently by *U.S. News and World Report* within the top public universities in the nation. Yet, one of Dr. Stevenson's greatest regrets is that his academic colleagues for the most part refused to even consider his work scientific, even though his published material fit the most stringent standards of research protocols.

As we shift our tendencies to "ask" and defer to someone else about the nature of our experiences, contactees will begin to grow in confidence until our collective voice simply and naturally elicits a shift in what the "normal standards" are considered to be. But as this shift begins to happen, remember who was pushing the envelope all the while! Keep moving in confidence; keep noticing how contactees foretell of our species' shift to that of a universal inhabitant.

As we move in that direction, we're going to have to start meeting our neighbors, and that's all that's going on. There's no bad guy; there's no insidious plot threatening humanity; there's no need to buy into the political voice that asks us to believe that we must stay militarized and fearful to be safe, separated from our peace within and our connection to each other. We can be thankful to those pioneers such as Dr. John Mack, Dr. Steven M. Greer, or UFO investigator Joe Nyman, and to authors such as Whitley Strieber who were, and are continuing to be, willing to consider approaching contact from a different perspective. As we grow in our individual spirituality, our ideas expand and grow too. And so, even the stubborn researchers will come around one day.

Step 5, Be the Expert, challenges experiencers to demonstrate confidence in their convictions by listening to the voice of their own soul for answers, for they are the ones being contacted. Experiencers are the experts, for they, not the researchers who are studying them, are blazing the trail. It takes courage to begin calling on extraterrestrials and greater courage still to confidently state the greater meaning behind contact when it speaks against the cultural fear paradigm.

But in the meantime, let's agree that it's not always easy to think differently from everyone else. And sometimes we do fall back on our society's tendency to be afraid, to forget who we are in the scheme of a wondrous universe. But when reminded and encouraged, we can help each other to feel safe and to feel at peace.

For when we shift this way, we recognize the truth of our status as spiritual beings living within a spiritual, wondrous universe. Only within a context of a sense of safety will our experiences expand; not from within the framework of terror and isolation.

I posed this question to the ETs:

So what is the purpose of all this newfound confidence? Why is it imperative that experiencers recognize that they have the ability and "credentials" to consult with their own higher authority about the nature of their contacts?

Your idea of yourself will determine who you become.

But most of us don't perceive of ourselves as having any of the answers. In fact, that's why people are reading this book in the first place. They don't think they know how to call their own contacts. That's why they're referring to this book.

Yes, but we are serving as reminders to your readers that ultimately, they need no other authority. Like your relationship with us, your readers have placed themselves in a position to be *reminded* of who they are. You are not wanting to perpetuate the idea that your readers need rely or become dependent on your ideas, or ours, or anyone else's ideas, but that they themselves can access the same higher realms that you have. This book is helping them to do just that.

Okay, so how can the average person begin to perceive of himself as an expert in anything, when there are so many opposite messages bombarding us daily? We're not supposed to be trusted and left to our own devices. We don't even think of ourselves as being able to heal ourselves physically, which is why we consult practitioners and doctors. We don't see ourselves as being able to heal our emotional and psychological issues, which is why we consult therapists. Heck, we don't even trust our ability to know how to exercise our bodies right, so we have personal trainers. As individuals, we just don't have much practical experience in the application of the knowledge that we get to be the bosses of ourselves. So there's not much to support the notion that we should now trust our own intuition about what our ET contact means to the growth of our own soul.

That is why you now might *practice* perceiving of yourselves as such. And "UFO phenomena" is the perfect arena in which to do so; there is an opportunity here for growth.

But the experts among us who do think that contact from ETs is possible have already established a barrage of media noise that may have permanently polarized the idea of "abduction theory." Who are we as "ordinary" nonprofessionals to suggest that our views might hold more merit than the "currently accepted scientific assumptions"? How do we, the non-experts, sometimes the least educated among us, develop the gall to perceive of our own personal "norms" as more accurate than theirs?

It takes no worldly education to remember and adopt ideas that are relative to the higher realms, only practice. This does not imply that ideas of those higher realms are better than others, only that there are many levels of awareness, and expansion and growth suggest that one is willing to expand one's current level of awareness. Each of us is moving upward and outward in our spiritual expansion, in a direction that slowly peels back the layers of the onion to reveal the core within. In fact, the more worldly education you have, sometimes the less likely you will be able to perceive of the higher realms, for the intellect has elected itself as the higher authority, so that you have no reason to look outside of your own ego.

And as far as this expansion requiring "gall," it does take some chutzpah to state the unpopular, when that unpopular idea involves openly expressing ideas that are considered ludicrous or faulty by the standard perpetuators of "accepted norms."

The most important idea you can contemplate is to recognize now that the ridiculous ideas of today become the standard norms of tomorrow. So, all that is required from you is patience. But even then, some of your souls are, in lifetime after lifetime, showing up in embodiments following embodiments, in which you agree to show up and plant the seed of new ideas. In essence, many of you recognize that time and again, you are one step ahead of your culture although from the depth of your illusion, this does not seem to be the case. You're often placing yourselves within a context that asks your soul to herald new ideas so you are frequently helping to "open" a new society, much as a new management team is sent to a new retail chain store to "open" a new outlet. You just get there first. That's the definition of a pioneer. You plant an idea, a seed. You set up a *system*—an *inner* system—which others can adopt when and if they're ready.

But often those ideas that we're pioneering are so opposite to the ideas of our most respected and powerful. Really, at the heart of this message is that we might begin to approach our cultural assumptions differently. But that's easier said than done. Even experiencers get sucked into the trap of perceiving of each other as the enemy, rather than beholding each other as part of a universal family. Our species must be a big disappointment to enlightened beings elsewhere in the universe.

We, and others like us, wish you well on the road you choose to take, whichever road that is, just as when a friend or loved one departs upon the long journey and you might lovingly wish them well.

We have no preference for your future, save the future that you best choose for yourselves. This means that we are not attempting to produce an outcome on your behalf. We are simply asking you what outcome *you* are attempting to produce, and then we can suggest and assist *you* in achieving that.

Are you saying that you're neutral as to whether or not we end up in World War III, blowing ourselves up?

A peaceful state of being is the only platform from which you can achieve those ideals that you are constantly talking about. And so, peace is not simply a goal but a state of being that can produce more of the same. The zone of a peaceful countenance is where you can birth all of your dreams. This is why, when you finally decide that there is no justification for continuing hate or war, it will be because you recognize that taking yourselves to war continues to delay your arrival to peace. You will have ceased assuming that through war you will gain peace. That is an illusion. From your peaceful countenance, you can begin to strategize the style of living that you say that you are yearning for, and if you hold that state of being, the rest of your unhealed masses will arrive there too.

It's not that easy to stay peaceful and gentle when others around you are attacking you and the ones you love.

But this is ultimately the only way your whole group will reach mass awakening. Enough of you have to hold your ground, but the "ground" that you are holding is one consisting of gentle peace. The rest can be healed from this platform.

But as a group, we're not very good at refraining from being induced to rage or at least, becoming angry and mistrustful. We don't have a lot of practice in the way of the peaceful Tibetan monk.

Liken this peaceful stature to that of the well-toned swimmer. Once trained, that swimmer can cross the English Channel, but until then, without that training and conditioning, one is in jeopardy of "failing" at the attempt. Adopting the stature and mindset that will produce your moving into a permanently peaceful state of being will mean that you have trained yourself there. This training means you will have exercised the muscle of your awareness. Expanding your awareness takes practice because dropping your cultural assumptions daily strips away the dross, which ultimately requires moving through your own personal fears. This training, then, produces the platform from which you will achieve mastery. Mastery really is a state of being that recognizes that there is no further need to hate anyone or to retaliate anywhere.

Someone there will lead by way of example. Who will it be among you? Where are your current leaders leading you? Where have your masters led you? Ultimately, where do you choose to be? Be there now. Do not adopt the illusion that suggests that you can arrive at your destination via a path that has the characteristics opposite to that of the path that you are choosing. This is a very basic spiritual tenet. You will know the tree by the fruit that it bears. You will know the path you are on by the trees that line the road. You will know your journey by the characteristics that make up your path. Just look at where you are heading, and you will know where you are going.

The training of which we speak is what many of you are now undertaking because you will be required to process your worldly events in a completely different way. This training also allows you to begin processing your *otherworldly* events in a different way as well.

This is why many of you refrain from receiving your daily input from the media, for now you are learning to access the voice of your soul as your authority and indicator of which path you are on. It requires practice to hear that voice.

Finally, recognize that tomorrow you have an opportunity to behold a different paradigm, but first you must choose and decide what type of being you would like to be. If you choose to be one who fears little and feels peaceful, then your activities will look and feel different, and you will be drawn toward different outcomes. More of you can choose this reality, and you may find yourselves in yet a different reality from those who choose the paradigm that they are choosing.

We are suggesting that you notice how you contribute to your immediate future on this planet. You are setting up that which you must address in your next embodiment. Notice in which areas you can contribute and birth an environment that suits your evolution. And so you are not merely participating in life at this moment. You are generating the experience of your next moment because your soul is participating in the grand scheme that allows each one of us to experience the results of our own creations.

Therefore, the responsibility for your next adventure rests with you. That is why it is said that each soul is producing its own experience in its next embodiment, because that which is not complete this time, or that which has not been addressed fully this time, can be addressed fully next time.

How you contribute to your planet's future is being noted by the soul.

What are you saying?

Your responsibility is not only to your world and yourself, to your children and to your children's children, but ultimately, your *next* world's experience has been generated in part by you, too. That is why all of us bear some of the responsibility for the state of our worlds at this moment. Were you to recognize how easy it is to join in and provide encouragement to a different experience, you would cease delaying your first step. You would then wonder why it has taken you all so very long to change your collective agenda.

As long as you hold the illusion that you can find peace and love through killing each other, or through demonstrating your hatred through attack, then you will delay a change in your paradigm. It is impossible to love and to hate simultaneously. If you choose love, then love will be your choice. You will not choose to hate, reasoning that by choosing to hate, you are actually producing love and peace.

When you steadfastly hold to peace, mass consciousness shifts, despite what your cultural ideas of fear suggest. There is a fear that the meek, while in their loving state of being, will be victimized and brutalized. Yet your greater inroads will be made by recognizing that, no matter the actions of a few, emanating love and light will achieve your goals in a tenth of the "time" and with a fraction of the bloodshed. Just look at your history. Nothing much has changed.

Does this mean that at the moment most of us agree to be peaceful and loving, others around the world will join us in short order even if they're terrorists?

No, not necessarily at that "moment" but in much shorter order than they would if you responded in anger and retribution. This transition would still occur much more quickly than if you kept up your current methods of thinking and politicking. In your current model, the one that has been around for millennia, you constantly delay the arriving at peace, for there is always another reason to be angry and to be designating someone else who needs to be held accountable. It is much like your game of dominoes. The dominoes have been reacting to one another in your cultural history for thousands of years and continue to do so. The trick is to be the domino that stands, and does not allow the domino next to you to seduce you into toppling towards that of your usual angry response. Instead, you might actively withdraw from reacting and responding as you normally do, by refraining from falling into line with the other dominoes, in the direction of the illusion.

Rather, simply stand even as your neighbor taps you; having fallen so many times before, you're now ready for your new cue. Say, "No, I will not succumb, for I know where this toppling will lead me, and I want to try something different to see if I get a different outcome."

And there may be bloodshed, but that bloodshed will cease sooner than you may know, and will cease more quickly than the alternative. And once it ceases, it will be permanently halted.

That seems so simple. Why haven't we figured this out yet?

Actually, many of you have figured it out on an individual basis, and where you have done so, you have arrived at this as a result of deferring to your own higher truth. The soul won't mislead you, but the collective voice of "rational" thought often does. That is why it is so important to practice perceiving of yourself as the expert in "paranormal" phenomena, because the more of you who can do so will start the trend at recognizing that higher truths are not usually arrived at by the holders of standard cultural norms.

But practically speaking, how does one begin to recognize that one has at one's disposal the answers to all that one seeks? How can we perceive of ourselves as experts if we don't feel like one at all?

By reminders such as this, over and over, until it sticks.

It's kind of you to be so patient.

When your toddler couldn't find his own mouth with his spoon, did you give up on him?

So you're spoon feeding us?

No, we're loving you. That love is potent with reminders of the nature of your soul—and of your very next evolution, which you are about to experience.

You cannot most effectively utilize universal energies until you are ready to surrender to the idea that you—in tandem with the God force—are creating it all. When you begin to demonstrate this in your day-to-day life, and begin to consciously understand and know this with respect to your paranormal experiences, then and only then can you confidently shape your future with us. It is in this way that you will be able to get a peek behind the curtain of extraterrestrial life. There is a plethora of universal experience that many of you yearn to know firsthand—and you can.

Your world will change when you begin to recognize that you can even manipulate the weather. This is why we are helping you practice your ability to comprehend your power base, for until you recognize your own inherent abilities as a creative being, you will not be able to create a different individual or global experience.

We must be a disappointment to enlightened beings everywhere. We sure are making a mess of things on earth.

We prefer neither your sleepiness nor your awakening. We recognize that the soul will always progress in the direction of growth, even when you don't seem to be, but many of you are ready to head more enthusiastically towards enlightenment right now. This is why we are offering these words. There is no award in striving; the pleasure is in evolving, in feeling alive. This is where we can help. To feel truly alive is what opening to love is all about, because you're no longer in isolation among the living dead.

Practicing opening to otherworldly communication is a very powerful step towards becoming more of who you are, because the next step is to begin claiming your own meaning from these communications. This is not merely a game or a parlor trick that you're learning to impress others. Your ability to open first to contact with us or others is a symptom of your awakening, and your next step is to feel comfortable in owning what those encounters mean to your personal growth. You're beginning to recognize that there is much more to your universe. By even considering that you can personally know and experience more—rather than waiting for others, such as your government, to give you permission to experience more—you are demonstrating your leadership. You can demonstrate the vision that you hold for your future, as exemplified by your ability to communicate to your universal neighbors. You can speak of what is possible.

I have indeed received so many letters from people who are on the brink of expanding to contact of their own. They sense that their dreams or snippets of strange memories indicate that something wondrous is under way, and they want to grab hold of it. In the early stages, that contact feels so elusive. Here's a typical letter that I received, describing this very thing:

Dear Lisette, I have never had any encounter experiences nor have I ever witnessed a UFO. However, I remember vividly when I was about seven years old (I'm now 37), playing with my dog, Rex, in the forest behind our home in Washington State and seeing balls of fire or orbs hovering above me. As I recall, they entered the branches of one tree and then reappeared out of another tree, then disappeared again, leaving me with a burning sensation along my spine. My dog was able to perceive them as well, but did not seem in the least bit alarmed. I told my older sister about it, but she thought I was just joking around.

Ever since then, I've had a number of experiences involving fireballs while walking in the forest, especially during the period of the waxing moon. However, once I reached adulthood, the fireballs ceased hovering about and instead would shoot past me overhead. The most recent one manifested on August 9 at approximately 6:15 P.M., as my girlfriend and I sat under some alders listening to Mozart. Unfortunately, she didn't see the fireballs, since they appeared behind her and disappeared quickly.

Most interesting of all, later that same evening, I dreamed that I was in an old cemetery accompanied by a man dressed in a black frock coat. It was daytime and we were searching frantically for my daughter's grave. (I have never been married nor do I have children.) When we found the grave, there was an elongated human skull on the grave plaque, which was inscribed with what I knew to be magical symbols, but they were not anything I had seen before. At that moment, the man in the black coat suddenly collapsed before me and a being resembling a "gray" appeared and placed silver coins over his eyes. It then picked up the skull and entered a nearby cave. When I attempted to remove the coins from the dead man's eyes, that's when I awoke from the dream.

Oddly, this dream has occurred repeatedly ever since, with only slight variations. But the otherworldly gray entity is always present, at times appearing with other entities who are so ethereal that they are difficult to make out. In one dream, the entity communicated the following to me: "Lepus zeta ta (or Lepus ze tata)." I have not been able to discover the exact meaning of this phrase although I know that Lepus (the Hare) is an ancient constellation found under the feet of Orion (the Hunter), while *zeta* is the sixth letter of the Greek alphabet. In mythology, the hare is associated with the moon.

I intuitively sense that the dreams convey my deep desire to communicate with interdimensional beings and that these dreams are perhaps the manner in which they have chosen to interact with me. Indeed, in many ways, it feels like I am undergoing some sort of initiation into the mysteries of death and rebirth, and that the beings in my dreams are adepts who reveal the gnosis (esoteric/secret knowledge) which lies hidden in the unfathomable depths of my soul.

At any rate, I shall continue to turn inward and probe the depths of my psyche, for I'm drawn to transcend our natural and conventional limitations and experiences, even if only for a moment. I'm convinced that humans can function outside the spatio-temporal law of causality and become multidimensional.

Is this writer tapping a deep memory of our connection to others who live elsewhere? It appears that he's being nudged to embrace our connection with universal beings.

Join in the chorus with others and admit to what you know and have seen. You open to knowing us for reasons of the highest order. Imagine when our worlds meet on a more global scale. You will certainly recognize that your early dreams, visions, memories, sightings, and contacts are the early steps, imperative to leading your whole culture towards that eventual occurrence.

The young child becomes more confident at learning to stand on her own two feet, and she then begins to walk tentatively, then grows to the youngster who is scrambling all over her world. So too will you maneuver. So too will you enthusiastically go forward into your universal home.

Step 6: Energize

The human body is capable of rapid transformation, despite our scientific understanding of what is possible. As our ideas change and evolve, our expanding awareness will sponsor a change in our physical world. ET contact enables our bodies to be "tweaked" by electromagnetic frequencies from the higher realms, enabling us to energize. Physical healing is possible and the material objects around us will also be affected. Evidence of having been energized is symptomatic of our evolution speeding up in which we will more readily access and know otherworldly realms.

We humans are poised to awaken to the new, improved version of ourselves, and we don't have to wait for several more lifetimes. We can stretch and change right now if we allow ourselves to. But the obstacle that looms largest, preventing us from moving through this transformation quickly, is our fear, because what often shows up as we open to contact is just plain *weird*.

Just as soon as we meet up with the "symptoms" of our expanding spiritual growth, we often close down again, uncertain of what we've exposed ourselves to. We worry that we may fall victim to the "bad" version of paranormal phenomena, and so we're afraid to be exposed to anything. We're suspicious we'll catch the next paranormal plague. Whatever negative version of phenomena is out there, we don't want it. We're so familiar with the barrage of media noise about the bad ghost, the terrifying poltergeist, the victimizing "alien," that we stay shut down, left out, seemingly safe. So we stay stagnant, too timid to brave the tide of an evolving paradigm.

We will feel the sensations of our stretching energies and vibrational bodies, ready to undergo changes that will allow us to better navigate our universe. All we need do is allow our vibrational "body" to be tweaked.

The manner, and degree of that "tweaking" will vary, depending on many factors. In addition, there are many parties involved in the supervision of that energizing: our own soul and the soul or souls of those others with whom we are opening to contact. This is a partnership, in which our soul and the soul of other enlightened beings who are assisting us work together to bring about our expanded awareness when adjusting to new and expanded frequencies.

Consider that we are big walking and talking radio receivers, capable of tuning in to other channels or dimensions in the universe. But we're presently getting a lot of static when we try to get our favorite FM station. Or perhaps we're hardly getting any reception at all, only that one talk show that bores us to tears. The speakers of our radio are a combination of our sight, hearing, taste, smell, touch, and our intuitive sense, and so from all these, we currently experience a very limited version of the radio signals of our world.

As a result, we now want to upgrade to a satellite. We're ready to "energize." Given that our blueprint, and the blueprint of thousands of others like us, ensures that we are now ready to tune in to the other stations in the galaxy, we will be provided with help to do just that. The "technology" which will facilitate this transition is nothing more than the universal timing made manifest through us, individually. It's already in place to support our upgrade. The timetable of our next evolution is upon us.

Since timing is everything, we're ready, individually and as a species, to call to ourselves our next new and improved version of human being. Notice that we're not a human "staying," we're a human "being." That state of "beingness" can and will elicit a state of calm in which we can "grow" ourselves literally into our next evolution and thus, our next experience, if we allow it to. This growth often has an energetic feel to it, literally. At times, our bodies seem to "buzz" as they become energized by the higher realms. (Such energies have made it easy for me to sustain water fasts and juice fasts lasting up six weeks.)

Yet sometimes, it seems scary or strange when you're confronted with evidence that you're expanding your awareness. There are those signature bright lights that can descend on you when you're least expecting it. Or, more likely, subtle flashes of light, energetic "charges" of electricity, zap you in your sleep; or perhaps bursts of different colored lights flash in front of you like fireflies on a summer's night. Or maybe you hear etheric music in your ear, wake up to a mysterious "tattoo" etched on your arm, or find what seems to be an implant placed somewhere in your body. Potentially, there are a thousand and one variations on this theme, and they alone would fill a book. Some of the "evidence" of your expanding energies and expanding *awareness* to those expanding energies can be quite unsettling. Other times, it seems downright comical. But in either case, it can often be disturbing if you have no context in which to perceive it.

When we understand that opening to the expanded energies of the higher realms has a different feel, look, and sound than the energies relative to this realm, then we can proceed in confidence with the childlike wonder of kindergartners first beholding Disneyland.

When I initially opened to contact, it seemed that nothing remained unaffected. My body certainly could feel the dancing electrical energies as it came in contact with my skin. My eyesight went all wonky at one point, and I literally almost went blind for an afternoon. I ended up in the emergency room, the physicians having no idea what was wrong. Depending on the type and manner of contact, I would experience everything from a bloody nose to acute nausea. And if I wondered if I was imagining it all, the appliances and machinery around me began malfunctioning.

Some of my things would break outright, and all the while, my mind was wondering how all of that was impacting my health.

Opening to the energies of the higher realms is not harmful, although the stretching involved in such an expansion can be challenging. Not only did I open to clairvoyance and clairaudience overnight, I began to suddenly "see" places and events as a remote viewer. When my ET contact began, I was continuously zapped by an electromagnetic charge that accompanied the bright lights. Such energizing becomes part of the process whereby the human body is prepared to access multidimensional realms.

Obviously, this discussion must not take the place of good medical care, since it would be foolhardy to assume that physical maladies must mean that ET contact is beginning. So if something is physically wrong, get medical attention.

My emphasis is on the fact that physical changes occur as a result of tapping into the higher realms, and those changes can be "managed and survived" by you if you recognize that you are a spiritual being capable of healing and transformation.

As I've begun participating in more and more media events, particularly radio, there's a remarkable opportunity for this expansion to be demonstrated, since the human body is not the only area that is impacted by expanded energies. For example, more often than not, during the hour or so when I'm a radio guest, either the radio station's phone lines, or other equipment relative to the technology of the show, are affected. This can occur not only as a result of my own differing vibrations as a result of contact, but also, at times, the extraterrestrials themselves produce an impact as a result of their vibrational presence. People and things in their sphere of influence become energized by their presence.

In other words, as I'm present, attending to the radio interview, often so are the ETs. They regularly assist when and where they are needed through the influence of their suggestions and ideas. As a result, time after time while I'm on the air, either the show's phone lines go dead, or there is some type of equipment failure. I can only smile as the host apologizes to his listeners for the surprising technical difficulties.

Recently I was a guest on an internet show, a Canadian webcast called *NMB Live, The Intelligent Radio Broadcast.* The host, Norman Mikeal Berketa, had me on for a couple hours as he interviewed me about my UFO experiences. We had also discussed on the air how strange things can happen in the presence of multidimensional frequencies. The show went well and ended after about two hours.

The next morning, I received an e-mail from him:

> Dear Lisette, Just a quick note to again say thanks for spending the two hours on the show last night. Another note of interest here . . . call it what you will, but after the show, as soon as I had reset my server from "live" to "rotation," my computer crashed!

I immediately wrote Norman back, inquiring more about it. He replied:

> It would be unfair to say that my computer has never crashed before. After all, I am running Windows; however, what I did last night was a very simple procedure that usually has no repercussions of any kind. It really surprised me when the whole thing just froze. In fact, I couldn't even "ctrl-alt-del" to restart the machine. I had to switch it off cold. To make things even more curious, a program that I've been running for months now will no longer run and I'll have to reinstall it. When all this happened, my first thought was, "they're (the ETs) letting me know in no uncertain terms that something's coming." I just hope I'm spiritually and mentally ready for it!

After chatting back and forth about this, a few weeks went by when I again heard from Norman:

> Just a quick update. After three days or so, the computer started working as though there was never a problem in the first place. But something else happened. A few weeks ago, my wife and I were putting some dishes away when suddenly one

of our drinking glasses exploded. I have never in my life seen a glass shatter like that. It was as if someone had smashed it with a hammer. It shocked us both, I'll tell you.

Then, this past weekend was our Thanksgiving, and my wife and I spent it at my wife's parents' place. I was helping with the dishes after a meal and, believe it or not, after putting the dishes in the drainer, another drinking glass exploded! This was a different glass, in a different house. It was just as though, one more time, someone had hit it with a hammer. My God, we were all stunned. There was glass everywhere.

My mother-in-law says that old glasses can shatter like that, but I have never seen that until it happened here. Could it be that, in inviting guests with paranormal connections, I have also invited other things? I'm freaked, and my wife is too.

At moments such as this, there is an opportunity to notice that what is shattering is our beliefs, which is symbolized here by the shattering glass. When we're exposed to the energies of the higher realms there's an effect on our bodies and the things around us. As step 6 suggests, if I can be willing to energize without being spooked by it, I will grow and expand. Opening to contact starts us on the journey of being willing to consider that the world is not put together as we think that it is. The manner in which emerging phenomena impact our senses is what we might begin to pay attention to. And so there is not a "correct" way to measure or determine if we have been contacted, but there are often signature "calling cards" left in our world that hint at the possibility that our awareness is being expanded. During those times, we often feel that something is indeed being communicated to us. This is often an accurate assessment, and depending on our willingness to stay open and receptive, we can and will experience the next "version" of contact.

When we begin to share our own experiences with others, we find out just how many of us are having strange things happen to us or around us. This following writer discusses a phenomenon that I have often heard of, in which household objects seem to vanish and then reappear.

Dear Lisette, I don't have anyone to talk to about this sort of topic, although I am married to a wonderful woman. I have two perfect, healthy, and highly intelligent children, a girl and a boy. I believe I have been abducted before. How can I be sure? I have anomalous electrical abnormalities that occur between me and electrical devices and street lamps. Lights turn on or off as I pass by, and objects that I own disappear and then reappear from time to time. I have always felt like a stranger in a strange land throughout my life as though I don't belong here.

Here's another reader's story:

Dear Lisette, I live in an isolated part of the United States on a ranch in the Pacific Northwest. Spacecraft are seen frequently in the skies by the locals. I have been on their ship three times that I recall. I have multiple sclerosis and these ETs have done two procedures on me. After returning home, I found I was much improved. This was noticed immediately by all those who are close to me. I remember the tools they used and they explained, somewhat, what was happening. Upon returning home, I found a strange substance on my forehead where they had inserted a tool through my brain. During the contact, all communications were perfectly clear yet total silence surrounded me. The only word I have ever heard them speak was my name. They have large eyes, which I refer to as "grapefruit" eyes. I have always felt safe with them and I can tell they go out of their way to help me feel comfortable. Everything in my life has been touched by these experiences. Nothing about me remains the same. They seem to come and go, and sometimes months will go by with no contact, then they just show up again in my home; yet they always ask for my permission. In fact, I expect them shortly.

Again, notice how the experiencer senses a tremendous benefit after contact is established, although sometimes it's difficult to precisely determine what the benefits are, or even to recall specific details about the encounter. After calling on extraterrestrials, experiencers often report having received spontaneous healing or receiving sudden physical enhancements. Often, the end result of contact is splendid, yet elusive; sometimes a bit frightening at first, but almost always ultimately beneficial. It's as though our soul has signed us up to have an otherworldly helper, yet the intellect cannot believe it. So we hear of regular people everywhere being encouraged, challenged, supported, and sponsored by gentle, enlightened beings from beyond.

But even when this help is positive, there are still challenges as we attempt to integrate our intellectual processes and concerns with our soul's higher agenda. For example, this next letter articulates the ongoing challenge with accepting the benefits of contact as it enhances one's professional pursuits. Often we doubt or question if we are able to handle the magnitude of some of the projects that have been seemingly suggested to us by residents of the higher realms:

> Dear Lisette, I became an environmental activist, in part due to a dream experience in which I spoke with a powerful presence that I believe may have been an extraterrestrial. This being, who was seven feet tall, informed me that his name was Bhumi Putra, which I later learned meant, "Son of the Earth" in Sanskrit. He told me that I'd have "continued success" with the environmental work that I had recently begun. I also had what researchers describe as a typical UFO encounter with a "gray" a few years earlier.
>
> Following those experiences, my environmental efforts have resulted in numerous successes in establishing and leading coalitions of environmental organizations in victories against various polluting industries and government agencies. Some of these successes defied all odds, and as a result, I sometimes find myself wondering if I'm unwittingly channeling the ideas and strategies of entities who are discreetly working behind the scenes for our benefit. Or, perhaps this is just my overactive imagination.
>
> I'm also worried that the intensity of this work is going to seriously affect my health and my ability to be in a relationship. I'm wondering if the ETs would push us beyond reasonable and healthy limits.

I posed this question to the ETs.

Is this possible? Would our otherworldly mentors push us to the breaking point?

No soul takes on more than it is prepared for, although within the "rules" that you live by culturally, this may not seem to be the case, so you call this "stress" or "problems." Your soul is up to something here, in this life, in whatever role you find yourself. And so, whatever challenges that you face, those too have been called to you by your soul. Granted, this does not mean that there is lack of what you label as "difficulties." To the contrary, depending on what you are addressing in your own growth, there may be considerable difficulties.

Despite these challenges, we invite you to seek your higher truth always; to go inside to where your heart whispers the truth for you. This is the key. It is not about your doing *our* bidding. We are helping you to do your soul's. We are, in conjunction with you, assisting you in addressing *your* stated mission. If you are feeling stress, if you are feeling challenged by that mission, then it is your responsibility to determine the solution for you. If you feel pulled or conflicted, this is a sign that there is still more for you to understand. But feeling conflicted is not necessarily a symptom of wrong direction in your work, but rather, suggests that there is further understanding required of you. So look towards this direction. Look to the true source of your conflict or your stress. What is this saying about your life's decisions in the context of your soul's choices?

And so, the more accurate question is would your *soul* ever push you beyond what you are capable of? Would God? Your conflict may not arise from an erroneous choice of the soul, but rather, the conflict stems from the issues *surrounding* that choice. Since you have free will, you are free to discern and to determine the best path for yourself. Despite seeming stressors placed on oneself as a result of a chosen path, those challenges and heartaches will invariably lead you someplace. Let them take you by the hand to lead you into the innermost center of yourself; to that place where you can more precisely define just what it is that you choose to be engaged in. Then you can begin to assess what is *truly* troubling you.

From this perspective, you can begin to understand that it is *you* who are asking you to grow, and to expand, not us. We do not use you for the purposes of our own agenda. It is *you* who have decided upon a path, and that path may challenge you. Just as the coach may challenge and guide his athletes through a training regimen, what has occurred first is that the athlete has decided upon that path, has he not? If the inherent rigors of the program are too much, the athlete is free always to reconsider his choice; to reconsider this line of work, or this particular life path. The soul is always free to choose again. But it would be erroneous to "blame" the coach for assisting the athlete in generating the strongest body possible; in learning the "highest" and most efficient techniques of the game, etc. If the mission is too unpleasant or difficult for you, select again. There is no punishment, there is only opportunity. If you do not enjoy the challenges for growth that it provides, you may follow a different path; or you can stretch, one day at a time, until you meet up with the completion of your mission to the fullest.

But how can we be certain that what we're experiencing in the first place is actually our highest calling? Using the example of this reader's question with his environmental work, if his relationship is falling apart and his health is suffering, then how can it be his calling?

You may be confusing the word "difficulties" with "problems." What seems to be a set of "difficulties" is more accurately an indication that growth is occurring, or that life is unfolding the way that it wants to—the way that your soul wants it to. This is why it is so important to have your ear to your soul. When you can hear the voice of your soul—when you notice the various and numerous ways that it asks to be noticed and heard by you—you will know. You will know because you will feel joy at the heart of your work. The "stuff" that occurs around that soulful work is for you to unravel and to heal.

But often, your assumption is that such "stuff" would be absent if you took off down a different path. If your soul is inviting you to address issues of your physical health, or issues of your intimate relationship, then "issues" will arise. They show up because you are ready to tackle them and heal them once and for all.

In any case, it is you who must decide what is true for you. And this is where the contemplation must begin. We only offer the awareness that the grander the nature of your trek, the greater the challenges, or seeming obstacles. If your soul is asking you to develop a stronger body, mind, sense of resolve, or whatever, you will need something on which to practice. That's what the "stuff" is about. So the greater and grander your role, the more challenges you may face. It all depends upon your soul's individual agenda, and how that agenda weaves through and impacts upon the greater agenda of your soul and your species' souls.

The key is to recognize that you have set it up this way, not us. We have only agreed to meet you here, in this time, on this day, to lend a hand. It is our pleasure to do so, but not one that we insist upon.

It would seem, then, that the key is to stay light on one's toes, to flow with the emergence of some strange "stuff," to stay calm and confident as that strangeness begins happening around us. There seems to be no limit to how that strange stuff manifests.

Just prior to my first contact, I began to see the face of extraterrestrials in the most unlikely places. One afternoon while visiting with a friend, we were chatting together, when suddenly, her face seemed to "morph" into the clear, unmistakable face of an extraterrestrial. She did not appear to be aware of it at all. As my jaw dropped, I blinked my eyes, and my pulse quickened. I felt alarmed that my eyes would play such tricks on me. I have since come to understand that opening to our connection with our otherworldly family can be surprising and startling. I received this letter from a woman who had a similar experience:

> Dear Lisette, In February 1992, when I lived in Houston, I had what I can only refer to as a paranormal experience with a close friend. Together, we saw other faces superimposed onto each other's faces and geometric symbols floating on my bedroom wall. I so much want to remember what the symbols meant, but can't for some reason. I think I was contacted by extraterrestrials that night.

What is particularly interesting is how these paranormal memories stay with us, long after, sometimes decades after they have occurred. The mind returns to them, over and over, wanting to make sense of them when it can't; or pausing at the wonder or the humor of the event.

I recall to this day sitting in my third-grade class in a state of wonder and excitement. I was staring out the window, my thoughts far away from the classroom instruction that was occurring. Over and over again, I said to myself, "Never forget this day. Never forget this day." Something incredible had happened, and it had had a significant impact on me, but I couldn't remember what it was!

I received a delightful letter from a young man who had had a similar experience. Like so many of us, he has a lingering, albeit partial memory of something wondrous happening long ago, but the "main event" seems to be erased from memory.

Dear Lisette, I have no memories of contact with extra-terrestrials except a memory from when I was very young, perhaps five or six years old. Something neat was happening—but I don't remember what it was—and I was saying to myself, "I'm gonna remember this!" and "someone" who was with me (who appeared to be female for some reason) responded, "Oh, no you won't," and I said emphatically, "Oh, yes I will." Then she said again, "Oh, no you won't."

I guess she was right because that's all I can remember. Since then, there have been a lot of strange things that have happened to me over the years. For example, one day I was at a gas station filling the tank of my car. It was as normal a day as ever, at a perfectly "normal" type of gas station. Suddenly, a woman of about sixty years old, accompanied by a man of about thirty, pulled up next to me and asked me quite earnestly, "Is this a gas station?" After I responded that it was, I watched him in amazement as he then had trouble figuring out how to gas up his car and where to place the gas nozzle. It was as though he had never done it before, although he had obviously driven into the station. They both spoke clear English with no accent. I have often wondered just how far out of town they were.

These stories consistently hint at the fact that something strange and wonderful is going on behind the scenes, and that many of us are just beginning to be invited backstage. This is why I am including so many others' stories in this book. It's important for us to hear that we're not alone in this strange and wacky, wild ride.

> Dear Lisette, I am a 40-year-old working woman living in Mexico and the mother of four children. The reason for this letter is that I know that something happens to me during my sleep, but I do not know exactly what provokes it and what to do with it. Sometimes I wake up but I can't move. I am conscious, but I'm unable to move or to talk. Sometimes I feel okay, and other times I feel anxious or frightened. The last time this happened to me, it was a little different since I began to hear the loud sound of a guitar, not a song or a note, but just the sound similar to that when you run your fingers over the strings of a guitar.

When I first opened to contact I too would awake suddenly to every conceivable occurrence that appeared to be generated from another dimension. Becoming energized by the higher realms influences not only the sounds we hear but all of the senses. When I began to have contact, overnight, I could "see" spirits who had passed over to the Other Side, and who would visit me. I too have awakened to strange music or other sounds that were clearly not coming from my house or neighborhood. When my son was very young, he also could "see" some of these phenomena, but the next morning he would often process them as though they were merely a dream.

These stories indicate just how many of us are having dreams and other experiences suggesting some type of contact with otherworldly beings, although, admittedly, we're not sure if they represent anything at all.

In fact, these dreams and memories *do* come from some place and that "someplace" is not our overactive imaginations or wishful thinking. These fragments are meant to nudge us awake. The higher energies with which we come in contact call on us to ready ourselves for something as we become exposed to a different electromagnetic frequency. They are not accidental, nor are they coincidental. These very happenings—strange vibrations and electrical pulsings, dream fragments, visions, extraordinary, unexplainable events that burst upon us—are what the union of souls—our soul and the souls of otherworldly beings—use to remind us of our journey. They are precisely what gets our attention and they foretell our next step, if we agree to take ourselves to that next step.

If we are emotionally and spiritually ready, I believe that we can graduate to our next role, our next version of ourselves. We can take ourselves from high school to college, then, if we choose, on to graduate school. But this program is not for the squeamish. It probably will not suit you if you're addicted to the fear model that says that, at any minute, the "bad guy" will get you if you trust, if you love, if you willingly open to more.

I don't have the answers for every single, individual "example" of what is occurring to you. But I can tell you that you're not alone in your process, although up until now, you may have believed that you were. That is the point of my writing this book. I want you to know that our entire species is about to take that leap, but some of us are heading the tour, leading the group, braving the unknown. By definition, a pioneer is one who is first among the earliest in any field of inquiry or enterprise.

Another consistent, yet controversial aspect of encounter phenomena is the issue of the use of implants by the ETs. This subject was addressed in more detail in *Talking to Extraterrestrials,* but it warrants further discussion since I've received so much mail asking about it. For example, I received this letter:

> Dear Lisette, I was told by "them" that I have an organic, crystalline transceiver-like implant in my pineal gland. I was told that I was "read" into the implant and then "translated" through it into my body. Apparently, this is something like a "walk-in" process but more technologically based. Through this implant, they guide my progress with my human potential, for want of better words. I've been looking for others with similar details with their experiences. I have

seen this implant on an MRI. The doctor assumed it was a tumor but said it couldn't be removed because it would kill me. So I just freaked for a while and now I'm trying to figure out if I can activate it and communicate with them in a more proactive manner from my side.

Implants are often assumed to be used by the ETs in order to keep track of a contactee. Yet, my understanding is that implants serve just the opposite role. Evolved, enlightened beings, who are familiar with navigating multidimensional realms, do not need us to wear something to find us, any more than our guardian angels, or spirit beings, need us to wear something to find us. What is usually happening is that experiencers themselves have decided to utilize certain applications or procedures to keep in touch with the ETs. Although we may not remember making such arrangements, it happens all the time, at pre-birth, in which we choose certain themes and blueprints to most effectively help our soul address our own particular agenda. These agreements continue to be discussed and evaluated by our higher self during sleep, meditation, or during the contacts themselves, often without our conscious awareness.

Not remembering these arrangements doesn't mean that we've fallen victim to an accident. A medium, for example, does not need to "wear" earrings, a collar, or have any other device placed anywhere in order for "spirit" to find the medium and to have communication. It is we humans who are evolving, who are in need of "help" or assistance as we navigate our own emerging potential. Enlightened beings can find and locate us, I assure you, without our needing an implant inside our bodies.

Instead, the implant is a device for *our* use, since *we* are not yet evolved or enlightened. It is a tool chosen by the soul to help us on our stated path. To suggest that beings who can navigate the solar system need us to wear a homing beacon on our body is silly. Otherworldly beings can detect the signature of our own unique vibration, just as the spirit world detects it. That alone is our signature thumbprint, and it is readily sensed and detected by beings who have evolved.

In my previous book, the ETs suggested that we need not be frightened by the idea of using implants and tagging devices. We humans use them all the time with the animals that we consider to be endangered species. We track certain rare birds with leg bands, and we place collars around the necks of wild lions. We can even visit our local veterinarian and have a chip placed inside our dog's ear so that we can identify it when lost. This is a use of technology that we understand. Now, simply expand the idea of that use, but reverse the scenario to that of us humans using technology to keep us "connected" with otherworldly beings.

It's rather humorous when you think about it, how we humans perceive from our own limited box. For example, in the movie *Signs,* starring Mel Gibson, the evil aliens have come to attack Earth. One of them enters a home and gets locked in a pantry. It seems that they can traverse the galaxy, but can't get out of a cupboard. Even as screenwriters, we subscribe our own human limitations to that of technologically evolved beings because we can't ourselves imagine how it all works.

It is erroneous to assume that without an implant, contact is not possible, any more than you would conclude that, without a pacemaker, your heart cannot function, or without a hearing aid, you will not be able to hear. It depends on the characteristics of the individual as to what path is chosen by the soul. Implants serve that individual need of the soul—of the body of a particular soul—but implants are not necessary for contact. It is only one avenue open to certain souls who have deemed it necessary, just as certain souls bring themselves to receiving certain physical remedies, enhancements, or adjustments in this realm as provided by physicians or other clinicians. It is a matter of utilizing available tools relative to your particular agenda.

Just as we need not fear the idea of receiving a root canal or a hearing aid, we need not assume that procedures as offered by otherworldly beings are evidence of manipulation or wrongdoing. Only from the context of our limited perspective, spiritually and universally speaking, do we jump to the conclusion that what we don't understand must be evidence of victimization or evil.

Often, what seems so bizarre to us at first glance is merely evidence of universal "technology" being made available to universal beings. Even on this planet, we have evidence of the weird and the arcane. There are fish, such as the northern snakehead, that can literally "walk" out of the lake and on down the road, and can survive four days out of water. Or, there's the story of the duckling in Russia that was born with four legs. I heard about this duckling while I was a guest on a radio show in Ireland, and the host was commenting that strange things were going on all around us.

Initially, reports of freakish happenings scare us because we don't know how to frame them. But when we recognize that all of the beings in the universe are pulsing forward into their next evolution, then we begin to more consciously relax our boundaries of what is "normal."

I asked the ETs about the possibility of danger in initiating contact with them.

People are wondering if contacting extraterrestrials is safe. Although such an expansion may indeed be normal, sometimes this phenomenon impacts our physical senses to the degree that it's uncomfortable, and sometimes, even painful. Are you sure that we're not in danger as we open to contact?

The swimmer develops aching muscles when he first begins a rigorous routine of swimming laps. During the first weeks, months, and sometimes years, you too will be strengthening the muscles of your expanding electromagnetic frequency. The process of this change in vibration may have a feeling to it, so patiently allow the expansion to take place. This is a naturally occurring phenomenon for all those who evolve and is available to all beings that choose to raise their vibration and to step more broadly into the universal neighborhood. Fear not, and have confidence because you are not the first who has crossed this threshold, nor will you be the last. Great care is taken to not propel you faster than you are capable of going. Trust in the perfection of the cosmos.

Imagine a human being becoming more developed, spiritually, physically, emotionally, and intellectually. Spearheading the movement of your species into its second generation will require thoughtful consideration as you comprehend just where you are leading your culture. We have evolved physically and spiritually to a physical countenance which is better suited to that of a universal being. We are able to transcend limitations of your so-called space and time. We can access multiple dimensions at will. We have broadly expanded our souls' experience to that of multiple levels of being. But we began as you are beginning now.

For example, we were not always able to exist at a level where we require no food. But we no longer need food, nor do we need to toil as you do to survive. Where do you think this change began? How do you think we first began to evolve? First we decided that we chose to.

Imagine a human who has the ability to survive without food and water. Imagine leaving your stressful lives behind and instead participating predominantly in your joy. When you begin to associate with those who have more experience in living a life as an expanded being, then you too will be able to "copy" those behaviors and characteristics that you find admirable. We're not suggesting that you become clones of us, but even the chess player increases his skill by playing with a more experienced partner. This way, now you understand the spectacular nature of opening to know us.

First we might become associated as brethren. Then, for those of you who would like to, we can mentor you into your next evolved status as universal inhabitants, although in the highest sense, you are already universal participants, but you do not know that you are. Just as the child who believes she cannot walk may remain crawling for some time, you are becoming aware more broadly of who you are. We can inspire you to reaching your highest potential, for you are truly on the threshold of experiencing and knowing so much more.

Between your lives, you have imagined this outcome. You have blueprinted this evolution. You might think this is the first time you are hearing this but, in fact, you yourself articulated these ideas long ago, and now you are ready to play a more specific role in your, and your species' evolution. The benefits of such evolution are not in simply knowing us; they are a more pronounced understanding of what actions and behaviors will best lead you out of your mess. More and more of you will begin to recognize that you are the leaders of your next cultural experience, not those of you who presently hold yourselves up as leaders.

As you become willing to step into the role for which you

have volunteered, you will find some startling changes beginning to occur.

Your body is more magnificent than you imagine. It is capable of great transformation, despite your scientific understanding or perception of what it takes to survive. As your ideas change and evolve, so too will your body. For example, we do not use our mouths to take in substance, nor do we use them to speak, for we live on the energy available in the universe and we communicate telepathically, yet our mouths are still in place, as a reminder to us and others of how quickly evolution is possible.

Your bodies are capable of transcending their present seeming limitations. Leaving behind illness is one possibility, despite your oftentimes polluted environment. There is a way to shield yourself from pollutants. This is done through a broadening of your being's evolutionary status. To do so means to increase the rate in which your physical body is vibrating and emanating.

As you proceed through this transition, it can be uncomfortable at times, both physically and emotionally. The discomfort may go as slowly or as quickly as you are designing it to. These are exciting times. There are physiological abnormalities that you can correct as you change biochemically and electromagnetically.

Others of you with more of a scientific background can best understand this process only by ceasing to attempt to, for your ideas of science lock you into limiting beliefs. Suffice it to say that the body is capable of growing into its evolution in *this* incarnation. Like the tadpole evolving into a frog, you too can change marvelously. Why do you suppose that such animals' evolutions are occurring right under your nose? As you broaden your understanding of what is possible, you can be inspired by the unhatched chick within the egg. You can be awestruck by the caterpillar that unfolds its wings to fly. These transformations are God's inspirations to you. They are gifts from nature to encourage your understanding of what you and your body are capable of.

Jesus demonstrated abilities in order to inspire you. Some denied those abilities and others instead worshiped him for having them. We recognize humans' tendency to deify that of which you yourselves do not feel capable. This is also one of the reasons why we are very careful to limit our communications with you globally. Until you grow to an understanding that we are not superior to you, nor need or require your worship, we will proceed with care. Eventually, you can come to accept that we are in fact you, evolved.

As you begin to recognize this, as you begin to see yourselves in us, you will cease perceiving our relationship with you as miraculous, for we simply have decided to unbridle our capabilities. So too can you. So be the flower whose petals open to beauty. Be the sunflower that stands tall, having burst forth through the rocky soil. You are capable of much more. Let no scientific "standard" dictate to what you aspire. Begin to perceive yourself as the magnificent spiritual being that you are.

But how do we make this step practical?

Begin by repeating thoughts in which you envision knowing us. This includes setting up a journal in which you begin to document and become more sensitive to all of the visceral input from the universe to include subtle energies, vibrations, bodily sensations, and flashes of light. With whom do you think these energies are associated?

By journaling your adventures in this way, you also imprint the idea in your heart that you are embarking further upon a *spiritual* adventure in which you know us, otherworldly beings, which are really not "other" worldly at all, but rather, are part of the greater world which is the entire universe.

You may not have previously considered us to be part of your same world, but we are. It is you who are expanding your idea of where the boundaries of your world are. So, not only are you considering that we are members of your beloved family, but that also, we're in the same category as your spiritual guides or mentors.

This is not suggesting that we deserve, or are requesting, your humbled praise or worship. We only ask you to begin relating to us as the divine beings that we are, so that you can begin to view yourselves as the same, for we are merely you, evolved. If we are part of the universal one soul, so are you. We both share in the divinity with angels and spirit guides. We too are part of this group. Because we have traditionally been seen by your culture as the enemy, deserving of your wary suspicions, this may be a leap in your perception and a huge leap at that. But all universal inhabitants come from the divine one soul, despite their varying degrees of spiritual evolution.

Our message is consistently one of non-judgment, loving acceptance, and encouragement to make changes where you will, while simultaneously holding the ideas of non-violence and compassion.

So this step asks you to recognize that as part of the one soul, there are aspects of you who are already familiar with who we are, which is no doubt why you have picked up this book in the first place.

Adopting a posture of sensitivity in which you begin to notice input that you observe, taste, smell, and feel through all of your senses, including your sixth sense, you will begin to see what you have not seen. You begin to understand that there's more. And that observation is expanding now. If you see flashes of light, rejoice. You are now beginning to expand your ability to perceive of subtle energy differences. This will be helpful as you begin to sense when electromagnetic frequencies are changing around you. This way, you can invite further contact with those frequencies, and begin to utilize them to your benefit. Do you see how marvelous your days can become when you are no longer simply motivated to get ahead in your job, but now you can add to your list of goals that which has you enjoying your universal camaraderie with us?

And so, be sensitive now to the changes in frequencies. Be cognizant of different lights that light up around you. These are telltale signatures of energies before you.

These are exciting times, in which you are now beginning to open to communication from beyond. And that communication between us can be more firmly established once you recognize us as your family.

Step 7: Discern Readiness in Others

Experiencers who first begin opening to contact by extraterrestrials are often conflicted by the need to talk about what is happening to them, and the realization that their experiences will frighten most people. In the early stages of contact, it is imperative to discern readiness in others and confide and seek advice only from confidants who espouse and attempt to make practical spiritual principles. The initiate is not served by receiving counsel from those whose world view is supported by our cultural illusion, which states that fear and mistrust are necessary for survival.

Back in 1989, my then-husband and I decided that I should admit myself to a psychiatric hospital for an evaluation. At the time, I had been having contact experiences for about two years, but I didn't know what was happening to me since I only saw explosions of light enveloping me, harrowing bolts of energy in my bedroom, and the occasional bloody nose and memory fragments. In short, my world had turned upside down and although I hadn't confided in my husband about all of it, I had alluded to some of it. And the response that I got from him with the little that I did admit to was not encouraging.

Although my first contact had begun when I was married, I

refrained from telling my husband all that I had seen, heard, and felt because I was concerned that he might think I was losing it. I was afraid that custody of my then infant son might be jeopardized.

So I kept my mouth shut, but this exacerbated my dilemma. The act of keeping trauma a secret from those around me doubled the magnitude of my upset. In the end, trying to keep such a secret made me close to crazy. On the other hand, I suspected that I would have to be careful in whom I did confide.

There were some nights when my husband would come home late at night and find me huddled in the bedroom closet, shaking and fearful, unable to offer any explanation as to what was occurring. This alone convinced him that I was losing my sanity. Eventually, we felt that the only people who could make it right were the doctors, and the "best" kinds of doctors for this type of thing were the psychiatrists found in the ward of a psychiatric hospital.

So one fateful night, I actually became a patient there, and a few days later, I was served divorce papers and notification that I had lost custody of my son.

The good psychiatrists wanted to know the details surrounding my upset but I didn't tell them either. I knew that seeing bright lights and hearing weird things go bump in the night didn't bode well for their version of sanity so, as I had done with my husband, I mentioned a few minor things just to see their reaction. All I knew was that I needed some kind of help for the lights and "hallucinations" that had shown up in my bedroom, and I was even willing to consider taking medication if that would make them stop.

So, on the one hand, there was no one with whom it felt safe to share my burden, which resulted in a tremendous sense of isolation. On the other hand, if I didn't talk to someone, I felt I would snap. Step 7 encourages the experiencer to Discern Readiness in Others before discussing the details of an encounter experience.

This quandary is typical of the challenge of many contactees worldwide. Emotionally, we have a need to connect with others about the life-changing events that have burst upon us; on the other hand, it's not always easy to find the right person in whom to trust such a confidence.

Certainly, the particulars surrounding this dilemma will either be exacerbated or ameliorated depending on the beliefs held by your current circle of friends, family, and co-workers. Whereas one newly contacted experiencer may easily be able to discuss anything with their spouse, another person would never dare to.

The point at which this perplexing dilemma surfaces is often at the most critical stage in the process of opening to ET contact. Step 7 helps prepare us for this dilemma by having us calmly assess readiness in others who might be potential confidants. It is crucial to refrain from sharing the details of an encounter prematurely, if the act of confiding will not serve you. Particularly in the early stages of contact when experiencers are often wide-eyed and in shock, reaching out for help becomes a tenuous option. If the contactee chooses a confidante whose own fearful belief system triggers them further into a tailspin, how has this served the experiencer?

On the other hand, trying to keep secret such an important life event from the people closest to you is excruciating. The very act of withholding often drives a wedge down the middle of your intimate relationship. There's often a feeling of guilt when you know you're holding back important information, particularly when your partner keeps asking, "What's wrong?" but you deny that anything's upsetting you, over and over again. As I have found, the process of calling on extraterrestrials can present challenges to a relationship, particularly if only one of you is opening to contact.

At one point in my own process, I had eventually confided in a medium, and she immediately told me that I was being "attacked" by evil spirits. According to her, I was being possessed by a demon and, if I read the Bible fervently and lit a dozen candles around the house, I could keep the nasty thing at bay.

Her "diagnosis" was hardly comforting, nor did it ring true for me. But I solemnly considered that she might be right, and so I began to repeat biblical passages while smudging the house by waving burning sage throughout each bedroom. If all I needed was an exorcism, by golly, I was up for the task.

In any event, a short time later I was in the psychiatric hospital.

It can be helpful to seek out the wisest elder, shaman, friend, therapist, or minister possible before you spill your guts. Since we are continually being reminded that we will know the tree by the fruit that it bears, look to your potential confidant's life and demeanor as an indication of the type of help that you will receive. This is how you will discern readiness in others. Look to the quality of their message, or the quality of their own life, or the degree of love that emanates from their heart space, and you will know if they attempt to apply spiritual principles to the events of their own life. Although most of us have not yet achieved mastery, some are applying spiritual principles to their daily lives more judiciously than others. Seek a confidant who is motivated by the call to love. Since love heals all, there is no thing that cannot be touched by its healing balm.

Had I been willing to notice, I would have observed how the medium whose advice I sought operated from an almost fundamentalist paradigm of good versus evil. In her world view, her safety was constantly threatened.

The problem with this perspective is that we so often manifest the very reality that supports our belief system—no matter what it is—and so she will continually have her beliefs reinforced by her life events. In addition, we usually are not aware of how our beliefs originally emerge as a result of our fears or some other limited or negative type of thinking. We are all just inventing our philosophies by the seat of our pants, so we might as well invent ones that will end up serving us, not thwarting us, since our personal philosophies will sponsor the details of our life. We do this as individuals, and we do it as a culture.

Suddenly we begin to notice that each of us is just making it up on the spot as to what we find acceptable, tolerable, legal or illegal, good or evil. And then we suggest that others agree with our version and adopt it as their own. In truth, there are many versions and philosophies, and so it behooves us, when we're seeking help or advice, to choose a confidant who at least speaks to our emerging desire to apply spiritual principles to the events of our life. This is the essence of step 7, to Discern Readiness in Others: determine their *spiritual* readiness. Just as it probably won't serve me to take financial advice from poor people, I don't seek wisdom from those who are spiritually asleep.

So if you are wanting to imbue your life with the tenets of spiritual principles that have been proclaimed by the masters since the beginning of time, choose "experts" who adopt spiritual principles in their own life. Read what they have to say about a thing, or listen to them speak. You will know immediately if they subscribe to the fear paradigm or the love paradigm.

Step 7 calls on us to invoke our inner knowing of how to balance knowing when it will serve us to keep quiet about what has occurred to us and seeking the gifts of transparency that honesty can offer. The process of calling on extraterrestrials can be greatly enhanced if we are spiritually centered as we open to contact. It is crucial, then, that we "discern readiness in others" in determining who is a suitable spiritual mentor.

No longer do we need to stumble outside blindly in the dark, bouncing back and forth between complete secrecy and confiding in anyone or everyone who claims to be an expert. In addition, we recognize that even our closest friends may have little or no comprehension of the agenda of our particular soul. Now, we are noticing that we get to have requirements as to who would best serve us as partner in the unraveling of the mystery. And until we determine who that person or group might be, we may indeed be best served to choose silence.

In the meantime, there are books, groups, and individuals who are not immersed in the fear paradigm. Sometimes, just reading about ideas as expressed from the higher realms will calm your heart and soothe your soul. That's why it's so wonderful when we can all help each other, lending the voice of our own experience, particularly when that voice attempts to overlay spiritual principles whenever possible. Most of us are not yet perfect, but we're motivated to find a way to heal ourselves, each other, and our world through love, not the furthering of fear, hate, and revenge.

One man wrote me this letter after reading a few sample chapters on my web site.

Dear Lisette, I am comforted to know that I am not alone and perhaps I am not crazy. I'm a college-educated male in law enforcement, so you can understand my concerns as well as apprehensions regarding this whole topic, although I have always been open-minded. In fact, I have had some other "paranormal" experiences prior to one night in 1999, when a being communicated to me. This being never identified itself or where it was from. However, it was very clear that it was not from this world. It was very matter-of-fact and spoke of a coming change in our world that is cyclical in nature and has happened many times before, every few thousand years or so. It was interesting that after being "paralyzed" I heard a tone in my head, followed by a message that was something to the effect of, "Prepare to receive communications." Then there was a "lecture," lasting about three minutes, regarding our situation here on this planet.

I have told very few about this encounter, and you can understand why. It's just nice to have someone that I can relate to, since it can often feel very isolating with respect to this phenomenon.

This letter summarizes the relief that experiencers often feel when there's someone else who shares what Alcoholics Anonymous describes as our "experience, strength and hope." And this need to reach out and share and confide with others like us is palpable. For in that sharing, our dilemma can be halved. The key is to find the most healthy and supportive individual or group possible who is worthy of our trust and whose philosophy is founded in higher ideals and concepts.

However, I cannot overstate that this motivation must come from an unemotional understanding of the nature of our culture, rather than a sense of fear that someone is "out to get us." Step 7 asks us to discern others' readiness, not become paranoid. Again, remember that we're now attempting to overlay spiritual principles on top of paranormal phenomena, to include our otherworldly encounters. We are now consciously choosing to cease perceiving of our world as unsafe, or our brothers as "evildoers."

Recognize that we can invoke the life of our choice and also choose to be around others who do the same. The *quality* of the life events that show up for us will burst forth from the holding area of the *quality* of our thoughts, words, and actions.

It is the same as when a computer programmer reminds us that the quality of the original program will determine the quality of the entire system. The phrase "garbage in—garbage out" becomes our new understanding.

We begin to unemotionally observe that *we* are the harbingers of a new reality, which means we will not be able to receive direction grounded in the higher realms from supporters of the old paradigm because they don't comprehend it yet. Just as the newly sobered alcoholic seeks the mentoring of an organization and sponsor who deeply understand the process of evolving beyond alcoholic addiction, the new contactee must forge through the masses of friends, family, and "professionals" who, although quite opinionated about "alien abduction," may have little or no understanding of the process of opening to an elevated spiritual expansion.

Most humans on the planet today view life through the fear paradigm, in part because our governments and those in authority encourage us to do so. Looking through the lens of this illusion, we rightly feel disempowered, ineffective to make changes, and victimized by individuals and groups whom we perceive as bigger or better than ourselves. In essence, we then give away our power to those who are telling us that we need them to protect us. As a result, if we seek help from those who have our interests at heart, yet have little understanding of the pattern or desires of our soul's growth, we may become more troubled, not less so.

Even if our experiences are troubling us, we can surrender to a sense of trust that, one day at a time, we can come to peace and understanding about what is occurring to us. Eckart Tolle states in *The Power of Now: A Guide to Spiritual Enlightenment* (Tolle 1999):

> It is the quality of your consciousness at this moment that is the main determinant of what kind of future you will experience, so to surrender is the most important thing you

can do to bring about positive change. Any action you take is secondary. No truly positive action can arise out of an unsurrendered state of consciousness.

Surrendering to the moment does not mean that we must immediately be able to make sense of the events that are concerning us, nor must we seek solace from those least able to provide it. Surrendering does mean that we are consciously ceasing to respond with fear and negativity. Eckart Tolle says of surrender:

> Surrender is perfectly compatible with taking action, initiating change, or achieving goals. But in the surrendered state a totally different energy, a different quality, flows into your doing. Surrender reconnects you with the source-energy of Being, and if your doing is infused with Being, it becomes a joyful celebration of life energy that takes you more deeply into the Now. Through nonresistance, the quality of your consciousness and, therefore, the quality of whatever you are doing or creating is enhanced immeasurably. The results will then look after themselves and reflect that quality.

But it will be very difficult to adopt a perception that life is "a joyful celebration of life energy" if we are consulting with others who seduce us into colluding with their fearful ideas of the horrible and unsafe nature of things.

When we begin to trust in the perfection of all experience and are able to allow that there is a "power greater than ourselves" in whom we can trust, our individual life and our collective cultural experience will change for the better.

Thus, the recovering alcoholic with long-term sobriety implores his newly sobered recovering alcoholic protégé to choose carefully the environment in which he places himself. His new "mission" of sobriety will not be served by spending an evening in a bar surrounded by alcohol. Nor would he find support in baring his soul and his experiences to the bartender or to other bar patrons who are in the active stages of drinking. He's going to have to move completely outside of that realm to receive inspiration in his continued sobriety, and to share his newfound "experience, strength, and hope" with a new circle of comrades. Then, once further into his own sobriety and healing, he can return to his old buddies, now acting as the inspiration to *them* to step onto their own path of greater awareness.

Learning to see ourselves and our world through spiritual eyes will take practice. Exposing ourselves to an ongoing barrage of "noise" that perpetuates the old fear-based paradigm may constantly thwart our growth and undermine our spiritual progress.

Experiencers who are just beginning to open to contact, like the fledgling recovering addict, must recognize that the atmosphere in which we place ourselves, and the philosophies of those to whom we expose ourselves, will, to a large degree, dictate the manner and degree of our progress.

And that *progress* is our spiritual path, demonstrated by an ability to expand our awareness to other "layers" of our spiritual universe. Contrary to an ongoing myth, those layers are not inherently "good" or "bad" but rather, are perceived by us according to what we are deciding about them from a subjective nature. Since quantum physicists have already proven that the experimenter in the laboratory can actually produce an outcome based on his assumptions about what that outcome will be (in other words, thought creates matter), then we might as well hone our emitting frequencies so that we can attract the like-kind energy of the higher realms. Junk in, junk out. Negative, angry thoughts in, negative, angry results will be produced.

But you won't find a lot of support for these ideas in the standard UFO literature, or from the experts and professionals who most purport to represent UFO research.

Ironically, what had once seemed to be the most likely avenues of support to us are no longer healthy options to our "recovery." As we progress in our ability to observe how deeply entrenched the current fear paradigm is, we will notice how the most established beacons of the UFO phenomena seldom adopt spiritual values as the basis for their philosophies or theories.

Without a platform grounded in spiritual principles, the hierarchy of our present assumptions will preside and take precedence, forever seducing us to view others as the enemy, and to spread hate and fear. As long as we remain fearful, we are not in touch with our power base. Hence, we are more likely to continue deferring power to the current "controllers" of power, who have convinced us that we're unsafe and in need of their protection.

Once freed from that illusion, we are unstoppable, able to transform our own lives and the nature of life everywhere. Together, we are bonded in spiritual principles, which will change everything.

In the meantime, it is ironic to finally recognize that you may not find spiritual inspiration through UFO conventions, UFO-related books, videos, television shows, movies, or UFO-related radio shows. You may be hard-pressed to find a spiritually based UFO-related chat room, web site, conference, or support group, that does not perpetuate the cultural illusion of our separateness and powerlessness.

Joe Nyman, the courageous UFO investigator who contributed appendix 2 to my first book, relates how, for years, he was practically booed out of professional conferences when he would stand up to share that many of the contactees who were coming forward did *not* feel that they had been brainwashed. He found to his surprise that when he suggested that the claims of such experiencers suggested that opening to contact is part of a spiritual experience, he has been harshly criticized. He has been accused of naïveté and told that his subjects have merely been brainwashed by the aliens who abducted them. And Joe Nyman is not the only person who has received this reaction when offering a viewpoint grounded in spiritual ideas that fall outside of the purview of the standard "abduction model."

After hearing me on a national radio show, a woman sent me a letter. After having opened to contact herself, she formed a support group for experiencers. She too, like myself and Whitley Strieber, has been beset by harsh criticism from certain members of MUFON (Mutual UFO Network), simply because she offers a different perspective to the fear-based abduction model. She writes:

> Dear Lisette, Aren't MUFON investigators supposed to be unbiased researchers? I have been called a brainwasher,

cult leader, insane, or just a plain liar, simply because I am offering a different perspective from what is often an initially difficult experience of having contact. I have found that some people hate me for my goodness, but I have chosen to ignore them. I have even received death threats when I first began my on-line support group in 1997. One man joined the group during a live chat and began posting anti-alien propaganda on my sites, sending e-mail bombs to the members, many of whom quit in fear. I was accused of being an "alien lover," intent on brainwashing my members, and I was told that if I didn't stop the group, he would kill me because someone needed to. I have since been told that this is the usual method used for infiltrating spiritually based groups. When his efforts increased, I was able to hold him somewhat accountable for the computer viruses, and he was jailed for a short time. Apparently, he is a member of a fundamentalist religious group who believes that aliens are trying to take over the Earth and make slaves of us.

As a result of all the difficulties associated with simply offering spiritually based support, I decided to close all my groups and I went into a depression for a while. After being off-line for about two months, I became angry at myself for allowing anyone to coerce me into giving up, and so I started two new groups. But this time, we met privately and away from public scrutiny. I currently have 32 members who keep in contact when they need to. At one point, I confided my concerns to a high level MUFON staff member, who admitted that it was common to be beset with criticism when offering positive messages about UFO contact.

In actuality, this type of anti-alien group does not merely function as skeptics, but rather they are part of an active group who sell bumper stickers, tee shirts, and have a huge following replete with propaganda not unlike that of the Ku Klux Klan. Their tone is very similar. It seems as though some contactees get on their list, and then they become targeted by them, much like during the 60s' civil rights movement. Don't be surprised if they show up at your own presentations.

There's a massive stream of disinformation out there in

order to frighten people needlessly. I feel so bad for the newer experiencers who are looking for information and then stumble upon this sort of message. I have even heard of an incident where a contactee took his own life for fear of being contacted by the aliens of this group's paradigm. I have worked with members in my group who have found me after having been so indoctrinated by the fearful messages that they have been convinced that they're possessed or insane, and then slowly, through the support of our groups, they've come to feel better about themselves and their experiences and are finally able to sleep at night. This is what it's about, isn't it?

Currently, I view skeptics and debunkers as lost causes, at least for the moment, and simply ignore their attacks, no matter how cruel. This is why I am writing you this letter. I wanted to encourage you to never stop spreading your message. Never allow their cruel criticisms to inhibit you. Their malicious behavior simply masks their own obvious feelings of fear and powerlessness. Nonetheless, like you, I'm intrigued how so much hate is directed at those who most spread messages of peace. Remember that most harsh criticism is sent in order to hurt your feelings and to shut you up, but do not allow it to do so. Your work is far too important. You are obviously doing something right, or they would ignore you. In actuality, they fear anyone who speaks of peace.

It's time that the experiencers who are lost be shown the light so that they may find their way. As Steiger states in his own book, "Now is the time" for the truth to be known. Time for those who preach darkness and fear to have the light chase them from the shadows. In other words, You go, girl!

This type of encouragement is beneficial to each and every experiencer, when we recognize that often those who most hate our ideas of being part of a grand spiritual awakening are the ones who are the most lost, and the most confused and afraid. We need not hate them back, but merely continue to progress in our spiritual growth, and cease exposing ourselves unnecessarily to negativity—or to their advice.

However, once we become stronger in our own convictions, and when the soul of the universe begins to move more strongly through us, then we become stronger in stepping out more broadly. This is when we are able to shift from student to teacher, capable of offering ideas on a broader scale that can help heal and transform. This is how more and more of us will join hands in unison, holding fast to ideas of spiritual connection and the abundant nature of life, no matter the gnashing of teeth around us, as perpetuated by the most fearful and hate-filled. And we can forgive them, for they know not what they do, because they are asleep.

Here's another perspective:

> Dear Lisette, I am a 50-something white male, married to a super lady. Professionally, I do regular hypnotherapy work, UFO investigations, regressions for abductions and/or past lives, etc.
>
> I was part of MUFON back in the 1980s and, as part of my own UFO research and hypnotherapy work, I was beginning to see and follow the thread of a spiritual aspect to these phenomena. But at the time, I found out rather quickly that MUFON was only interested in a "nuts and bolts" explanation of the phenomena, although I have no idea of whether or not this still holds true today.
>
> I do know that years ago, there were often government informants and/or agents that attended UFO meetings. Once, in Dallas, I attended a UFO meeting, and there were many plain sedans with government plates in the parking lot. The occupants were photographing the people and their license plates.
>
> I do not necessarily believe that such a narrow vision as is exemplified by MUFON is in any way exclusive to MUFON. I recognize that ufology is rife with personality clashes, prejudices, and even fraud. I try to avoid these with a passion and I will not engage in debate with people who insist that they have all the answers.

I include these letters because it's helpful to have an understanding of how much backlash you may receive if you begin to speak of the spiritual nature of your contact. I invite you to lead the world by your own example, *but not before you are prepared to do so.* That preparation does not include your level of education, money in the bank, an accumulation of munitions, or even the passage of time.

This preparation comes as a result of strengthening our alignment with the God of our understanding, and believing with all our heart that, when we're connected to our spiritual base, no harm can befall us. Ironically, when we finally recognize that we're safe, we understand that we always were, even before we thought that we were. And so, really, no other person or group can harm us, for we are spiritual beings, but we may not yet recognize that we are. Eventually, we can trust that divine truths will be made manifest through us for all the world to see.

Or, you may have no wish whatsoever to tell anyone anything about your encounters. In your case, you will face fewer challenges than the person who is routinely confronted with others' ideas about what's happening to them. But there is still virtue in silence, assuming that you don't feel that you require support outside of your own inner guidance. My hat goes off to those of you who are already strongly connected to your own inner wisdom.

Otherwise, until we arrive at our center, we're like a hockey puck batted around the rink by the opinions and prejudices of whoever comes into our space. As a result, it may help you on your journey to notice that you can tell the tree by the fruit that it bears. If you want to move in the direction of spiritual growth, move towards those people who support ideas that reflect spirituality, not its opposite. Then, once strengthened by our trust in the soul of the universe to lead us home, we can expand our territory because we are no longer vulnerable to others' attack, for we recognize that we are safe, no matter what. And we are even safe from our harshest critics: the point is merely to notice that we may be better served to strengthen ourselves first, before we place ourselves in a position of attack.

Eventually, our souls may ask us to share our truth with the world, especially when our truth radiates ideas of love and connection to the one-soul. The more hands raised in testimony of a grand spiritual awakening, the more quickly our entire species will move to a shift in mass consciousness. But first, it helps to be confident of our own truth, before we expose ourselves to an onslaught of controversy.

Attending a support group is not the only way to connect with others who share our experiences. There is always a way to stay connected, or to make a connection with others, even under the most isolating of circumstances, as exemplified by the writer of this next letter:

Dear Lisette, As you can see from my return address on the envelope, I am incarcerated in a prison in the southeast United States. I know why I am here, at least in society's terms: I broke the law. But I don't know why I am here in terms of my soul's choices. I must be learning a valuable lesson of some sort.

I have just started reading your book, which I heard about while you were a guest on Art Bell's *Coast to Coast*. I'm moved to write you at this moment to say something, although I'm not sure exactly what. Perhaps it is to thank you for agreeing to do what you are doing. That was a brave choice, and honoring that choice may still be a brave and costly experience for you. I, for one, appreciate your efforts.

For years, I have wanted to participate as you have, in preparing humankind for an adventure in increased awareness, but evidently, the Grays did not select me to aid them. I still await such an opportunity. I am an old, arthritic man in prison, for eight more years, but maybe there is something I can do to help from here. For the highest and best good for humankind, I place myself at their service. With my free will, I freely choose to help. My prayer is: "I am a human becoming. Help me to become." I offer this prayer to God who is within me, and to my galactic brothers and sisters.

Perhaps when I get out of prison in eight more years, I too can be prepared to do something to serve the cause of enhancing our collective conscious awareness. As I heard your words on the radio, and as I'm reading your words in your book, I seem to remember them from before. I feel that I have awakened, and am now ready to learn again all that I have forgotten.

I welcome contact with our galactic brothers and sisters,

in whatever form it may take, and accept their love and offer mine in return. Jesus told us that we are *all* brothers and sisters, the operative word being *all*. From now on, I plan on being a part of the New Paradigm. I am up to my ears in people whose fear is very great, and who feel unloved and rejected.

My invitation is thus made. I await their approach and my opportunity to do whatever I can to facilitate the Great Awakening. Thank you for writing your book and for sharing your experiences with those who will hear. (Psst! Could you please refer me to your ET friends?)

This letter moved me so much as I ponder how precious is our connection to each other, and I'm humbled to have played a tiny part in inspiring him to expand his awareness. Notice how this man discerned that in his immediate environment, he is surrounded by those who are fearful, which is why he chose to connect with someone outside of his immediate circle.

What is amazing to me about this gentleman's letter is how he suspects that, even in his own incarceration, his soul is up to something. And even within that isolating environment, he is still able to find connection with others by reaching out and writing letters, or by reading material that inspires him.

I posed this question to the ETs:

> *It would seem that this is our responsibility to ourselves: to steadfastly maintain our inner peace, no matter the chaos, attitudes, or opinions of those around us.*

Yes, as each of you begin to expand in an upwardly direction toward the higher realms, you are in essence mentoring a new paradigm, not only for yourself, but also speaking of what will be coming to others who will be following you. The process of expansion involves allowing your trust in God to bring you to a new awareness. The challenge arises when you seek assistance, emotionally, physically, or spiritually, from others in your immediate surroundings, and those others are not yet ready to take that leap.

You will often find yourselves in a position of attempting

to glean support from those who are least likely, the least able to provide it. There is a habit of seeking counsel from those we love, from those who are most involved in our day-to-day lives. Yet certain people for their own soul's reasons, have placed themselves in a position to be on the cutting edge of experiencing otherworldly dimensions. How then can you proceed if you are asking another to help you prepare for this, when that feedback is predominantly one of fear or concern for your safety?

When you move forth into the higher realms with as clean a vibration as possible—meaning you are moving forward with thoughts of peace and love—you are imbuing your motivations with the Christ consciousness. Then you will more likely attract that which you are.

However, one of the greatest hurdles to expansion still does involve the challenge of moving into a new paradigm without benefit of the support of most of the people in your immediate circle of family and friends. You will find yourselves needing to go outside of that circle, not for lack of trust, but for the simple recognition that the neighborhood little league coach may not be able to guide you to the Olympics. You may need to obtain the help of a specialist. You may need to expand your contacts or associations beyond your immediate comfort zone: the immediate comfort zone of your family or your neighborhood.

The existence of us is evidence that your species' tomorrow is already upon you. This concept is much more difficult for others to accept than you may initially realize. You will receive guidance through your dreams or meditations, which will assist you in moving the boundaries of your comfort zone out further and further.

This way, you will begin to know us and your awareness of all things universal. Deepen your understanding that you yourself may be poised to take a momentous leap in your individual spiritual growth but those around you may not yet be ready to join you.

You then are sponsoring a magnificent leap for many of you. The higher realms will guide you in this transition, and will help ease your discomfort, if you have any. By the same token, relax into your knowing. To the degree that you are comfortable expanding and spreading your wings, will you be able to fly. Those destinations await you. The longing of your soul symbolizes this call. Not yet remembering in detail that you have chosen to play does not mean that you will not remember. Deep inside each of you there is a spark that symbolizes the memory of who you are in the totality of the universal experience.

This is the spark that we are addressing, for it remembers us. Allow it to light your way. The purpose of this step is to invoke your understanding that it would not be surprising for you to need to move outside of your current circle of family and friends for inspiration as you broaden. Go, then, and learn of all that you know. There is perfection to the passing of the seasons, and so too is your spring upon you. Your next evolution awaits you.

Step 8: Be Here Now

Extraterrestrial contact does not encourage the initiate
to escape the rigors of Earth life or Earth's planetary
changes. Instead, enlightened beings inspire us to transform the paradigm on Earth and "be here now" emotionally and spiritually in order to do so. No matter our
Earthly problems, ETs serve to remind us that there is
always a spiritual solution.

It's exciting to think that as we grow in awareness and spiritual understanding, we can begin to know and relate personally to
otherworldly life. In conversations and letters from other contactees and would-be contactees, one fantasy that I often hear
expressed is a desire to be assisted in leaving this planet altogether or in escaping our worldly life and problems. As the state of our
cultural affairs worsens—as we gear up for more war or face
threats of terrorism or environmental demise—there can be a tendency to wish that we could be taken away from it all, to be magically transported to another space-time continuum free from the
trials and tribulations that we're confronted with on Earth.

As we begin opening ourselves to contact, it's helpful to
remember that the contact we desire is with enlightened beings.
Spiritually evolved beings deeply honor universal law. They con-

sciously make practical spiritual principles and willingly make them part of their everyday life and decisions. As a result, they honor each of our souls' mission statements, and so their assistance and mentoring must be consistent with our souls' desires. Just as Jesus did not effect a healing on every single sick person with whom he came in contact, enlightened beings recognize that each soul has chosen circumstances to further its own growth. For example, some souls who are ill seek instantaneous healing, and other souls seek the wisdom that only prolonged illness can bring. Some souls choose to be born into third world countries and other souls are born into more "modern" locales. Then once incarnated, all of us have an opportunity to "grow into" the role of a master and to impact our world beneficially within the roles we have chosen.

Since calling on extraterrestrials and opening to contact are part of an inner journey first, it will be helpful to know from the outset that extraterrestrials and other enlightened beings will assist us in ways that are consistent with our souls' blueprint.

In many cases, we have forgotten that our souls' blueprint is not to escape the rigors of Earth life, but rather, to Be Here Now, to evolve to our next spiritual level while we're here. This will enable us to play a more effective role in changing our paradigm.

This is why contactees potentially play such an enormous part in the planet's healing, because we can now consciously choose to be mentored in order to help change our world. If we have agreed to play this role as part of our pre-birth arrangement, then it's easier when we're aware of this agreement, rather than to be "drafted" by circumstance. Being "drafted" can appear any number of ways. Often when events seem to happen to us that first appear to be devastating, such as illness, being fired from a job, or being dumped by our lover or spouse, we're often shocked and surprised at the sudden change of events, not recognizing that we've strayed from our path and that our soul has called to us circumstances in order to bring us back into alignment with our destiny.

But in so doing, we have assumed that we can be most effective if we operate from within those other dimensions and altered states of consciousness in which otherworldly beings reside. We forget that our souls' goals may instead be to stay right here and learn how to bring the higher energies to us while being sponsored from "there." I posed this question to the ETs:

Shouldn't one of the goals of having ET contact be to get the heck off this planet while we still can?

That depends on whether or not you've decided to be a leader of the new paradigm while on Earth. Although you're not always aware of it, this shift in the consciousness of the peoples of your planet is one of the top three missions in scope in your sector of the universe. That's why there's so much "otherworldly" attention upon you right now. You don't recognize the magnitude of what you've undertaken.

But many people have expressed a desire to leave this dimension in favor of permanently escaping to another altered state of consciousness or physical reality. We're tired of it here.

You don't recognize that your agreement to depart from your most natural state of consciousness—while temporarily agreeing to take up a mission right there on your planet—has been your highest choice for your life.

The physical density of Earth is not your most natural environment, since you're spiritual beings living a physical life. You are not physical beings trying to live a spiritual life. You've placed yourselves there to impart an outcome on behalf of all of you as part of your growth towards spiritual awareness and to awaken from your forgetfulness.

So you're saying that Earth life is not something our souls are wanting to escape from, but rather, something that our souls are wanting to transform?

Yes. In the context of your most challenging "graduate program" there, at this point in your evolution, you don't recognize that this dimension on Earth is your ultimate altered state of consciousness, not those others. In actuality, the Earth plane is the realm that's most "altered" and that you're most "alien" to, not the realm where we reside.

Remember, you've all decided to be part of the general movement back home to God as part of the One Source. The key word here is to "return," which implies that at one time, you're been part of the One Source. And now you're going back to the awareness of your part of that One Source. This suggests that you've started out as all-knowing spiritual beings, and that you're simply playing a part, donning a role in order to participate in the wonderful "game" called human evolution. The next "time" you might be elsewhere in the universe, playing your role differently.

It's hard to believe that we're actually spiritual beings when we're so messed up and our species is so messed up.

This is a temporary situation, part of the process of your evolution.

That is why we say over and over again that our roles are simply to remind you of yours: a connection to all that is. Your relationship with us can trigger your memory to that connection which is universal in scope. But we would not "fix" everything for you, because you have not asked us to do so.

At some point in your youngster's growth, she refuses to let you tie her shoes since she wants to do it herself. At such times you smile at her lovingly as she does so, even when her attempt makes a big knot of the shoe laces. In so doing, she is expressing her independence from you, having recognized that her soul is encouraging her to become self-reliant.

So in essence, the greatest love that we can demonstrate to our children is to render ourselves as unnecessary?

This is the same role that we play with you. There is nothing for us to do for you, because you are wanting to learn to tie your own shoes, to heal your own shores, to love each other back to full knowing. But you might call upon us to encourage you from the sidelines to remind you of all that you're capable of. The youngster might watch her parent tie his shoes in order to remember how to tie her own.

The dimension in which you currently reside is the one most "foreign" to you. As such, you are merely finding your way back to those other realms of which we're part, that you actually know well from before, but have forgotten about. That is why your present domain seems so difficult for you, for it is the "altered state of consciousness," not another. And all of you throughout millennia have participated in the altering, but will, through your remembering of who you are, alter it back to what is more closely aligned with you.

Are you saying that we've all had some responsibility in messing up our planet through eons of incarnations, and so all of us are ultimately responsible for the solution in healing the planet?

Precisely. That is why there is no "escaping" the process of that healing, for your soul has deeply desired to be part of it. Imagine dismantling sections of the house in which you live in preparation for the remodel of your dreams. For years you have wanted to expand your kitchen to accommodate your growing family; or you'd like to update the furnishings to be more in line with the environment. You've torn out the asbestos that you've come to find out is harmful, and you've torn down some walls that no longer serve your ideas of a more suitable floor plan.

Out in the garden, you may have to uproot some of the flowers to replant later when the scaffolding has been removed. You have laid the drop cloths in preparation for painting and have donned a face mask to keep the dust from your nose.

Now that you have prepared yourself for your overhaul, do you want to quit now? Do you want to walk away at the moment of your home's rebirth?

The home of your planet also awaits a remodel, for you have participated in the preparation of the overhaul by the very lives that you have lived before now. Only your intellect convinces you that participating in the fixing of it should be done by someone else, not by you personally.

From the perspective of your soul, there's joy in the resurrecting of your world, although your mind says it's frightened to be part of it.

Currently, you point an accusing finger at your politicians, or at a certain group, ascribing blame to someone else or to another group for getting you to this point. You don't remember that *all* of you have been politicians and members of that "other" group at one time or another, And so, contrary to your indignation, you've all had a personal hand in bringing about the state of your world to where it is right now. And like your home awaiting its remodeling, your planet awaits its own. But you are the ones who have wanted to participate in this healing process, because your soul recognizes that you've played a part in its temporary demise.

But so many people are frightened about what those changes might entail. We recognize that we're in the throes of a changing paradigm, and many are afraid that we'll die before we see those changes. If we don't blow ourselves up as a result of World War III, many people wonder if we'll survive the purported Earth changes through the shifting of the poles or other phenomena such as the supposed passing of various planets close to Earth. How do we prepare for all of these potential catastrophes? Will the ETs rescue us and whisk us off the planet?

Historically, there have been large groups of you who have moved beyond this plane to another through the events of your history, whether from planetary sources or political. The truth is that at any given time, millions of you are in the active stages of transitioning in, or transitioning out: as a group, and individually.

You are all in constant flux, traveling back and forth between your realm and other realms. Nonetheless, you often forget that you are doing so, and instead call it "death." You also forget that this is in an "ordered" universe, in which there is no such thing as accident or error. Currently, those souls who are traveling in either direction are part of a transition in which a new paradigm is being heralded. This changing of the guard, so to speak, is not bad news, but merely a shifting of souls who have decided to either be here or elsewhere as a result of what their own soul has called to them.

Yes, but we're referring to masses of us dying as a result of Earth's cataclysm or nuclear wars. This is our question.

First of all, you need not "prepare" for the last day of this embodiment, in the way that you deem that you need to, for you have *already* prepared, we assure you. From your soul's perspective, you are well prepared, and you have set it up this way. Were your mind to routinely recognize and comprehend the manner in which you will return home, whether that return is "scheduled" by your soul next week or in the next decade, most of you would be paralyzed beyond your ability to function. And so, why do you assume that in *this* case, you will have the benefit of knowing when your last day here is upon you? For even that departure is likely to be temporary, and you may return yet again, beginning the process anew.

The truth is, you cannot know, at least on one level, for it is not yours to comprehend at this moment, even though you wonder what the chances are of individual survival in the case of major Earth cataclysms.

It is difficult, we understand, to discuss what you call issues of death, because by your definition, your intellectual understanding assumes that it's an end. Even while your higher ideas recognize that it's not an end, you still have much fear about when that day might be. For this reason, it is not an accident, nor is it a coincidence, that the universe, within the context of your present awareness, has not included more specifics as to which day you will arrive there as a newborn, and which day you will depart. That departure, no matter the day, is not bad news from the spiritual realms. It is only bad news from yours. And so, this discussion is difficult because, in essence, you are asking for that date, as to when you might be "disembarking," or when you can expect many others to.

It is not up to us. It is not our responsibility, nor have you awarded this responsibility to us, to be the communicator of that information. If you are asking about Earth changes and transitions . . . my friends, you are all constantly in the throes of Earth changes and transitions. Are you not noticing them? In addition, currently, great numbers of you are passing in and out. It is the "out," we understand, that you are concerned about, but that is already occurring, and so what is there to fear, for you are presently existing within a changing universe; within a planet that breathes in and breathes out. The inhale and the exhale, and where you are in relation to it, is what the soul is deciding. These are *personal* issues, personal to each soul.

What specific and/or overall planetary changes are antici-
pated to occur in physical terms in the near future?

Again, if it is your understanding that there are *currently*
no changes happening, then you are in denial, plain and simple. You inhabit a planet that is undergoing untold changes,
although we do understand your question. For your question
implies, "Will there be mass chaos and death as a result of
future Earth changes and the shifting of the poles?"

We will undoubtedly dismay you by suggesting that a shift
in your poles is *already* occurring. Change in your planetary
backbone is already underway. A transition of your entire
species has already begun. You have expected that, like a light
switch being pressed, that one particular hour of the day,
everything will shift. Notice the shifting that is occurring at
this moment on your planet and with you individually. There
is tremendous change taking place, stirring so many of you.
There is a tremendous shifting emerging within your ranks.

This is not a "cataclysm," but rather an *evolution*, for the
cocoon is ready to unveil a transformed being. The paradigm
by which this will happen is unfolding before you in due
course, and in due time.

When your young children approach you with questions,
you recognize that the answers must be provided in a manner that can be comprehended and understood according to
the child's age and development. Certainly, we are not suggesting that you cannot grasp whether or not you will be
"alive" a year from now, or if your neighbor will be. But,
within the context of your current understanding, you would
still perceive of such a date as the bad news that you're convinced that it is. And so, it is challenging for the young mind
to discuss this, even when such events and occurrences might
be the greatest events in the history of your planet.

You might understand that it is not our intention to be the
bringers of fear. Nor is it our intention to encourage you to
look for such answers outside of yourselves.

Our mentoring of you, like that of others before us, exists
to remind you of what your world can become. This is an
empowering relationship and an empowering message. And
so, really, you ask the impossible question, for the answer
cannot be given to your satisfaction, for you are seeking
specificity that would not help you. You are asking us the
dates you have agreed to live upon Earth at this time.

What is helpful is to, instead, prepare for yourself to evolve, no matter what your tomorrow looks like. Ironically, it would be "harder" for you to be left with your current state of affairs for the next 50 years, would it not? The "easier" way is to behold a cataclysmic end to your paradigm.

As a result, *the answer to your question does not matter*, for either way your soul is choosing the path that best suits its agenda. Keep in mind, even if great cataclysms were to take place in six months, there are still millions of you transitioning home in the next twenty-four hours who would miss that circumstance altogether. Conversely, there are millions who are arriving in your world weekly, arriving at this very moment; and why are they still arriving? Souls are arriving because your world is still a worthy destination, no matter the month, no matter the year. It is a time for each of you to recognize that the answer to your question is irrelevant, given where you say you want to evolve to. That statement of intent suggests that you are choosing to become aware that you are a spiritual being. As such, there is no need to analyze and forever dissect and describe the process by which you may transition, in or out, on this day or that. It is a quandary for the mind, but the soul has other interests, and so we ask you what is your soul up to at this moment? Does the other really matter?

To ascertain the state of your poles, look to the state of your being, for your Earth is changing and shifting as you are. In fact, they mirror each other. If you do not like what you see, find what it is that you wish to be doing differently, or how you wish to be behaving differently and then move in that direction, in your daily thoughts, in your daily conversations, and in your daily activities.

Ultimately, the answer to your question is none of our business, nor is it yours, for the "business" of the soul is of living, of evolving, and this consternation has stopped you from doing so. You are mired in the issues of survival. Have you forgotten that there is order to the universe? Remind your fellows of *that*. Have you forgotten that there is synchrony to all of the events on your planet and off?

When you are able to trust your life to the process of life itself, then you are ensuring your survival. Instead, you think that you are attempting to ensure it by studying, analyzing, and focusing on the suitability of your planet and how it will accommodate the life-forms there at any given point. Naturally, as guests on the host planet, you are concerned about the status of that planet. Yet, if you truly comprehended how a species survives cataclysms, or what you call "tragedy," then you would prepare yourself in a different way. That preparation involves becoming fully aware of who you are. And then, "coincidentally," when you recognize who you are, you recognize that there is nothing to prepare for, there's nothing to fear, for you are all *participants* in the grand orchestration, even though you've forgotten that you are. And so you are not being left out of the secret. There are not beings who know one thing, but have not told you. This is your fear that somehow there is knowledge that you are not being given, the knowing of which will save you. But contrary to your thinking, the simplest understanding will prepare you for anything. That awareness of your potential, of your highest placement as a spiritual being, as a member of this universe, designates you as a member of the One Soul. This recognition then is part of your survival plan.

Your focus is misplaced when you fear transitioning. From our standpoint, your fear is as misplaced as is the fear of your five-year-old who fears stepping onto the school bus. "There is nothing to fear," you gently remind your child. "You are safe," you might smile lovingly.

You need only awaken to who you are and no matter the outcome, no matter if your homecoming is tomorrow through illness or an event in traffic, no matter the cause, you are well orchestrated, because you are simultaneously the conductor as well as the orchestra. You are a spiritual member of the society of beings within the universe. This is an important shift in your understanding that would benefit you, for then, dear ones; you *are* prepared for anything and everything. For you recognize that you are well versed in the mechanics of survival. Your soul will always live on, and it is not necessary to become bogged down in the minutiae of how that survival will play out with respect to the ins and outs of this incarnation or the next.

What would be the spiritual significance to the passage of Planet X or any other cause of catastrophe?

When you recognize that there is "spiritual significance" to the passage of a small child across your front lawn, then you will best understand how we might answer that question. There is spiritual significance to those events that you deem horrible. There is spiritual significance to everything and anything. It is only you humans who have decided to label all that is spiritually significant, with names that imply that they are not spiritual at all. The more appropriate question might be, "What event, if any, is *not* spiritually significant?" And the answer is, there are no random, insignificant experiences. All events and circumstances are playing out and existing in the context of an ordered, synchronous cosmos. The fact that you cannot believe that this is the case does not make this statement false. What you have done culturally is describe as spiritual some event and circumstance that you "agree" with or find has some "value" to you. But value is everywhere, with every event and every occurrence in your life, even if you disagree with it.

You may accuse us of playing with words and avoiding answering the question, but we are answering the question from the level that will most benefit you. Isn't this your request then? Are you not seeking the answer that will most benefit you? Then you can understand why it is that we refrain from answering your question the way that you are hoping we will answer it, which in fact, would achieve the approval of your cultural mind. But that type of response does not necessarily benefit you.

If there were to be cataclysms, would there be assistance, in the form of evacuations from ETs, and if this help is given, what approximate percentage of the population will be receiving assistance in this manner?

My dear, dear friends, what would you say if we told you that more than a billion of you have already received assistance in some manner, in some degree or another, by extraterrestrials or otherworldly beings as of this date in time? Do you think that just one event would happen and then assistance would be granted? This is a very naïve perspective, for there is more going on already behind the scenes than you can comprehend. There is assistance, the likes of which would shock you. There are those of you who have received healings from us as called to you by your own soul and much, much more. There have been many of you who have been taken off your planet temporarily for myriad reasons, and all of this has been going on for years. And so, you now ask if it will continue to go on next year? Yes. Some of you are aware of these relationships and some of you are not.

Your question more accurately is asking if this assistance will occur in plain view, for all to see. And again, we would suggest that even if it did occur in plain view, many of you would still not see it. That is the definition of being asleep. Those who have eyes to see will see. Those who are not yet ready will not see. So, although again, you may feel that we are skirting the question, you are asking it from a context of "rescue." We do not agree that we are rescuing, have rescued, or will be rescuing you from anything. In fact, just the opposite is the case. We are empowering you to notice that there is nothing to be rescued from.

If you move or relocate from Colorado to Florida, does that mean that you're being rescued by the move to Florida? In one paradigm it may mean that to you, but within a higher paradigm, you recognize that there is nothing to be rescued from. If your soul's intention is to exist in a certain way, in a certain time, it will do so. The mechanics of that transition or move are available by many different means. But the context in which you ask the question suggests that you yourselves cannot be entrusted to evolve when, in fact, you can be. We have evolved and so can you. If, in the example of moving cross-country, you rent a truck and ask your brother to drive the truck for you, is he rescuing you or have you caused him to help you? This is a seemingly small nuance, but is not as minor as it sounds. The nuance is that empowered beings understand and recognize that there are numerous avenues of orchestration available to make any transition at all to anywhere at all. This, at the seat of your soul, you know. Your mind thinks that you need rescuing, but that is an illusion.

If your soul has determined that it would like to be someplace, it will be there. No amount of scrounging, worrying, analyzing, or scrutinizing will make that transition easier for you, for you will not be operating from that level. If your soul's intention is to finish here and continue elsewhere, the details of orchestrating that, we can assure you, are handled. The preparation that would best suit you is simply to practice remembering *that*.

What is the most significant beneficial piece of information or perspective that can and should be relayed about potential Earth changes?

You, as spiritual beings, are all sharing a characteristic and that characteristic is that you are constantly changing and that you are confronted with changes around you. If this is so, then do not fear that you will not be prepared for a certain change down the road.

Life is always about changing. Change is going on around you constantly. Believe in your soul's ability to know the best way and the mechanics for evolving. The mind would like to help you, but how can it? The mind knows nothing of what we speak, and so it is floundering, admittedly. The soul will always be safe. You are well cared for, because as participants in the process of life, you have access to the greatest insurance policy of all time, which states that you will survive everything and anything, because that is what evolution is about. There is no end to your life. The mechanics of how you skip from one life's embodiment to another have you fearful. But why? You have skipped thus hundreds and thousands of times. Why are you worried now? You can trust in the process of life itself. It is neither stupidity nor naïveté, but in fact demonstrates your mastery, for you are recognizing the true nature, the true characteristics, of your soul and those of the universe.

This answer, this message, is what will best help you and those you love, for this is universal law and does not change, although your mind says it's irrelevant or that it's not helpful. It is the most relevant and helpful reminder that we can send to you.

Is there really another physical planet that could disrupt the poles of the Earth?

Again, your emphasis is on one object creating a shift in the poles, but the poles are already impacted and are shifting, as are you, by the way.

But is there an actual object of which they write?

The most correct answer is yes and no. We will explain thus: If you ask us, "Do thousands of people die of starvation every day on this planet?"—we would agree that yes, this is the case, at present. Then you would clarify, "Then it's true that the condition of starvation exists on this planet and will exist to a greater degree in the next few years?" And we would respond, "No, not necessarily, for it is not necessary that one thing means that the other must occur."

Because even if there is in existence a planet, it does not necessarily mean that a full cataclysm must occur. Was it your thinking that you are insignificant to the state of your world? There are some beings on other planets who are able to control their weather because they understand that it is their birthright to do so. Because a planet exists, traveling in a certain way, does not mean that it is a requirement for it to end up in a certain location. This is the case for many different reasons, the least of which is that there are other beings in your universe who can impact certain events because we understand that our birthright allows *us* to do so.

Do you understand the distinction that we are making? We are suggesting, we are reminding you, we are compelling you to remember that creative beings can employ creative outcomes. Consider your Native American shamans who took part in the rain dances of yesteryear. Do you think that they were merely partaking of entertainment? In fact, they were calling upon their right as heirs to the universe to impart an outcome. That is what intention is about. Change your course if you don't like it. Change your entire life. As your mythical Captain Picard would say, "Make it so." This is the nature of powerful, creative beings; they understand that the events and circumstances of their life need not be trivial and meaningless, but rather, are part of that which we all have set up and orchestrated. And so the weather then falls within your own domain, as does the shifting of the planets, for you and the planets and the clouds are made up of the same stuff, and therefore, can impact each other by redirecting your energy. As such, tweaking is possible and "legal" in the context of the universe.

And the same goes for your very life. Tweak all of it, if you so choose, while also recognizing that all will unfold as it is deemed best by the souls of you who are participating.

Step 9: Shapeshift

Extraterrestrials vary the outer "garment" of their physical appearance by choosing to shapeshift into various forms. When we're aware of the nature of limitless beings, we're able to recognize and be mentored by phenomena that can inspire us to know our magnificence.

There is an old saying that states: "If you believe you can, or if you believe you can't, you're right."

If you believe that it's possible for you to begin calling on extraterrestrials, you're right. If you believe that it's impossible, you're right. When it comes to your perception of what is possible, including your chosen outlook on life, there are no "wrong" perceptions or attitudes, and the subject of ET contact is the perfect example of this. It's just a matter of how you choose to perceive life, or in this case, paranormal life. If you know in your heart that contact is not only possible but probable, then this belief will be supported by your experience. Your choice of perception is no small one since however you choose to perceive will determine the "type" of life that will show up as your experience. Your beliefs will be supported by the types of relationships and events that make up your experiences and the quality of your relationships with anyone, whether from this world or another.

If you believe that most humans are evil, then you will attract and come into contact with just the right mix of humans to support that particular world view. If you believe that "aliens" are evil and manipulative, then your own contact, or any ET contact that you hear about, will most likely match your preconceived ideas about it.

In addition, if you believe that humans share an identical thread of life that pulsates through all of life, then your experience will also match this belief. Step 9 suggests that otherworldly life is teeming around us—and it shapeshifts to appear in all shapes and sizes—and all we need do is to observe what is already there.

Once we understand that we have at our disposal every single potential experience out of the grab bag of universal experience, then we realize how important it is to hold firm to the outcome we desire, which will then most likely become our experience. The only (seemingly) "temporary" exception to this is when the soul has a specific agenda for its own growth, and therefore, the soul will call forth a particular experience that does not seem to be of our liking. But even in this case, years after the event or circumstance, we often look back upon the former unpleasantness and recognize how "perfect" it actually was for our growth. And even so, it only appears that the soul was not getting its way, when instead, the soul is always moving in the direction of growth and expansion, no matter how slowly, and even when we say that it doesn't feel that way.

Since experiencers are explorers extraordinaire, we are daring to invoke every single universal law at our disposal through the force of our intentions in order to call forth the ageless wisdom and power of extraterrestrials and otherworldly beings. But this invocation starts with our belief in a power greater than ourselves, and our ability to invoke it at our own discretion. Once invited, otherworldly residents begin to show up in the most surprising ways and in the most unlikely contexts. This realization is the cornerstone of shapeshifting. Why? Because they're everywhere, literally.

Consider what astronomers currently estimate about the possibility of life elsewhere: The known universe is huge, so it's likely that there's life out there somewhere. For example, it's so vast that to cross it traveling at the speed of light, astronomers say that it would take approximately fifty billion light years. And there aren't just a handful of likely planets that might hold life. Astronomers estimate that there are a trillion planets or satellites in our galaxy alone that could be inhabitable, and more than fifty billion galaxies. If you do the math according to the Drake Equation, a mathematical computation used by astronomers, that's one trillion planets per galaxy multiplied by fifty billion galaxies, which equals a number so high it's hard to even imagine it. This represents the total number of estimated planets in the known universe where life could exist. Again, that's one trillion times fifty billion! And it stands to reason that many of the species that inhabit those planets are intelligent beings who can develop the technology to travel and communicate with us.

It's estimated that there are five thousand billion, trillion stars that are like our sun in this part of the universe and that we can see. So it stands to reason that surrounding those suns are inhabitable planets. It also stands to reason that if there are *that* many inhabitable planets out there, we're bound to run in to some of those residents. In fact, it's crowded out there and although we're not capable of getting out much, it stands to reason by all the UFO sitings that *they* get out a lot.

And all that's required from us is a willingness to notice them. The catch is we usually don't.

We assume that if they exist, they'll ring our doorbells and ask to borrow a cup of sugar. Or, that they wouldn't want to meet us *personally*, but would prefer to do the communicating with the suits and ties via our governmental agencies or NASA's satellites and technologies. Although they're smart enough to get here, we give them no credit for discerning which individuals might make for a more suitable ambassador, which, by the way, is exactly what contactees are: ambassadors heralding a new paradigm where we can know our neighbors from beyond the sky.

Extraterrestrial beings get in touch with millions of individuals and are making their contact *personal*. Of course, governments know this, which is why they're so jealous that they thumb their nose at experiencers by insisting that we're making it all up and that there's no evidence to suggest that ET life exists. Face-to-face contact is potent, and produces the most meaningful type of communications, for them and us.

As these communications take place, experiencers are in the process of helping to create a new version of reality for humans, as we speak about what is possible. Today, stories of ET contact serve as our present-day folklore for those who are still skeptical. In mythology and folklore from years past, in records and carvings from thousands of years ago, there is mention of strange and exotic beasts and creatures. We've heard of unicorns and dragons, the phoenix and Sphinx, fairies and gnomes. Are they make-believe? Or do the rumors through our myths help us to become more comfortable with the idea that otherworldly beings come in all shapes and sizes?

The discussion and consideration of mythical creatures allow our culture to slowly digest new ideas. So we relegate such beings to "myth," which allows us to do something with the "gossip" of phenomena, yet not officially buy into it as a reality until we're ready to do so.

Yet, there's something meaningful to be gleaned from mythology. From the safety of "legend," we can consider the diversity of creatures large and small, creatures whose appearance is far different from our own, which makes our acceptance of them more challenging.

Rather than remain relegated to myth along with other legendary creatures, ETs can no longer be easily dismissed as products of a fanciful imagination, fantasy, or lore because more and more contactees are refusing to be silenced by the "critics committee" of our culture. Thousands of otherwise normal people are talking about having met them in some form or another.

It is my understanding that extraterrestrials can look any number of ways and can "arrive" in any number of packages since they, like us, are made of energy. The "clothing" of their physical form is easily changed and shapeshifted. They are not limited to any one physical description or characteristic, but unlike us, they know that they're not. This means that they can change their form at will by shifting the "shape," or the form, of their energy.

By shapeshifting this way, they are not transforming into a different form, but are merging with other forms that are already part of them. This is a critical nuance, and makes the art of shapeshifting possible in the first place: the ability to shapeshift requires a recognition that all living beings—humans, trees, animals, rocks, clouds, insects, extraterrestrials—are part of the same One Soul. The same thread of energy runs through all of life, all sentient beings, no matter the shape or form. This makes it possible then for one to show up as any part of the greater One Shape.

Evolved beings, whether extraterrestrials or Mayan shamans, don't change into a different form when they shapeshift; they recognize that they already are part of that differing form, and simply merge into it. Their form then appears to be changed. They choose whatever part of the larger "it" they prefer at the moment. And that "it" may be any number of physical forms, from an orb of light to a rhinoceros.

Perhaps the Mayans demonstrated this when they disappeared long ago, by making practical the ability to instantaneously shift the way that life was being lived by them, by shifting their forms from humans into something else. Even today, archeologists, anthropologists, and historians have attempted to explain this phenomenon by erroneously concluding that their disappearance can be attributed to environmental factors or wars. Yet suppose all that had happened was that the Mayans simply shapeshifted to another form of the one soul, whether to the trees or the animals of the forest, or "extraterrestrials."

Like certain Mayan and other shamans who may have been able to shapeshift at will, extraterrestrials are capable of shifting to any number of different forms in order to blend in with their environments or to experience another environment altogether. They do so in order to help bring about change by sponsoring others to learn the same techniques so that they too can help change a paradigm.

But rather than permanently escaping to the metaphorical Amazon of the galaxies, many evolved beings, whether Mayan shamans or otherworldly beings, choose to shapeshift into the heart of the most extreme "alternate reality" of our present existence: life on planet Earth at this time and date. Remember we are spiritual beings first, trying to learn how to live and grow spiritually while living in a dense physical plane. From this perspective, it is an "alternate" reality for spiritual beings, who originate and are most comfortable in the spiritual realms. Rather than fantasizing about how they can escape our threatened planet, wise beings from all over the universe are shifting their shapes and are choosing to come here and move among us. Today they take on many different forms and shapes by being willing to become part of that which many of us say we loathe: life as it is evolving presently on Earth.

Enlightened beings continue to arrive here, imparting their energy to help bring about a great change. By involving themselves in our mess, they have chosen to make Earth an important destination in order to be part of the healing of our world. That healing can be initiated through all of the systems that are part of our society—our institutions, policies, our politicians and laws, our systems and procedures.

We hear reports of ETs who are small-framed and gray, or who are ten feet tall and orange. We hear of mysterious trails of light, or a humming bird that acts "strange." Their appearance is less important than our understanding that, just as we humans have differing shades of hair and skin color, so do all the creatures of the universe. But we no longer need be frightened by their varying appearances because we will feel the tone of their vibration. That tone will bear the imprint of their consciousness, whether evolved or not, and we can trust ourselves to know the difference and respond accordingly. The master shaman can shapeshift into a tree or a rock, a raven or a doe, and so too can other beings in the universe, including those we label as extraterrestrials.

With all this life teeming around us, we begin to recognize that the same spiritual thread has united all beings since the beginning of creation. And it's not only likely but very probable that as humans we will be in contact with the beings who are t ed to us by that spiritual thread. That connection can be called any number of things: it can be called "contact" or "communication" or "telepathy" or even "face-to-face" contact, or it can be referred to as a "sighting." No matter what label we give it, we are simply coming into contact with the souls who are part of us, even if they sometimes look different.

As we become more comfortable with these ideas becoming a reality in our day-to-day experience, we can stay open-minded as to how that contact—or evidence of ET shapeshifting—comes to our attention. Rather than whining that we haven't awoken on a spacecraft, we are content to allow our relationships to be guided by our soul and the soul of the world. And sometimes, that contact initially begins with an exposure to the evolved *frequencies* of beings who are part of the higher realms. Since all of us are composed of energy, it stands to reason that energy can easily change form in the twinkle of an eye.

Although most of us have assumed that UFO contact must fit one type of description only, we will be well served to allow life to show up as life knows best how to do. What this means is that, initially, we may be contacted by the ETs' energy form that takes the shape of an animal or a tree, a human or a "gray," a "reptilian" or a "Pleiadian." As we slowly become comfortable being exposed to all the differing energies of the universe, we will begin to witness more versions of the One Shape that are part of the One Soul.

Even today, a decade and a half after my initial face-to-face contact with the ETs whom I'm in contact with, they continue to communicate and encourage me from the sidelines because my soul has chosen to be mentored by them. If this is the same for your soul, you too will be contacted any number of ways that best suit your current level of awareness. Higher energies move through everything, whether animate or inanimate. Yet we need not be frightened by these energies, any more than we need be frightened by witnessing our own shadow. When we make the intention to be sponsored by these energies in any way that best suits the agenda of our soul, there is no limit to how we can be assisted or inspired.

For example, just last night my teenage son and I were watching a television show together and for no apparent reason, he "impulsively" decided to switch channels. Normally I would object that he switched channels without at least checking with me, but this time I didn't because I sensed the ETs' presence. As he did so, he came upon another show that he preferred over the one that we were watching.

For reasons that are difficult to describe, I just knew without a shadow of doubt that there was something of importance or of relevance for us to see in the "new" show. My scalp began to fire as though it had been jolted by a lightning bolt. Then, sure enough, a few minutes into the show, in which the main character was giving a heartfelt explanation of something, a message was provided that greatly assisted me in a troubling dilemma.

Precisely the right words were delivered to me in a manner that, although arriving differently from what I might have expected, had been delivered nonetheless. Simultaneously, an electrical vibration filled the room, and next to me, my son's bag of potato chips shifted on the table on its own. The sound of it moving caught my attention, and my head snapped to the right to peer at it more closely.

After this moment passed, I mentioned it to my son. Like some of my friends, he sometimes complains that "phenomena" do not happen to him as they do to me. But my understanding is that it happens around us all the time, but usually we don't bother to notice it, or if we do, we explain it away as having some logical explanation. Case in point: when I mentioned the movement of the bag of chips to him, he admitted that he had in fact heard movement on the table next to us but had assumed that I was doing the moving.

His response is typical of so many people's. When we are confronted with communication that sometimes comes packaged in different ways and in various disguises, we make all kinds of assumptions and ascribe something "normal" to what may well be extraordinary.

Now a potato chip bag that moves on its own may not fit your description of extraordinary, but if you demonstrate that you can notice *this* type of contact or communication, then more will be made available to you. The reason for this is that beings from other realms want to check your tolerance level and your preferences. If you notice and appreciate the way that subtle energies can be displayed around you, then as you nod in acceptance, they'll know. It's as though someone out there in the sky yells, "Okay, Tommy handled that without any trouble, so let's move on to stage two." But first, you must demonstrate your readiness and willingness to stomach and notice "stage one" contact.

In my case, I continue to receive both subtle and overt contact and communication because I openly invite and encourage it. I'm calling on extraterrestrials day and night and then I notice it as it is occurring. This is what step 9 is asking of us: to notice the shapeshifting energies around us. When we choose to place ourselves in a ready position to be willing to observe all that's going on around us, we will begin to *notice* what's already going on all around us.

And there are virtually no limits as to how contact and communication can be presented and demonstrated.

Many contactees have reported strange and out-of-the-ordinary face-to-face encounters with animals in which the animal demonstrates behaviors that seem unusual in some way. Since ETs reside in the higher realms, but are composed of the same energy that we are, they, like us, are able to take on different shapes, sizes, and forms according to their needs at any given time.

Not only can they shapeshift into any shape or form desirable, but they also commonly take on the form of an animal when it's suitable to the moment. As a result, it's quite common for experiencers to have some type of unusual contact with animals as they open to otherworldly contact, since evolved beings are able to choose the garment that best suits their purposes. That garment can be varied in appearance and style.

Humans have classified the animal form as subordinate to the human form. Enlightened beings do not kill, eat, or subjugate animals, but embrace them as sharing the same spiritual thread that runs through all creatures of the universe.

Extraterrestrial influence often comes in the form of animal communication, and my experience has borne this out. The following story is just one of many, many examples in which I have come to recognize that once we are exposed to more finely tuned energies of the higher realms we are no longer limited by our physical bodies. In fact, we begin to recognize that physicality is a tool that we can use for myriad purposes and soul experiences, and that physicality can also be used as a tool by *other* physical beings, including ETs, animals and all of the beings normally associated with legend and myth.

If we tend to resonate to animal energy, then animals will come to us as teachers or helpers, often initiated by the mentoring role of otherworldly beings. Often, the eyes give away their identity, since the eyes are the window to the soul. If you find that an opportunity presents itself in which you are peering deeply into the eyes of an animal, consider yourself blessed, for the hand of God is assisting you through the shared energy of the universal One Soul. And that One Soul can take the shape or form of anything available and will provide help or assistance at a crucial or important choice point in your life.

Approximately six months ago my partner and I came upon a lovely cabin located in the foothills of the Blue Ridge Mountains, and the owners had offered it to us since they needed to relocate quickly out of the state. My dilemma was twofold: First, I intuitively sensed that we wouldn't be living in the house for very long, and as a result, although I loved the cabin, I was concerned that perhaps this meant that we shouldn't move in at all. Second, and more pressingly, I was nervous about taking on such a big financial commitment with my partner. It seemed like every time I relaxed and felt confident that a relationship would work out, it didn't, and next thing I knew I was being urged to move on in order to continue the next layer of my life's work.

As a result, I was nervous about making such a substantial change in the relationship that would further cement us together. In the past, every time I had come to be attached to a piece of real estate or to a particular relationship, it would seem to be uprooted, and I would be reaching deep inside myself to find a way to stay centered and trusting even when it "looked" like I was getting nowhere in my personal relationships. In the final analysis, I was scared silly to enter into a commitment with my sweetheart and with the cabin, since he made it abundantly clear that he would never have previously considered buying the cabin if it weren't for me.

My waffling and my indecision whether or not to go forward with the house symbolized for me all of my issues with "relationship." As a result, over the course of the month in which we were visiting the house and planning where all the furniture would fit, I was starting to feel edgy. Okay, I was downright somber. I had begun moping about the house, wondering if I was helping us to make the right choice, or if I was leading us into the move that would prove to be our undoing.

Every evening for weeks I would take my dog for a long walk in which I would attempt to unravel the dilemma. And every evening while on my walk, I'd pass a lemon yellow pick-up truck parked near our house whose license plate seemed to taunt me by its message: The license plate read, "Moping." As soon as I'd pass the truck, I'd chide myself, "Yes indeed, I do have to stop moping. I've got to shake myself out of this. Really, this is so silly, all this consternation over a little bitty commitment like buying a house together." What I had come to recognize was that, every evening that I passed that truck, I used it as a little pep talk to myself in which I attempted to talk myself out of my moping mood.

So, on the fateful day in which we were heading over to the house to finalize the paperwork, I had been awake half the night tossing and turning, wondering if I should say or do something to stop the process. Even as we got into the car I was a breath away from just staying, "Stop. We can't do this. I'm too afraid of commitment!" But before I could utter those words, and just minutes into the drive, we passed the yellow truck with the "Moping" license plate. But there on top of the cab of the truck, sat a stunning wild hawk, sitting there as nice as you please as though it had been waiting all morning for someone to pass by and notice it.

"Stop the car," I almost squealed, ordering my boyfriend to pull the car over.

When I pointed out the hawk, he was as amazed as I was, but after a few seconds of respectful gawking at Mother Nature, he began pulling away from the curb saying, "We're gonna be late for our appointment."

"Wait, don't leave yet," I insisted, pointing behind us to the hawk who had been left in the dust as he was anxious to get to the house and sign the paperwork. "I can't leave yet," I told him.

Reluctantly, he did a U-turn, and returned to the truck with the bird still perched on top. He shut off the engine with a loud snort. "Now what?" he asked me impatiently. "Do you want me to call National Geographic, or something?" he chided me with a grin.

"No, silly," I responded, ignoring his impatience. "I need to get a better look at it. I'll be right back."

"Wait a second," he protested. "We're going to be late. They're expecting us at 10:00 A.M."

"I've got to see it up close. It's got a message for me."

"What?" he asked, "What do you mean?"

But I couldn't explain it at the moment, and I closed the passenger door on his ongoing protests.

I just needed a few minutes to indulge my intuition.

Slowly I walked forward to where the truck was parked. Several cars drove by, also gawking at the beautiful bird. A few people came out of their houses to get a better look. A neighbor emerged with binoculars. Within a few minutes, I was standing just two feet from it, without its having flown away.

From the car, my boyfriend called to me, "Is it injured?"

"No," I responded, smiling at how we so often fail to recognize the wondrous ways that the universe's creatures show up to offer encouragement or hope, a message or an answer. The intellect automatically assumes that if we come upon an animal in a way that seems unusual or out of the ordinary, the animal must be injured. We've gotten to the point as a species of being so industrialized, that we wrongly assume that animal life would only place itself at our feet if it were in need of medical care. Once again, we're habituated to find the logical explanation in anything that seems out of the ordinary.

To me, this was no ordinary hawk.

As I continued to slowly inch forward, I was able to look deeply into its eyes as I was just inches from its face. As I did so I became mesmerized by some inexplicable force. All activity around me blurred, and I knew without a doubt that I was connecting with extraterrestrial life—or *this* life, or the "life" that implies that all of us are brothers and sisters, myriad beings connected by the cosmos.

From down the sidewalk in the distance, my boyfriend began to snap pictures with his Nikon, while a message was transferred from the hawk's eyes to my own. My scalp felt as if it had been plugged into a generator.

The relocation into the mountain cabin was necessary for my soul's, and for my partner's, growth, and we were correct in our desire to go forward with it. My fears, on the other hand, were rearing their ugly head, and I need not honor them, nor give into them, but to recognize that I was on-target with the house, and that it was definitely the highest choice for both of us. Even the sellers would benefit by making the transition. In short, it was written, and all we needed to do was show up and participate, not allowing my fears and shortcomings to get in the way.

As this message came to me from the depth of the hawk's gaze, tears began streaming down my face. I was overcome with humility. I had asked for a sign, for a message from on high to help me at this choice point, and sure enough, help was provided. As we become willing to notice how otherworldly beings share the universal life thread of *all* beings everywhere, then we can stay more connected to it, through all types of contact.

Extraterrestrial life is teeming all around us, but we don't recognize it when it shows up in packages that look commonplace. To many observers, I was simply bird-watching a hawk that had landed on a truck. To me, I was communicating with the higher realms, and those realms had sent me an enlightened being who had taken on the form of a hawk. Tomorrow this same evolved being might look like an "alien" with large black eyes, or any number of other physical forms suitable for its, and my, purposes. When we remember that all divine beings everywhere are doing the dance of life together, then we relax and allow all of the higher energies to take on whatever physical form suits the moment.

Often, those forms that are presented to us and that best suit the moment are actually part of our own soul's multifacetedness.

Since time is only relative to our realm, we are not aware of the lives that our soul is living out, even on our own planet simultaneously. For a further discussion of this topic, refer to the last chapter of my first book, *Talking to Extraterrestrials*. And to take those ideas one step farther, when we evolve to a more expanded state of being, we become aware of those other lives that we are embodying simultaneously and we do so through the natural abilities available to all souls everywhere—that of shapeshifting.

Evolved beings are not only aware of the other aspects of their soul, but they perceive those other aspects not as separate physical forms but as part of their own soul. As a result, they are able to move back and forth between forms at will, which looks as though they are switching disguises. In reality, they are simply partaking of the abilities that are available to beings who are comprised of energy. Whether a butterfly or an oak tree, an "alien" or an old man at a bus stop, energy is what unites us, for we are all made up of the same stuff. And that stuff of energy makes it possible for the outer garment of our physical form or shape to change and to shift at will if we believe that we can.

This is why experiencers often report that rocks, shells, or gems that they have collected and keep in their homes seem to disappear and reappear shortly after or before ET contact. The ETs are not taking and then returning the rocks; they *become* the rocks. For even what appears to be solid, such as a rock or a tree, is actually made up of energy. The human form appears to be solid but it too is made up of energy. "Aliens" are also made up of energy. Hence, all of life—driftwood on the beach, the sea gull in the sky, and the toddler playing in your front yard—are all composed of the same energy, so it's not surprising that we can learn to become more aware of that connection by sensing it on a daily basis.

We can liken our emerging understanding of our commonality to other "forms" of energy by considering how limited our experience would be if we erroneously thought that we were only capable of wearing one type of clothing. Suppose that no matter what we did or where we went, we believed our clothing must be limited only to a white cotton gown. Then suddenly, we are introduced to other fabrics. There's wool, silk, and cashmere, in untold colors and styles. Suddenly we've opened to a cornucopia of "garments" that become available to us, and so we wear them because we can. We utilize all that is available to us, not because we want to trick anybody by doing so, or to disguise ourselves, or to pretend that we're one thing when we're really another. We simply are no longer limited to *being or appearing* as only one "look." And so we happily choose other "looks," depending on the energetic "mood" that we're in.

Even now in our daily lives, we accept this desire to vary our outer garments when we change our clothes in making fashion statements or adjust our clothing to outside temperatures or changes in culture. We don't think a thing of it. But suppose that we become evolved to a level in which we recognize that not only can we vary our outerwear, but we can vary the outerwear of our physical form. We're no longer limited to "being" just one physical form at one "time" of the day. Or at one "time" of a life. We can be "into" the different aspects of the souls of us *literally,* and those aspects can look any number of ways depending upon our choices.

But when we encounter those differing aspects, we don't have to assume that they're trying to get one over on us, or that they're trying to trick us, simply because we ourselves are limited and we don't recognize them. The "problems" we encounter when we become surprised at different forms of life are due to *our* lack of awareness for not realizing that life shows up in many different ways—not with *them* for partaking of all of the ways that are available to residents of other realms.

These are my questions about the subject and the answers that I received from the ETs:

> *To continue with this idea that you touched upon in the last book, we humans are not presently living just one life, in one embodiment, and apparently, neither are extraterrestrials. Is that correct?*

> As human souls, you are not relegated to one physical embodiment during any given "time." And so as a soul evolves, one does become aware of those other embodiments and is aware of living them out simultaneously, yet in a more integrated way.

As do extraterrestrials?

Yes. We can, at one moment, appear to be one being, and the next, another. In some ways it is very similar to what you yourselves are experiencing, but are not aware of. You are currently residing in one locale and another aspect of your soul is residing and embodied in a physical body elsewhere. But right now you are not usually aware of that other or the "elsewhere."

In our present level of awareness, which is what enlightenment is, we can embody each of our incarnations simultaneously, just as you are doing, but we are aware of those variations while you are not.

We cannot exist, nor do we choose to, as just one physical being at a time. It is not necessary, nor does it pay homage to our highest abilities. This is why we simultaneously exist in more than one place. We are simultaneously more than one body. So are you. You just don't know that you are. You are just not aware of the multifaceted nature of your soul.

But how will we recognize you if you're constantly changing form? How do we know what to look for?

You can resonate to who we are through our tone, our vibration. Just as you recognize your dear friend on the other end of the telephone, you recognize his voice, or if you close your eyes, you can feel someone approach you from behind. You can feel that presence. If you are in tune, if you are aware, you can often correctly guess specifically who it is. This is because there is a part of you that senses and is aware of the signature of the fingerprint of each soul.

We, as multifaceted beings, come to you through various encounters, looking different. In fact, we can attribute our facial structure or other physical characteristics to those of a number of beings. In many "contacts," we choose to take a form that is the most easily identifiable by you as that of an "extraterrestrial."

So when I've seen you as having the physical appearance of the classic "grays" with the large, inverted pear-shaped head and large black eyes, you've come to me looking like this because you know that I would recognize you as an ET?

Precisely, although it is not just we who are doing the choosing. There is consent at the highest level as to which "type" of contact is appropriate. The "gray alien" form is a common form that is chosen when you and others become aware of other life in the universe. But we're not limited to this form.

But why would you choose to take on an appearance that so many humans consider to be bad? The "grays" have a bad rep, if you know what I mean. Why not choose a more cuddly demeanor?

What would you have us be when we meet you?

I don't know, but I'd have shown up looking like someone who at least enjoys more popularity, like a koala bear, for instance. You should have chosen that form, not those huge eyes and that frail, anorexic body and no hair. You're scaring the daylights out of people.

So you want us to Westernize our appearance for your sake or at least look like a teddy bear, so as not to frighten you?

Well, you already said that our soul is choosing, along with you, your appearance to some degree during these encounters. Why would we all choose the "gray alien" visage? It might help relations between our species if you could show up looking a bit more civilized.

Yet, you—by your standards—are the more "civilized" in appearance and yet are the group who is killing each other.

Touché. But your appearance is just too jarring.

It never occurred to you that beauty is in the eye of the beholder?

Are you saying that, in the universe, entities like you are winning beauty contests?

To the contrary, we have no need to measure up to one group's generalized idea of "right-appearance," precisely because there is so much diversity in appearance in the grander universe—and thus, no "right" appearance at all.

I'm only suggesting that if you want more humans to like you, you should show up looking a bit more like we do.

First of all, we *do* show up often looking precisely as you do. Second, when we do so, it is not to gain popularity or acceptance from you, but rather to participate as you are in the nuances of life, when such "encounters" are appropriate to your soul's desires.

When we appear as you have seen us, we are merely demonstrating diversity. In *your* culture, that diversity is met with prejudice.

So you do walk around looking like us humans?

The human body is not the "end of the line," "top of the heap," "thrill of all lifetimes." It is one aspect of the One Soul that is identifiable to that particular level of limited spiritual awareness. Your form will change as your awareness changes. And yes, at times, we "revert" to a "former" version of your shape for myriad reasons, the least of which is that some of you prefer to meet us this way, and some of us prefer to participate this way.

So you admit that you are seeking our approval of you when you show up looking human?

No, we are merely addressing you at a level where you can be reached. Some of you have demonstrated your readiness and ability to be reached (contacted) while we are in different forms. This indicates your readiness, not ours, for we have long been ready.

If and when you meet us while clothed in our diversity, you have indicated that you are awakening to a broader understanding of what is possible and characteristic in the universe. When the student is ready, more will be revealed, and so it is.

Most people who don't like aliens would not consider themselves to be prejudiced against you simply because of your appearance. They claim that you're the bad guys, and that's why they don't like you.

Yet this is precisely the definition of a prejudice: dislike generalized to an entire subset. Why would someone identify an entire species as undesirable?

Just because a group of you decide to "prejudice" those characterized by a particular skin tone or eye shape does not mean that we will change our idea of who we are, or who we can be.

But some people say that they've been contacted by aliens who look like you and who have been doing the victimizing.

That is no different than suggesting that if you're robbed at gunpoint by someone with a particular appearance, then all others with that same appearance are potential robbers.

Well, some people feel that the behavior represents an entire group of you. Like the Borg on Star Trek. *"Trekkies" would tell you that every one of them is evil.*

This type of thinking keeps you operating from the lower levels of spiritual understanding. This is a good attitude with which you might justify starting another war.

A little while ago you admitted that you specifically choose the alien form of a "gray" and not another during some of our encounters because so many of us recognize it to be that of an "alien." If so many humans consider aliens to be evil or manipulative, why would you not choose a form different from the classic gray in order to avoid eliciting this prejudice?

You assume that we would want to avoid eliciting your prejudice. In fact, the greatest gift we can provide you is to help you recognize those tendencies that do not serve you so that when you're ready, you can drop that "habit" completely. Championing prejudice in any form does not serve you or your species. Once this is learned and internalized at a deep level, you will catapult into your evolution.

So you're saying that you're actually inciting us to hate you for our own good?

We're invoking you to notice something about yourself. Hating us or fearing us—or anyone—is a personal *choice* and limits your spiritual growth. One day you will recognize that your fearful or hateful feelings about us are symbolic of the way you choose to target any group as your enemy.

But many ufologists would argue that your actions are what invoke their dislike or suspicion of you. People believe that you're using humans as lab rats and taking their genetic material. That's why you're feared. Not because of your appearance.

This is the same argument that is used to justify any prejudice, that a particular group of people or beings are all of one particular ilk that you deem as "bad." The very nature of prejudice attributes physical appearance with being bad, negative, aggressive, stupid, or in our case, victimizing.

If you have this capability to change your form at will, how do we develop this ability?

Start by noticing that presently you don't recognize how little you are aware of. If somebody passes you in the hallway at work, close your eyes and ask yourself if you even could recount what that person is wearing, even generally. Do you notice people's changes in appearance, their change in haircuts or styles; do you notice people's clothes? What can you say, if anything, about your immediate surroundings? Despite the fact that you've had the same office at work for a year, do you know what color the walls are? This is where to begin. Notice what you do not notice, what you have not observed, for you will also not notice us when we are right next to you. Who is standing next to you in line at the grocery store?

This is a very difficult intellectual confrontation because many people say that they choose to increase their awareness and experience more phenomena, but how can you when you are not yet ready or able to experience the phenomena that are right under your nose?

The levels of higher awareness are definitely easily accessed, but first, you must notice where you are presently on the ladder.

There is a process that you can embark upon. Notice how much you don't notice. If you've been visiting the same community bank for a decade, can you report on the color of the carpet in the lobby? Can you report on the type of roof of your office building? This seems trivial, but it is not. You cannot expect to be aware of higher realms if you are shutting out the subtleties of your own. This is a common characteristic of more of you than you realize. This is a more difficult step than you recognize.

Yesterday I accidentally wore two different shoes on my feet, yet of thirty people at the office, no one seemed to notice or comment.

Precisely, and did you yourself notice?

Not until I came home at the end of the day and took off the shoes.

This is a delightful representation of what we are speaking. It is simply allowing oneself to begin taking in all the input that make up your surroundings. Like the dog in your midst that can smell more easily than you, some of these faculties are indeed better suited to certain "builds," but not entirely. You may not be able to smell as well as your Labrador retriever, but you can definitely increase your sensory sensitivity in this area and in others.

We are often among you. More and more beings from other dimensions are among you in these times and days. Constantly there is movement. Constantly there are visitors and visitations from untold realms in your midst. Becoming aware of these subtle energies will require you to make a conscious choice to sensitize your senses.

Begin with the senses of your physical body. Start there. Notice what you have not seen. For many reasons of childhood, most of you have learned to close off your sensitive nature for reasons of your own coping. But now, what would happen if you chose to take it all in? Observe more. Feel more; sense more. What is happening under your nose that you are not aware of?

Metaphorically speaking, you might now remove the layer of packing foam between you and whatever else buffers you from your world. You will not be overwhelmed, although you have been afraid that you will be. In fact, more changes are likely once you begin to reduce the numbing that has occurred, emotionally and physically. When you begin to notice all that you do not, and have not noticed, you will be making a conscious choice to be increasing your sensitivity— your awareness—to all that is occurring and happening around you. Once you do this, then you are ready for more.

What more is there?

Since we do not need to relegate ourselves to one physical description or one physical body at a time, if you have called upon contact, you can imagine then how many opportunities there might be for contact. There are myriad ways in which you can be touched or visited or affected or impacted from beyond. The question is, do you notice? Have you noticed? Will you notice?

How do we develop these skills of observation?

You will have to first choose to *choose* to observe what is already taking place around you. You will have to choose to take your head out of the sand. You will have to decide that you no longer want to remain limited in your understanding of the glorious nature of the universe. It comes down to your choice to no longer live in denial; to no longer live in fear. What has stopped you is your fear. You haven't wanted to see us. You haven't wanted to know us, because you're afraid.

Once you notice that you have not noticed, you must arrive at this, you must give pause to this level of functioning; then you can begin to expand your level of sensitivity. Like a pumice stone upon the hardened skin of your foot, you can begin to dissolve the callused layer that has protected you from your surroundings. This removal process can occur as a result of your intentional thought about it.

Picture yourself wearing a rubber suit that encompasses your entire body. Attempt to feel the fur of a kitten while wearing a dish glove. You cannot, and yet you are asking how you can feel the fur with the glove on. First you must remove the glove. But you cannot remove it until you notice that you donned it. Once you notice this, then the next step requires you to remove the outer covering that is invisible to your eyes but exists very clearly to otherworldly beings. So this is why other beings know what you know and know what you can see. We sense what you can and cannot sense, for your outer appearance may have a very intact covering or layer, so to speak, which comes between you and other worlds, literally. This is very much a part that needs cleansing in some ways, although it is not dirty, nor is it evil. It is simply a barrier, although an invisible one to you, that once removed, will better establish your connection to the higher realms of which we and others are part. This barrier has been placed around you by your fears.

The dissolving of this covering or this layer is most easily impacted by daily affirmations of your desire to remove it. Many books already discuss and describe how you can visualize your way out of illness by imaging any sort of illness as symbolized by some object or thing. Then, the sick person is guided to imagine being able to dissolve that metaphoric version of the illness. If you have cancer, you may literally imagine it dissolving from your body. Humans have healed themselves this way. There are numerous books on the subject. In the same manner, you can begin to imagine this dense energetic outer layer dissolving so that you can reach out, physically even, with all of your senses, in which you can hear the higher vibrations more readily. You can see out of the side of your eye those images and movements that you thought you had seen but were not sure. You can sense the presence of a being or a spirit guide, when previously, you had assumed it was your imagination and that it wasn't relevant. Now you are recognizing that it is relevant. You are choosing to increase your awareness and sensitivity tenfold. This can be done if you choose it to be done by imagining that it is done.

Now, during your evening walk, you may see something. You may now attribute these nuances to other energies in your midst that your eyes do not yet see. But your eyes, your sight, will come along, once you allow it to do so. As you defocus your vision while in relaxation or meditation, you may be surprised at the forms that emerge. You may not receive perfect facial characteristics, yet you may see a form that seems to be comprised of smoke because it seems translucent. These are the early stages of allowing yourself to notice, allowing your sensitivity to be increased, knowing that there is nothing to fear.

You mention nightly walks. A few nights ago I smelled the fragrance of flowers despite the fact that there were none to be seen anywhere since it was mid-December and there was snow on the ground. I also heard a sound that didn't make any sense. Is this what you are referring to?

Yes. There is more going on around you than most of you are aware of. Some of you see craft in the sky and assume that they're only there once in a while. Others of you smell the fragrance of a rose or the smell of an alpine meadow, when it's a complete deviation from your setting. These are all indications of other life teeming around you.

When you say "other" life, do you mean "otherworldly" life?

Yes, although what you had once considered to be out of your world is actually very much part of your world, where you presently live. You need not even leave your neighborhood to experience what you had once considered to be "phenomena." Simply open to the possibilities of life, and you will experience the clouds above you as part of yourselves; the willow tree next to the brook you can now recognize as sharing your same cellular makeup; the bird that alights on your backyard fence brings you news from afar. No longer do you need to be frightened of the powerful connection that binds you to all of creation.

Part Four

See the Big Picture

Step 10: Fear Not

We cannot receive help from evolved beings in the universe if we don't recognize the helper. When we "fear not," we feel safe. This sense of calm encourages us to drop our prejudicial paranoia and set in motion our exposure to the higher realms and the inhabitants who are part of them in order to realize enlightenment.

I heard a story about a Roman soldier who was ordered to nail Christ to the cross. He truly believed that he was doing the right thing and wanted to punish him as much as he could.

When he got to Jesus' right hand, he carefully pounded the stake through the fleshy part of the palm in such a way that he knew it would cause more pain as it tore from the weight of his body.

As he began to pierce Jesus' left hand, another Roman soldier pinned Jesus' arm with his foot to hold it still. As the soldier was about to drive the stake into his palm, he looked over at his captive and saw that Jesus had turned his head and was looking intently at him. As the soldier caught his eye, Jesus said to him gently, "I love you."

It so unnerved the soldier that he threw down the mallet and ran away, sobbing.

Most of us are not prepared to undergo such a radical perceptual leap, an arrival at that state of mind that knows without a shadow of a doubt that no matter what, we are all safe; we are all connected; we are all one soul.

In this story, the behavior that Jesus modeled at his own torture and the response it engendered in the Roman soldier are testimony to the power of what might happen differently were more of us to replace our current perceptions of another. We would shock our enemies into dropping their guns because the potency behind the energy of love is far greater than fear and malice, although we continue to believe that it's not.

Most of us declare that we're entitled or justified to feel fear or anger. We don't feel it necessary or even appropriate to replace those perceptions with a response that is forgiving and compassionate. Had psychotherapists been on hand at the crucifixion, they might have suggested to Jesus that his gentle perceptions in the context of his circumstances were inappropriate and co-dependent at best, and symptomatic of delusions at worst.

This is one of the difficulties in undergoing a cultural change in our perceptions: we have constant approval in retaining our feelings of having been victimized or abused, and it reinforces our misperceptions that we're spiritual beings, living out spiritual lives in the physical.

When we replace fear or anger—that no one would fault us for feeling—and we instead turn it on its head by feeling its opposite, we invoke the magic of the ages. More of us will need to model this philosophy in order to bring about a complete change in our way of life. We have no business judging our government for taking us into another war if we're not getting along with our own co-workers or family members. We are going to have to find a way to be at peace with everyone we know, even when those with whom we relate don't meet with our approval.

Yet I'm not suggesting that we'll be immediately able to respond lovingly to someone who is slaying us—at least not yet anyway—but what we might begin to do is to practice snipping the fuse that leads to our knee-jerk response of fear or dislike in many areas of our life. One of the most notable areas of our cultural fear is when we behold those who are different from us. Whether we are speaking about the witch hunts of Salem, prejudice toward any minority group, or of the high-level fear attributed to the mostly invisible life of the other realms, we allow ourselves to be incited to fear. If we're not fearful of the enemy on the outskirts of town, we're fearful of some supernatural demon residing on the outskirts of our realm. It doesn't matter how you label it: if you've demonized some person, place, or thing as having the power to create problems for you, then you've not embarked as fully on a spiritual path as you think that you have. In fact, you can use the example of your own perceptions as a marker as to where spiritual growth is needed.

Agreeing to be fearful, or sponsoring the fear in another, of any group or phenomenon by buying into ideas of separatism is not a characteristic of enlightenment.

One question people frequently ask me is, "What do the ETs suggest that we do in order to save our planet, our environment, and ourselves?"

The answer is to respond unflinchingly to any problem, dilemma, attack, or upset without invoking fear.

No matter the dilemma, no matter the form of attack, no matter the quandary, when we choose to feel and respond with fear, or sponsor or encourage a fearful response in others, we are championing the single most potent way to remain stuck in our present paradigm.

The ETs' consistent answer to questions arising as a result of any problem or upset is to develop a habit of refraining from feeling fear or invoking fear in others, in order to remain in touch with your Source and thus find your solution. You cannot find the highest solution when you are seeking answers from the mindset of fear.

This book is a road map that can assist you in building relationships with beings who are other than human. It takes courage and independent thought when venturing into the territory of inter-species contact and communication. You cannot effectively pioneer this frontier if you come primed with your predecessors' fears, judgments, assumptions, and generalizations about extraterrestrials. Most of us would agree that the most rewarding relationships are approached from trust, not suspicion; open-mindedness, not prejudice; ideas that are grounded in ageless wisdom, not the opinions of our cultural intellect.

As experiencers, we have an opportunity to break the mold of what has been spoon-fed to us about the generalities and prejudices against otherworldly life, and to decide for ourselves what is so. If we don't like what we see, or whom we meet, we can trust that we need only choose again, just as we do in our interpersonal relationships on this planet. Analogously, because we have an unpleasant experience with any other human being, it does not indicate that all human beings must be suspect. Neither do we assume, simply because there's a book or a speaker, an investigator or a researcher who claims that "all aliens are up to no good," that this generalization is one that we need adopt.

In fact, not only might we decide that we needn't adopt fear, but we're predisposed to adopt it so we will be particularly challenged when we decide that we wish to avoid it. The challenge is to notice that in our culture most of us are addicted to being motivated by fear in our every endeavor. We buy products and services as a result of fear. We attempt to sell our products through fear. We attempt to motivate our children through fear. We attempt to motivate our employees through fear; and we erroneously believe that we can change our environment, politics, individual health, or planetary health by being motivated to do so through fear.

The reason there's so much fear going around is that millions of us are subconsciously looking for someone or something to fear because we're conditioned to do so. The "leaders" among us—our politicians, authors, speakers, publishers, networks, movie studios, producers, businesses, and religions—are happy to oblige because of what they are selling, so they identify, label, and demonize somebody or something for us. As a result, the latest addition to the list of bad guys is downloaded into us for our own good and in our best interests, and we're told who or what has been identified as the evildoer of the moment, and what we must do to protect ourselves.

As individuals trained in consumerism since the time we were tots, we usually gobble up the latest "evidence" as to who the new bad guy is among us, or out there, or within us, or around us, because without a demon of the hour, we'd have to settle down and notice that there's nothing to fear at all except fear itself.

But the "controllers" at the top of our cultural hierarchy would rather we not feel our power. It's better for their agenda if we continue to believe that we're inherently *unsafe*, because then we will continue to defer to them for answers. And those answers that they provide consistently lead us away from the voice of our soul, which quiet voice reminds us that only through peace, forgiveness, and love can we ever find everlasting joy.

Now before you protest that I'm advocating complacency, or that I'm a Pollyanna with a huge case of denial, I'm merely pointing out that there's a difference between observing something we choose to change and then changing it, and fearing or hating something we want to change and then trying to change it. The difference is that one mindset will reap everlasting results. The other will not.

When we notice and observe the state or condition of a thing that we don't like or approve, then calmly and gently take steps and take action to change it—when love and peace are the sponsoring motivations—then we will heal those states and conditions. Step 10 encourages us to Fear Not because there's no spiritual evidence to suggest that fear improves or heals anything. When we pinpoint the object of our distaste or objection but perceive that "enemy" as having the power to win, defeat, destroy, or consume us if we're not victorious, then we're already defeated by our sponsoring thoughts about it.

There's a huge difference in the two because the first scenario assumes that as all-powerful, sentient beings, we are capable of transforming our lives and the life on our planet. The second scenario takes us to a fear stance, since it assumes that we're helpless, victimized, would-be abused lambs-being-led-to-slaughter who need to try to stand up to the Bad Guy and duke it out. The sponsoring assumptions are worlds apart and as such, will invoke a world of difference in our experience.

Step 10 is about noticing that when we agree to assume that all extraterrestrial beings might be evildoers, we will in fact limit our experience to the precise type of contact that we fear. If we're calling on extraterrestrials, let's call on the ones that match the way we are resonating.

It's time that we begin to get the hang of walking a spiritual path. By getting the hang of life, we agree to cease being afraid of life. When we actively choose to begin walking a spiritual path, we cease allowing ourselves to be incited by fear, or to be motivated to incite others to fear.

One of the most common characteristics of a master is his consistent restraint from choosing to look at any life event or circumstance through fearful eyes.

A symptom of starting to get the hang of walking a spiritual path is to notice that our current cultural habit that we use to perpetuate fear is through gossip. We gossip to each other about another, and we gossip about what potential scary thing out there might be lurking in the dark to get us. This gossip assaults us hourly and daily through the gossip at work, the gossip of television commercials, the gossip of a new book that's selling fear, or the gossip of a new movie or TV show that's selling fear. In short, most of us are scared silly and there's always someone who will sell us the latest fear, packaged in some form or labeled as a different demon of the week.

This will be the single most difficult habit for most of us to break: to *cease the need to demonize anyone or anything*, and to cease buying into others' needs to sell us the idea that we must demonize anyone or anything.

Through our new and expanded awareness, we will notice who is selling fear. We will notice if the books we're reading are selling fear; we'll notice if the newspaper or the television show that we're watching is selling fear. We'll recognize if the person or project to whom we're giving our money is selling fear. And we will stop this habit of agreeing with the fear sponsors, since in the final analysis, we admit that this fear-philosophy doesn't work.

We're no happier, no more abundant, and certainly no safer as a result of our paranoia. In fact, we're not better off for agreeing to be so vigilant, but worse off, since we've agreed to become detached from our spiritual center, which recognizes that as spiritual beings, we can impart all manner of outcomes through our connection to the One Source. As a result, we need not fear anything except the very fear that is being sold to us.

We can make an objective observation about something that we don't like, such as the state of our dying environment, but this *observation* can motivate us into changing things. We can invoke our highest idea of ourselves as creative beings to engender a creative solution, without buying into the greatest illusion of all time, which denies our heritage as spiritual beings and instead pretends that all we see is all there is, and that greed, avarice, and competition will serve us best in helping to ensure our survival.

Changing the world, improving ourselves, or establishing blessed contact with our neighbors off-planet is less likely to happen when motivated by fear. Instead, when we're sponsored by our passionate recognition of our nature as creative beings sharing the thread of life that runs through all of God's creatures, we ensure the outcome of our desires. Since like-energy attracts like-energy, we recognize that we serve our highest agenda when we refrain from fearing anything.

These individual agendas are interwoven with our species' agenda.

Since so many of us have pre-birth agreements to be part of the first group on our planet to interact with extraterrestrials, there is a divine path set up for us personally, specifically suited for this transition in our evolution. But it will be very difficult to start a new paradigm if we're adopting someone else's fear as promulgated by the same old party line: "Someone or something is out there ready to get you, so be careful."

It is our species' destiny to evolve to the status of universal participant, and so the entire universe will conspire to assist in this peaceful expansion. Individuals will be readied and be sponsored not only by the extraterrestrials themselves but by the spirit realm in general. This means that our spirit guides, our angels, and the God force itself will support our movement in the direction of this expansion. In this light, opening to contact is less about our individual fascination or curiosity with ETs, than about shifting our cultural experience. Suddenly, we're not simply dabbling in a pastime or a hobby, but rather, we're being actively recruited from on-high to help move us in the direction of our own survival. The stakes are upped, as it were, and long ago many of us agreed to play a role in act 2 of this saga.

The second act in this drama of our evolution has to do with our recognition of who we are as divine spiritual beings and the knowing that we can receive help from other divine spiritual beings because we're all from the same family. But we are less likely to embrace that help if we don't recognize the helper. Despite what religions tell us, despite what ufology sells us, our spiritual helpers come in all different appearances, shapes, and sizes. It is only our egocentric, prejudicial paranoia that constantly assumes that what looks different must be bad.

Now you know why the ETs don't show up en masse. Because it will take brave individuals to break out of our cultural bias and to start to think and act differently. That's why this transition to that of a universal human begins on an individual basis first, because this shift must be experienced personally in order to be fully embraced. We're more prone to subscribe to the lower energies of prejudice, hatred, and the "pack" mentality. This is another reason why the ETs don't just land on the White House lawn as part of a presentation to the whole of humanity. Enlightened beings are extremely respectful of free will, and such a public viewing would compel acceptance of their existence.

Instead, individual free will mandates that all must come to recognize such truths from their own intuitive response rather than by public pressure. Then, when enough *individuals* (contactees) have reached this readiness, we will help shift the remaining masses towards ideas of oneness, through the experience of our own lives.

But the ability to arrive at this intuitive response in the first place will be set in motion by our ability to access higher dimensions through our free will, by consistently refraining from choosing the fear response. Time and again we hear of someone who has suddenly become aware of the spirit realm, the divine presence, or even ET contact that radically shifted their world view overnight. These types of conversion experiences are felt at the individual level, where it becomes more and more difficult to deny the spiritual and wondrous nature of life. In essence, conversion experiences inspire us to drop fear as a way of perceiving life. When an individual's life is jarred awake this way through a meaningful conversion experience, the person is often never again the same. Often, they report a greater sense of connection to a grand plan, in which they begin to feel watched over and protected, inspired by the recognition that they too have an important destiny that is interwoven with the destiny of our species. A shift in consciousness has taken place, all because fear was replaced with its opposite.

The movement towards planetary healing will require this shift in consciousness, which is initiated from within. It must be felt viscerally as part of our inner journey, for that is the only experience that has lasting meaning. Ultimately, that which moves us deeply compels spiritual growth. This is how we can move towards enlightenment.

The more comfortable we become at directing our focus inward, and away from the outer noise of the fear paradigm, the more likely we are to place ourselves at the doorways of multidimensional experiences that are part of the higher realms. Being exposed to those higher realms exposes us to our eventual birthright: realizing enlightenment.

Through our associations—our communications—with those who are more evolved and enlightened than we are, we can remember who we are in relation to them, in order to bring about the life of our dreams. But those associations are less likely to be initiated if you're frightened by all the "what ifs." Yet when you drop your fear, knowing that you're a spiritual being in a spiritual universe, then the divine communication plan is initiated. The particulars of what that communication system involves are personal to each individual according to the mission of each soul. That mission will invoke a custom-made bridge to access otherworldly dimensions. And the "bridge" can be contact with myriad different beings, whether those beings are angels, spirit guides, master teachers, or enlightened extraterrestrials.

But prior to any of this contact taking place, we have been participating in a warm-up exercise to get us in the mood and ready for contact. That preparation has been asking us to practice refraining from spreading fear in all its permutations. Upon reading this, you will know to what I'm referring.

You might recognize an opportunity you had in which, instead of choosing to feel fear or to further talking about fear, you purposely chose the higher road. Just a simple reminder to a friend or a co-worker that, "Everything's going to be okay. We're all safe as spiritual beings," can spearhead a change in thinking or a change in someone's life course. Those of us who consider ourselves to be leaders are being asked to help our brothers and sisters to cease feeling frightened, for we know that fear never led a people out of anything. Such leaders are being prepared to lead a whole species.

This preparation is taking place on our behalf, whether or not we're even aware of it. In fact, many times we are not aware of it at all. Step 10 asks us to become aware of those ways that we have been in the past—and will continue to be in the future—exposed and introduced to snippets of insight from the higher realms while simultaneously refraining from choosing fear as our response.

Many years ago, I was awakened by a man who appeared at the end of my bed. At first, I was quite startled, but I decided to give the moment a chance, to see what life was offering me.

I was immediately becalmed when he withdrew a beautiful token from a satchel and handed it to me. Although my mind was protesting that midnight burglars shouldn't be entertained, another part of me knew that the man wasn't an intruder at all, but rather a divine messenger.

He handed me an ornate wooden cross, inlaid with gold or bronze, and as I touched its smooth surface, I looked deep into his eyes, wondering about its significance.

"It's from the time of Christ," the man responded. "We want you to have it."

Prior to my contacts with extraterrestrials, nothing at all like this had ever happened to me. But once I stepped through the doorway the first time and was "exposed" to multidimensional experiences, I began to be contacted by beings, seemingly from other dimensions, who would appear, then disappear without a trace, and with little or no explanation. Yet always, the incident left me deeply contemplative and would stay with me for years. I more readily began to consider my options with respect to what was possible, and I definitely wanted more exposure to it. As a result, calling on extraterrestrials and those who inhabit higher realms is a delightful enhancement of my life.

The visit by this mysterious man at my bedside ended just after he invited me to follow him to another dimension—which I did, although I have no idea how—and he showed me the foods that would best suit my body: fruit, vegetables, and brown rice. The message he brought to me confirmed my intuitive under-standing that I should refrain from eating animal products.

At the time, it did not appear that I had consciously done any-thing to elicit this visit, but on looking back, I realized that I had. Once my ET contact began, my world view was dramatically expanded. I considered very little to be in the realm of "impossible." More importantly, I became willing to believe that my fear, or lack of fear, might dictate the type of experiences that I drew to myself.

As I began to expect interesting visitors and "paranormal" experiences, more became available to me. It seems that my very expectation became an invitation, but I couldn't have had this expectation if I was afraid that I might open myself to the devil or to Satan, or some Bad Guy who was waiting to prey on me. Instead, I trusted in the protection of the life force that I'm part of. This is the way that I had become willing to consider that, at any time of day or night, I might be able to "meet" those who inhabit-ed those different realms. And as if by magic, that was absolutely what happened. When I dropped fear, I beheld magical phenome-na that helped me to awaken to a better version of myself.

Once experienced, otherworldly encounters with divine beings become stepping-stones to our own awakening because our perceptions change forever as to what is and is not possible.

It is the consideration of what could be that will change our experience. At any moment, an opportunity for "out-of-the-normal" experience can open to us. The key is to recognize at the outset that these doorways exist all around us and that they are available to us. But not if we're sponsoring fear, because fear stops the opportunities dead in their tracks, or conversely, compels us to experience pre-cisely what it is that we say that we fear. Fear is creative, just as is any other feeling or thought that is passionately held. Otherworldly experiences with beings who are inhabitants of otherworldly realms can be invoked by a recognition that portals to experiencing "phenomena" exist everywhere, and can be accessed by us at every time of the night and day. But those portals will match the energy of our *feelings*. So choose wisely. Extraterrestrials tell us that the quality of our experience depends on it, although for years I resisted that this was true.

I asked the ETs for clarification.

Many people would claim that not all states of being are actively chosen by us. They just happen to us. We can't help our feelings, or how we feel about such-and-such. Feelings just are.

As long as you believe that you're not choosing *all* of your states of being, then you will not arrive at the other states of being that you say you would like to experience, but don't. It is not accurate that you are a leaf upon the river. You are the river itself. Choose where you prefer the leaf to be upon your current. To acquiesce to your cultural voice, which pretends that you're the leaf instead of the river, is part of your illusion.

I know that we're supposedly choosing even our undesirable perceptions and the conditions of our life, but it doesn't feel as if we are. It feels as though we carry on day to day, and stuff happens to us, and that stuff dictates how we feel.

We are speaking now of all the states of being and states of consciousness that are available to you. Currently, it's your belief that what you most experience—that which makes up the predominant part of your day-to-day life—is what is most "natural" to you. Anger, frustration, etc., would seem to be "natural" and yet it is not natural at all. What is most "natural" to you is sensing your connection to all that is, including each other. When your life demonstrates that you recognize this connection, it simply "works" better since everything imaginable in your life shifts.

Were you to feel that sense of connection to each other, none of you would be impoverished, or without a place to sleep, since such conditions would not be tolerated but immediately mended. You wouldn't be killing each other over disagreements. This means that your sense of connection would change your daily lives, and your planetary home. Crime becomes a thing of the past, a memory that symbolizes a time of barbarianism.

When your understanding shifts, each of your needs is being met, and so there is less silent desperation playing itself out in a manner that you name as crime, depression, and hostilities. The quality of your every perception is available to you at your invitation.

This invitation by you is what makes your recognition of these options of consciousness come alive. It's like becoming aware of your neighbor who lives right next door when you'd like to borrow a cup of milk. Until you recognized that option, you were less likely to choose it. Once considered as an option, it becomes a possible choice. In this way, you are exposed to the idea that your choice of perception dictates the quality of your life. This is also the way and the means by which you can gain entry to other realms, and you will partake of them more often. And once this occurs, the doorway to meeting and knowing us, and others like us, simply becomes commonplace.

Analogously, once you began to dream of navigating your globe through the advent of airplanes, you more easily exposed yourselves to each other on different continents as air travel became commonplace. In this same way, other galaxies and other realms become your next possible destination. What once seemed as unlikely to you as air travel did a hundred years ago, is now well within the realm of possibility. Through your air travel, now you are able to visit remote tribes at the farthest corners of Earth in a matter of hours. Exercising that option is now considered "normal" and part of everyday occurrence.

Similarly, you are able to navigate other corners of your universe through modern "travel," but that mode of travel begins with your being exposed to different frequencies that are part of other dimensions. But the attitude that best invites these differing energies is one of fearlessness. Then, as you bravely expose yourself to these energies, you become more and more accustomed to them, and then more "travel" is possible and comfortable. Accessing altered states of consciousness, other realms, and meeting up with otherworldly beings can jump-start your journey and can encourage you to begin the transition to your next evolution.

Step 11: Metamorphose

To transition from a human to a being who can navigate otherworldly realms is to "metamorphose" from our current habitat and easily navigate more than one "terrain." Experiencers are metamorphs, profoundly adapting to a new age when our next stage of life requires inter-dimensional mobility in order to transform our species and ensure our survival. When we metamorphose, we can walk between worlds.

Many humans have a hard time believing that we can shapeshift into animate or inanimate forms, change our cellular makeup, dematerialize and then materialize, float through the air, or move through solid objects at will. Generally, we don't believe that the human body can travel faster than the speed of light, embody more than one physical form at a time, and possess the skills and attributes that have been heretofore relegated to fantasy, myth, science fiction, or biblical miracles.

Although we humans purport to believe that we're at the top of the heap on an evolutionary scale that includes such "subordinate" life-forms as animals, insects, birds, trees, and rocks, in truth we don't think very much of ourselves. No matter what we pretend to believe about our characteristics and abilities, in truth, most of us do not recognize that humans are complex life-forms with intriguing biology and behavior who stand ready to metamorphose.

Future scientists will one day recognize that humans on Earth now during this critical time in our evolution are an important group for study because we will prove to be the forefathers of the first New Humans, the group making up the Second Generation. This generation of our new species will be able to emerge from our current habitat—both the habitat on Earth as well as the habitat of our limited cultural beliefs—and to know and relate to others both within and outside of our realm.

One of the first groups of humans to expand their awareness sufficiently to allow for universal connection with other life-forms in the universe is what we have been referring to as experiencers, contactees, or close-encounter witnesses.

But in actuality, none of these words adequately describe what we are and what we portend. We are not simply "experiencers" of phenomena. We are not merely "contactees" by "aliens." We are far more than "witnesses" to the existence of extraterrestrial life. In fact, we are none of those things exclusively, although we are all of them. In reality, we are much, much more.

We are "metamorphs," spiritual beings who recognize ourselves as such, and who claim our inherent supernatural powers that allow us to inter-relate with all forms of life everywhere within myriad venues. Those relationships can and will enhance and change everything as we know it.

Metamorphs who are scientifically astute are sponsored, and will continue to be sponsored, by beings from the higher realms. ETs will inspire the ideas for inventions and schematics, theories, medical breakthroughs, advanced uses of energy, and myriad ideas to assist us in healing ourselves. We will be taught how to save our dying animal species and return our planet to a state of well-being.

The time it will take for individuals on Earth to move through the spiritual, intellectual, emotional, and physical process of metamorphosis can vary enormously. Children, in particular, transition easily, having less cultural resistance to overcome. They often report to have met all sorts of beings in their private moments, none of which the adults around them have witnessed. Of course, adults usually dismiss their claims as childish imagination.

Other individuals begin to open to contact over a period of weeks or months, depending upon their ego strength and soul's code, which will determine how much, how soon. Others take several years or even many lifetimes to merge more slowly into a recognition of who they are as universal beings. And finally, some people will not only fail to recognize their potential as meta-morphs, but will lose their capacity to metamorphose through consistent denial of their inherent nature.

But even in this case, this loss of potential is not "forever," since each soul is always moving towards evolving, no matter how "slowly." It really comes down to a choice of how fast or slow one chooses to evolve.

A key event in the metamorph's ability to transform is the recognition of where he or she stands in the context of humanity. If the individual can believe in his heart that he serves a vital link to our future through his ability to make contact and be sponsored by all other life-forms under God, then an abrupt transformation can and will happen. The more of us who transform this way, the more metamorphs will be available to help shift our planetary paradigm.

Even so, metamorphs will not even be required to remain on this planet, for as bringers of a new dawn of possibilities, we can move at will through different realms. It all depends on the soul's desires and the stated mission or purpose of your life. It all depends on what you were born to do.

Are you progressing down the path that you were intended for? If it is your destiny to sponsor the evolution of life here on *this* planet, you will do so. If it is your destiny to sponsor the idea of how it's possible to move between life on *different* planets, you will do so.

No matter what details make up your soul's ability to meta-morphose, consider yourself the embodiment of the future of life-forms everywhere. Metaphorically speaking, we are morphing from the current stage of human "larva" to adult, wherein we are undergoing profound adaptations for our next stage of life. Some of those morphological changes are subtle, and some are not so subtle. These include modifications in physiology, behavior, and frequency or vibration that accompany the metamorphic process, whether through implants, modifications, or an adjustment in our inner belief system in adopting spiritual principles to apply to supernatural and paranormal phenomena. Whatever form these changes take, they are profound and far more remarkable than non-metamorphs can ever imagine.

The inner and outer journey to opening to otherworldly life does seem to render the metamorph vulnerable during this transition. But this does not mean that we're vulnerable to evil influence or satanic forces. Instead, we are vulnerable to the assumptions, opinions, and judgments of our greater society, or even our friends and family members who do not yet recognize the profound spiritual journey on which we have embarked.

Our greatest potential "predators" during this transition are our own doubts and insecurities, since metamorphosis is the time of greatest vulnerability. During this transformation, we can no longer fully relate spiritually or physically to a limited human form, nor can we yet fully embrace or relate to that of a fully metamorphosed universal being who is fully comfortable and well versed in his limitless nature. We're like the early amphibians, actively evolving from aquatic fishes to a species that can maneuver beyond its watery element.

Metamorphs are at the in-between stage, not quite tadpole, but not yet frog, and the duration of our individual larval stage will depend on our spiritual and emotional constitution, which hosts the timing of our development.

Metamorphs are the amphibians of the new age, but unlike amphibians, we don't divide our life between water and land; we can live alternately in our world and that of others. Although it's said that the metamorphosis for amphibians falls under hormonal control, metamorphs will transform according to spiritual law. We recognize that we are by no means merely limited to the human version of frogs or salamanders, but instead, our metamorphosis will be triggered by our intent to be one with our universal comrades and to know more of universal life. This process is about learning how we can be mentored by those who can show us about adaptation to life, both on, and eventually off, our planet.

These universal families inspire us to recognize that we're not limited to one fixed genetic "human" trait. This recognition is not easily arrived at, but is internalized and becomes available only at metamorphosis. As a result, the barrier to this shift is an inner one. This is why it's so difficult for "non-transitioning" humans to relate to these ideas, since, prior to the process of metamorphosis, a limited world view limits understanding.

And like some species of amphibians that have lost the capability to move between their realms of water and land, human metamorphs can choose to remain static in their current paradigm. Like various amphibian species who remain permanently aquatic and others terrestrial, humans do not have to embrace their potential to transition to other realms, but can deny their potential and stay as they are.

Metamorphs, like their amphibian counterparts, will grow to be successful at utilizing a wide range of habitats. Frogs and salamanders display a stunning ability to exist and move between the land and water realms despite their soft, smooth skin that is permeable to water. We're hardly surprised at all that such creatures on Earth can do this. They are remarkable, exquisite examples of sentient beings. Even scientists are beginning to agree that they have not deserved their previous label of "lower life-forms," but embody profound abilities and characteristics that have ensured their survival.

Yet, humans have assumed that such characteristics cannot be duplicated by us. We have not allowed ourselves to recognize that we too can adapt to more than one environment. The word "amphibian" comes from the Greek *amphibios,* which means "a being with a double life," and this is precisely what the extraordinary experiences of human metamorphs are heralding. Both groups—amphibian and human metamorph—play an extraordinary role in demonstrating the ability of living a "double life."

Just as the amphibians effectively transitioned from a completely aquatic life as fish, humans can also make the transition from the physical realm on Earth to multidimensional realms on Earth and elsewhere. Although the amphibians' evolution involved a radical reorganization of the skeleton and an ability to breathe air, metamorphs' immediate evolutionary responsibility will involve a radical reorganization of their belief systems and attitudes, to include an ability to breathe intention into a changing paradigm. This shift in our inner perceptions will be our link to our next evolution.

A metamorph is a being who also lives a double life, but that life is not limited to remaining on land or water. Rather, we can maneuver in this realm or others, on this planet or another, or with our fellow human beings or other universal beings. But unlike the double life that is the rule for most of amphibians that use environmental temperatures to regulate body temperature, metamorphs use the "thermostat" of spiritual awareness to dictate their spiritual temperature.

Herpetologists now recognize their heretofore faulty assumptions in shrugging off amphibians and reptiles as "lower lifeforms," as compared to animals and birds. Herpetology is as significant a specialty as is ornithology and mammalogy. In reality, all creatures, large and small, are sentient beings, although we all go about things differently, whether on this planet or another. This recently enhanced status of herpetology in the eyes of scientists symbolizes the soon-to-be-enhanced status of metamorphs, who will also one day be recognized as an important discipline of science. Right now, scientists and researchers have sponsored the denial that runs through most of our culture, and so humans who can traverse more than one world are flatly ignored.

Biologists agree that the ancestry of modern amphibians is unsolved because there are no fossils linking ancient tetrapods (from which living amphibians are thought to be descended) to "modern" amphibians, but despite this, they have attempted to answer the question: How did the transition from fish to amphibian—from water to land—originally come about? Possibly, the more youthful and agile fish gathered in shallow waters and eventually ventured onto land in search of food. In the case of these tetrapods, this transition took millions of years, but for reasons of the speeding up of time during the new millennium, such transitions for human metamorphs can happen in a moment. Early tetrapods that moved from shallow water to land had to evolve a physical structure that could adapt to gravity, for example.

Human metamorphs also have a physical adaptation to make, but that transformation is sponsored by the energies of the higher realms. Those energies, if embraced and not resisted, can be utilized by the metamorph efficiently, and so a long passage of time, as we know it, is not a requirement for evolution as it has been in the past.

The ETs tell me that their once dense physical bodies evolved to a lighter, more agile form, allowing them to more easily navigate multidimensional realms. They say that they are nourished by photon energy without need of food. Even today, although scientists vehemently deny the possibility, there are humans who are able to be nourished solely on light energy sources, and they are referred to as "breatharians."

But even scientists agree that there are many amphibians that are able to live on little food, and some salamanders can exist happily and unaffectedly in extreme cold and without food for a year or longer. So on the one hand, scientists applaud the human biological machine for its superior abilities, and yet the "lowly" amphibian demonstrates characteristics that scientists would argue cannot be shared by humans. Is it likely that as sponsored by all the glory of the universe, only a few animal species can evolve in such a way that allows for such enhanced abilities of evolution?

If more than twelve species of amphibians have adapted to survive freezing temperatures by releasing glucose into their blood to lower the temperature of water in the cells, then why is it so far-fetched to imagine that humans, like the ETs, can also adapt to extremes in temperatures, making universal travel possible?

If the California newt is able to stroll through wildfires by protecting itself by simply secreting mucus over its body, then what more has God intended for humans? Like the human body, ordinarily, amphibians are not suited to extremes in temperatures but have adapted to thrive in them out of necessity for survival. If frogs and salamanders have adapted to be freeze-tolerant or fire-resistant, what more is possible for human metamorphs in withstanding the elements? If frogs and salamanders exhibit seemingly magical qualities of survival, then why not metamorphs?

We as human metamorphs are upon that time of rapid evolution right now. As the astounding transformation of amphibians once took place, remarkable changes are also occurring in human metamorphs. But unlike tadpoles, who can transition only after resorbing their propulsive tails at metamorphosis, human metamorphs will be required to resorb their culture's once propulsive ideology that was thrust upon the species and considered to be gospel.

Human metamorphs, though, will not have to contend with the physiological metamorphosis involved with the resorption of tail fins, differentiation of eyelids, or changes in the thickness of the skin and its permeability to water. Instead, our initial metamorphosis will involve the resorption of a limited belief system, which will be replaced with new ideas of our emerging evolution as universal humans.

Like the emerging amphibian that met with many challenges in becoming terrestrial, metamorphs also have challenges in becoming extraterrestrial and exploring previously unexplored regions. Like the emerging tadpole that transforms and ventures from water to land, metamorphs will overcome numerous challenges physically, and also emotionally, intellectually, and spiritually, as we venture from our realm. The transition in our permeability will not be limited to the elements of water or fire, but will involve all of the differing elements, energies, and frequencies of the greater universe.

Recognizing oneself as a metamorph will be the environmental trigger that can instigate these changes. Whereas the emerging transition from fish to frog took millennia, metamorphs are learning to move between realms over the period of a weekend. As evidenced by metamorphs' face-to-face contact experiences with their extraterrestrial neighbors, we are ready, willing, and able to shift our locomotion to beyond our own realm, whether on this planet or beyond.

Our adaptation to new environments is happening right now and metamorphs will prove to be the missing link between the old limited version of human and the New Human who can emerge from one element to another. Our metamorphosis is upon us and it will not be long before our species will look back to these days and to the lives of metamorphs as the defining transition of our species. We are transitioning to a new human and to a new land, but that new land is right here on Earth, and any other place in the cosmos.

The amphibian is threatened by extinction and its population is declining at an extraordinary rate. Human beings also are threatened by a polluted environment and spiritual misalignment. What is needed for all species is an evolutionary jump in our spiritual awareness, which will enable us to correct immediately our past behaviors and to mend and heal our planet. The adventure of the transforming human to that of a metamorph is one of the most exciting transitions in the universe today, and a role that will assist us in returning our Earth home to the garden of Eden.

Lasting change begins as an inside job, as part of a shift within the individual. The great masters have known that the world will not change by shifting the culture, but rather by changing the hearts of men and women, who then become inspired to shift the culture and change the world.

The Christ modeled the ability to refrain from fear and judgment in any circumstance, because he knew that when he changed men and women from the inside, they themselves would go on to change the outward circumstances of their problematic cultures. Christ didn't take a man out of poverty, but instead took poverty out of the man, who then would take himself out of poverty.

The great masters of wisdom throughout time are on the same team, no matter their name, or their physical description. Today, the holy works of every major religion promise ongoing inspiration and mentoring during the return of their spiritual teacher. Jews await the Messiah, Christians are patient for the return of Christ, Krishna is expected by Hindus, and the Fifth (Maitreya) Buddha is anticipated by Buddhists.

No matter which name is chosen by these groups, each master is also a metamorph, as are the extraterrestrials themselves and the human initiates they inspire. Each teacher shares the common characteristic of the essence and quality of his message. That message inspires us to evolve spiritually beyond where we are right now, to find a way to be at peace with ourselves and each other by resting in the faith of On High, knowing that in this life or thereafter, all is well and there is nothing to fear. Like the beings that we refer to as "extraterrestrials," all great masters have known that by inspiring men, women, and children to change within themselves, those individuals will go on to change their culture and their entire world.

Enlightened otherworldly beings presently serve a role similar to the role of many religions' spiritual teachers who are believed to return to Earth to help humanity. The name of the Wise One doesn't matter. What matters is the message. For it is the message, not the messenger, that will save us. Only now are we beginning to recognize that the extraterrestrials' message bears the same quality of inspiration of every major religion's spiritual teacher. In the final analysis, the extraterrestrials, like other masters before them, inspire certain leaders—brave metamorphs who choose to spearhead a change in our species—to take the higher road beyond the fear and prejudice in our worldly habits and biases. They encourage us to make a shift within that can elicit the change of a lifetime—a change that can and will occur during *our* lifetime if only we believe.

We have entered a new age that has been prophesied by masters and prophets since the beginning of recorded history. *The prophets were right after all: these* are *the end times, but not the ones that we thought! It's the end of our misery—not of our world—once and for all.*

We humans are changing. In fact, the extraterrestrials tell me that *they* are humans, evolved. They have returned from our future to help us. In the absence of "time" as we know it, all experience is happening simultaneously. Thus, metamorphs are actually meeting ETs who are our future selves, since outside of our realm, time as we know it does not exist.

When I first began to have contact more than a decade ago, I had no idea that people worldwide who are contacted by ETs are actually "official" yet unrecognized members of our planet's space program. Metamorphs are already accomplishing what NASA hopes to without benefit of any special training, equipment, or billion-dollar budget. We are navigating our universe and meeting those who reside there. But technology has not made this possible; spiritual awareness has. In fact, if the *Columbia* space shuttle tragedy and others like it taught us anything, it's that science does not have all the answers.

ETs are contacting people around the globe and are providing contactees with ideas and inspiration for inventions and projects that can benefit all of humanity. They can show us how to heal ourselves and our planet. They can teach us their technology and help us to grow spiritually. The corporations won't save us, nor will our politicians or pharmaceutical companies. We will have to lead the way ourselves, not motivated by profit but rather out of a desire to be of service. We can share what we know and what we have learned, not allowing potentially transformative inventions and technologies to be suppressed. We can bring to humanity those ideas, inventions, and applications that can transform the world and her people. There are Einsteins and Edisons among us now who have been inspired and tutored by the higher realms, ready to offer what they know for all of our benefit.

When we have the courage and confidence to begin calling on extraterrestrials for help and guidance, we will be sponsored by God's helpers, which will ensure our evolution to the glorious tomorrow that is our birthright.

11 Steps to Inviting
Your Own UFO Encounters

Step 1: Call It Forth

In order to begin calling on extraterrestrials, you must desire to have contact.

Step 2: Remember Soul Connections

Activating our soul memory helps us reunite with family members who make up our greater universal family.

Step 3: Forgive the Pain

The evolution of our species to that of a universal being requires us to proceed gently with love, no matter how much pain and suffering have been part of our past.

Step 4: Celebrate Family Reunions

Despite physical and other differences that often initially frighten us, extraterrestrials and humans share a bond as family members although we have forgotten that bond.

Step 5: Be the Expert

The contact itself serves as contactees' "credentials," even though our insight may diverge from currently accepted scientific and cultural assumptions.

Step 6: Energize

ET contact enables our bodies to be "tweaked" by electro-magnetic frequencies from the higher realms, enabling us to energize beyond the dense realm of our physical world.

Step 7: Discern Readiness in Others

In the early stages of contact, it is imperative to discern readiness in others and confide and seek advice only from confidants who espouse and attempt to make practical spiritual principles.

Step 8: Be Here Now

ETs serve to sponsor us to transform the paradigm on Earth, not to escape from it.

Step 9: Shapeshift

When we're aware of the nature of limitless beings, we're able to recognize and be mentored by phenomena that can inspire us to know our magnificence.

Step 10: Fear Not

We cannot receive help from evolved beings in the universe if we don't recognize the helper.

Step 11: Metamorphose

When we metamorphose, we can acquire mobility in walking between worlds and adapt to our next stage of life.

References

Brennan, Barbara Ann. 1998. *Hands of Light: A Guide to Healing through the Human Energy Field.* New York: Bantam Doubleday Dell.

Grossman, Neal. 2002. "Who's Afraid of Life After Death?" *IONS: The Noetic Sciences Review* 21(1). Fall: 5–24.

Larkins, Lisette. 2002. *Talking to Extraterrestrials: Communicating with Enlightened Beings.* Charlottesville, Va.: Hampton Roads.

Ludington, Alan. 2002. "Appendix 1" in *Talking to Extraterrestrials: Communicating with Enlightened Beings* by Lisette Larkins. Charlottesville, Va.: Hampton Roads.

Nyman, Joe. 2002. "Appendix 2" in *Talking to Extraterrestrials: Communicating with Enlightened Beings* by Lisette Larkins. Charlottesville, Va.: Hampton Roads.

Stout, Martha. 2001. *The Myth of Sanity: Divided Consciousness and the Promise of Awareness.* New York: Viking Press.

Tolle, Eckart. 1999. *The Power of Now: A Guide to Spiritual Enlightenment.* Novato, Ca.: New World Library.

Whitfield, Charles L. 1995. *Memory and Abuse: Remembering and Healing the Effects of Trauma.* Deerfield Beach, Fl.: Health Communications.

Acknowledgments

To my friend and associate Dutchie A. Kidd for her invaluable help and input with the ET projects and for agreeing to be a guinea pig for this book.

To Grace Pedalino and Tiffany McCord of McCord & Pedalino Literary Consulting (www.literaryconsulting.com) for being my publicity gurus.

To Rebecca Williamson (awordsmith@earthlink.net) for her astute copyediting and manuscript polishing.

To Matthew Friedman at Marjoram Productions for book cover and web site design and assistance.